⚖️ NOLO   Products & Services

⇨ **Books &**

Get in-dep... at books and software programs for consumers and business owners. Order a copy—or download an ebook version instantly—at Nolo.com.

⇨ **Legal Encyclopedia**

Free at Nolo.com. Here are more than 1,400 free articles and answers to

SBA's funding should not be construed as an endorsement of any products, opinions, or services. All SBA-funded projects are extended to the public on a nondiscriminatory basis.

up-to-date source for definitions of legal terms.

⇨ **Online Legal Documents**

Create documents at your computer. Go to Nolo.com to make a will or living trust, form an LLC or corporation or obtain a trademark or

Find an attorney at Nolo.com. Nolo's consumer-friendly lawyer directory provides in-depth profiles of lawyers all over America. From fees and experience to legal philosophy, education and special expertise, you'll find all the information you need to pick the right lawyer. Every lawyer listed has pledged to work diligently and respectfully with clients.

⇨ **Free Legal Updates**

Keep up to date. Check for free updates at Nolo.com. Under "Products," find this book and click "Legal Updates." You can also sign up for our free e-newsletters at Nolo.com/newsletters.

1st edition

Employment Law

The Essential HR Desk Reference

Lisa Guerin, J.D.

FIRST EDITION	MARCH 2011
Cover Design	JALEH DOANE
Editor	RICHARD STIM
Book Design	TERRI HEARSH
Proofreading	ROBERT WELLS
Printing	DELTA PRINTING SOLUTIONS, INC.

Guerin, Lisa, 1964-
 Employment law : the essential HR desk reference / by Lisa Guerin. -- 1st ed.
    p. cm.
 Summary: "An A-Z reference encyclopedia, with more than 200 entries defining and explaining employment and labor law topics. The entries combine a summary of the law with real life case references, pop culture references, and statistics and trends"-- Provided by publisher.
 ISBN-13: 978-1-4133-1333-8 (pbk.)
 ISBN-10: 1-4133-1333-7 (pbk.)
 ISBN-13: 978-1-4133-1359-8 (e-book)
 ISBN-10: 1-4133-1359-0 (e-book)
 1. Labor laws and legislation--United States. I. Title.
 KF3369.G84 2011
 344.7301--dc22
                             2010042817

Please note

We believe accurate, plain-English legal information should help you solve many of your own legal problems. But this text is not a substitute for personalized advice from a knowledgeable lawyer. If you want the help of a trained professional—and we'll always point out situations in which we think that's a good idea—consult an attorney licensed to practice in your state.

absenteeism

Absenteeism refers to an employee's pattern of failing to show up at work or to the rate at which a group of employees don't show up for work. (For example, if a company or department has a 10% absenteeism rate, that means one in ten of its employees are likely to be absent on any given day.)

The term is usually reserved for employees who are absent so often that it causes problems at work, employees whose absences are suspicious in some way (for example, who routinely call in sick at the end of a vacation or long weekend), or employees who do not follow required procedures for absences (like calling in sick or giving notice of vacation). An employee who is out of work for a few days with the flu would not be accused of "absenteeism," for instance.

What companies do about absenteeism. Companies use a number of strategies to manage absenteeism, including adopting procedures employees must follow to take time off, disciplining employees who ignore the rules, having supervisors follow up with employees who call in sick, and combining vacation, sick, and other leave into one paid time-off entitlement, which means an employee who calls in sick at the last minute is losing a day that could otherwise have been used for vacation. Policies like these make it more difficult—or less appealing—for employees to take unscheduled time off at the last minute, which helps the employer manage its workforce and workload.

Who's Absent the Most?

According to 2009 data from the federal Bureau of Labor Statistics (BLS), the employees who missed the highest percentage of work hours to absences each year work in the health care industry. Government workers had the second highest percentage, followed by a tie for third among protective service employees, community and social service employees, personal care providers, office and administrative support employees, and production workers. (The figures are based on time not worked because of illness, child care problems, personal obligations, and so on; time spent on vacation or holidays wasn't included.)

No-fault attendance policies. Some employers use "no-fault" attendance policies, which typically penalize employees for having more than a set number of unexcused absences per year, whether the employee is sick, has a family emergency, or takes a last-minute personal day. (Some policies count even scheduled absences, such as vacations or time off for scheduled surgery, toward an employee's total, and allow a higher number of absences before discipline kicks in.) For example, a no-fault attendance policy might give employees a point for each unexcused absence, then provide that five points in a year merits a verbal warning, eight points results in a written warning, and ten points in a year is a firing offense.

Policies like these can lead to legal problems if the employee is penalized for absences that are protected under the Family and Medical Leave Act (FMLA) or the Americans with Disabilities Act. The FMLA allows employees to take time off if a serious health condition requires it, even if the need for leave was not foreseeable. For example, if an employee has a chronic condition that flares up and makes it impossible to work, that employee may use FMLA leave. An employer that counts that absence against the employee has violated the FMLA.

EXAMPLE: June Manuel began working for Westlake Polymers Corporation in 1986. Her absenteeism was an ongoing problem during her employment, and she was warned that her job would be in jeopardy if her attendance didn't improve. In 1991, Westlake adopted a no-fault attendance policy, which counted every absence against the employee no matter why the employee missed work. Manuel was warned four times in 1992 that her attendance had to improve immediately or she would be suspended or fired.

In October 1993, Manuel got permission to take a Friday off to have an ingrown toenail removed. She was expected to return to work the following Monday, but suffered complications, including an infection and swelling. She missed more than a month of work following this procedure. When Manuel took a few days off work sick several months later, she was fired.

She sued Westlake and a federal Court of Appeals allowed her lawsuit to go forward. Why? Because the FMLA became law in August 1993, and her month-long absence may have been protected leave under the law. If so, counting that absence against her under the no-fault attendance policy was a violation of the FMLA. Westlake argued that Manuel didn't give notice of her need for leave, as the statute requires, because she never mentioned the FMLA. The court found that this didn't matter: Once the employee gives notice of leave for a medical condition, it's up to the employer to figure out whether the FMLA applies. (The court didn't offer an opinion as to whether Manuel's ingrown toenail was a serious health condition covered by the FMLA.) *Manuel v. Westlake Polymers Corp.*, 66 F.3d 758 (1995).

Related terms: Americans with Disabilities Act; Family and Medical Leave Act; paid time off (PTO); presenteeism; sick leave; vacation.

ADA

See Americans with Disabilities Act.

A

ADAAA

See Americans with Disabilities Act.

ADEA

See Age Discrimination in Employment Act.

administrative employee

Although many people refer to secretaries and others who keep an office running smoothly as "administrative employees" (or "admins," for short), this term has a more specific legal meaning. It refers to a category of employees who are exempt from the minimum wage and overtime requirements of the federal Fair Labor Standards Act (FLSA). Even if they work more than 40 hours a week, these employees aren't entitled to get overtime.

Two requirements must be met for a worker to qualify as an administrative employee: a salary test and a job duties test. Under the salary test, the employee must earn at least $455 per week and be paid on a salary basis. Workers are paid on a salary basis if they receive their full salary for any week in which they perform any work, regardless of how many hours they work or the quality or amount of work they do. (There are a handful of exceptions to this rule, covered in "pay docking.")

An employee must also perform certain job duties to qualify. An administrative employee's primary duty must be office or other nonmanual work directly related to the management or general business operations of the employer or its customers. Examples include performing functions like tax, finance, human resources, marketing, regulatory compliance, auditing, or insurance. This work must include the exercise of discretion and independent judgment regarding matters of significance. This might include the authority to make decisions, set policy, carry out important assignments, or commit the employer to a particular course of action with a significant financial impact on the company.

Related terms: exempt employee; Fair Labor Standards Act; minimum wage; overtime; pay docking; professional employee.

affirmative action

Practices that are intended to promote opportunity for members of historically disadvantaged classes are referred to as affirmative action. Although most often associated with promoting opportunities for candidates of color and women, affirmative action may assist any disadvantaged group. For example, some affirmative action programs benefit people with disabilities or military veterans.

Affirmative action is most common in employment, government contracts, education, and business. In the employment field, the federal, state, or local government might implement affirmative action measures, either when the government acts as an employer or when the government contracts with, or provides grants to, private business. Private employers may also adopt their own affirmative action programs.

Affirmative action measures run the gamut from steps to make sure that candidates from historically disadvantaged groups have an equal opportunity to contend for jobs and promotions (such as posting jobs in areas with high numbers of minority job seekers, developing outreach efforts to find qualified female candidates, and supporting training programs for candidates or employees in protected categories) to giving members of historically disadvantaged classes an edge in employment decisions by taking gender, race, or another protected characteristic into account as a factor in the selection process.

The controversy over affirmative action. As noted above, some affirmative action measures don't take race, gender, or other protected characteristics into account in the selection process, but seek only to widen the field of qualified applicants through outreach and search efforts. When the employer in this type of program reaches the point of actually selecting candidates, the process is color- and gender-blind. These measures have not met with much legal or social resistance.

A

However, measures that give an edge to particular applicants based on race, gender, or another protected characteristic have historically been more controversial. These measures might include:

- using race as a "plus" factor in hiring (so that an African American applicant would be preferred over a white applicant with the same qualifications)
- using lower cutoffs for test scores for minority or female candidates, or
- setting hiring goals or quotas (that 30% of the workforce in a traditionally male profession be female by 2020, say).

Measures like these provide a benefit to members of one group that comes at the expense of members of another. Proponents of affirmative action argue that this is fair and appropriate, given our country's long history of discrimination, and is the only way to create truly equal opportunity for groups that are disadvantaged. Opponents argue that discrimination is unfair, no matter who it helps or hurts, and that (primarily) white men should not have to pay the price for historical discrimination.

Affirmative action for federal contractors. Executive Order 11246 requires certain federal contractors to adopt affirmative action programs. Among other things, contractors must analyze their workforce, target any areas where members of protected groups are underrepresented, and come up with specific goals to help address the problem. Contractors must make good faith efforts to achieve these goals, which might include outreach and recruitment programs, training, and other strategies to expand the pool of qualified candidates. Executive Order 11246 is administered and enforced by the Office of Federal Contract Compliance Programs (OFCCP), www.dol.gov/ofccp.

Affirmative action in other government settings. When a government uses affirmative action as an employer, it is subject to the Equal Protection Clause of the 14th Amendment to the U.S. Constitution. When governments make distinctions based on race, the Equal Protection Clause requires them to have a compelling interest that

"Reverse Discrimination" in the Supreme Court

The U.S. Supreme Court has decided a number of affirmative action cases in the last 40 years. Typically, these cases have been "reverse discrimination" claims, brought by potential students or employees who believe they were denied opportunities because a school's or an employer's affirmative action program favored minority or female candidates. Here are a few of the most widely publicized cases:

- *Regents of the University of California v. Bakke*, 438 U.S. 265 (1978), in which the Supreme Court held (by 5-4 vote) that the admissions program of the medical school at the University of California at Davis was unconstitutional because it excluded applicants on the basis of race.
- *Martin v. Wilks*, 490 U.S. 755 (1989), in which a group of white firefighters sued the city of Birmingham, Alabama, claiming that a consent decree the city entered into with African American firefighters resulted in discrimination in promotions. The Supreme Court decided that the white firefighters could challenge the consent decree even though they knew about the earlier lawsuit and could have gotten involved then.
- *Grutter v. Bollinger*, 539 U.S. 306 (2003), in which the Supreme Court ruled that the University of Michigan could consider race in deciding which applicants to accept, as long as it did not use quotas and the program was narrowly tailored to further the school's compelling interest in providing students with the educational benefits of diversity; the Court also noted that affirmative action measures should be temporary.
- *Ricci v. DeStefano* 129 S.Ct. 2658 (2009), in which the Court held that the city of New Haven, Connecticut, could not ignore promotion test results, even though white applicants generally scored so much higher on the test than African American and Hispanic applicants that the city feared it would be sued for race discrimination if it used the results. The Court found that the city could refuse to certify the test scores only if it had a "strong basis in evidence" to believe that they were discriminatory.

A

is served by the distinction, and the means chosen must be narrowly tailored to further that interest.

The U.S. Supreme Court has held that a desire to remedy the effects of societal discrimination is not a sufficient justification for race-based classifications, nor is a desire to provide nonwhite role models. Instead, a government entity that seeks to implement affirmative action must show that it has a history of past discrimination or perhaps that it has been a passive participant in societal discrimination, which the affirmative action program seeks to remedy.

Even if a government entity has a sufficient factual basis to adopt an affirmative action plan, the plan might still be illegal unless it is narrowly tailored to meet those goals. For example, a plan that lasts longer than necessary, confers benefits on people outside of the group that has been discriminated against (for example, benefits all minorities when there is proof of discrimination only against African Americans), or sets goals that go beyond the proven discrimination might be struck down.

Affirmative action by private employers. Private employers are not subject to the Equal Protection Clause, but their affirmative action plans must meet the requirements of Title VII. The Supreme Court has developed a three-part test to evaluate the legality of private affirmative action:

1. **There must be a factual basis (of discrimination) for the plan.** The employer doesn't have to admit that it discriminated in the past to adopt an affirmative action plan (although such an admission would meet this requirement). For private plans, statistical evidence might also be sufficient, if it shows a "manifest imbalance" in traditionally segregated fields or it would be sufficient to allow the group that would be benefited by the plan to bring a discrimination lawsuit.

2. **The plan must not "unnecessarily trammel" the interests of employees who don't benefit directly from it.** For example, a plan by which the employer would lay off workers to

make room for a more diverse workforce would be more detrimental to the laid off workers than a plan that addressed recruitment or hiring.

3. **The plan must be temporary.** Affirmative action measures may last only as long as necessary to undo the effects of past discrimination.

Related terms: Civil Rights Act of 1991; discrimination; disparate impact; disparate treatment; protected class; Title VII.

after-acquired evidence

After-acquired evidence refers to information an employer learns after firing an employee that would have justified firing the employee in the first place. After-acquired evidence may be used by the employer in a wrongful termination lawsuit to limit the damages available to an employee who was wrongfully fired.

You can be fired after you're fired? Here's how it works. Let's say an employer fires its chief financial officer (CFO) because it wants to hire someone younger for the job. The employee files an age discrimination lawsuit. During the discovery phrase of trial preparations, when the parties gather and exchange information and documents, the employer learns that the employee falsified her resume, which said that she graduated from Yale University and received an MBA from Harvard Business School. In fact, the employee dropped out of Yale after two years, never completed her undergraduate degree, and never attended business school. The company required all applicants for the CFO position to have a college degree and an MBA, and would not have hired the employee had it known that her credentials were false. Even if the employee has a slam-dunk age discrimination case, her damages will be limited to what she would have earned between when she was wrongfully fired (because of her age) and when the employer discovered the evidence for which it could have fired her legally (résumé fraud).

Copying Confidential Documents Leads to Limited Damages

The U.S. Supreme Court first recognized the after-acquired evidence theory in *McKennon v. Nashville Banner Publishing Company*, 513 U.S. 352 (1995), an age discrimination case. Christine McKennon, a 30-year employee grew concerned that she might be fired because of her age. She photocopied several confidential documents relating to the company's financial condition, brought them home, and showed them to her husband as "insurance" and "protection" against losing her job. The company terminated her employment, claiming that it was part of a reduction in force plan to cut costs; McKennon believed it was age discrimination and filed a lawsuit.

During her pretrial deposition, McKennon revealed that she had taken the financial documents. The company filed a motion for summary judgment, claiming that even if it had been motivated by age discrimination when it discharged McKennon, her misconduct gave the company good cause to fire her. Therefore, the company argued, McKennon wasn't entitled to win her age discrimination claim. The company won its motion, and McKennon appealed all the way to the Supreme Court.

The Supreme Court first found that after-acquired evidence doesn't affect the employer's liability for discrimination. If the employer had discriminatory motives for firing the employee, later evidence of the employee's misconduct doesn't change that fact. However, the Court also found that after-acquired evidence should be considered in determining damages. Back pay, for example, should be measured from the date of the discriminatory firing until the date the employer discovered the after-acquired evidence. Beyond that date, the employer had a legitimate reason to fire the employee, so it shouldn't be liable for her continuing lost wages.

An employer who wants to rely on the after-acquired evidence defense must be able to show that it would have fired or never hired the employee if it had known about the employee's fraud or misconduct sooner. If, for example, the company's past two CFOs didn't have MBAs or college degrees either, the company might have a harder time proving that it wouldn't have hired the CFO if it knew her credentials were false. If, on the other hand, the company's employee handbook states that résumé fraud is grounds for termination, and the company has fired other employees when it learned that they had falsified their credentials, the company would more likely be entitled to rely on this defense.

Related terms: age discrimination; wrongful termination.

age discrimination

An employer commits age discrimination when it treats an employee or applicant differently because of the person's age. The federal Age Discrimination in Employment Act (ADEA) prohibits age discrimination against those who are at least 40 years old. Most states also have laws prohibiting age discrimination, and some don't apply this 40-year-old age limit. A few states protect employees only until their 70th birthday.

Age discrimination can happen at any stage of the employment process, from hiring to promotions, benefits, compensation, and layoffs. Often, age discrimination cases include evidence of age-related stereotypes or comments that indicate a lack of respect for older workers, such as statements about "senior moments" or old dogs who can't learn new tricks; comments about wanting to bring in younger (or more "energetic" or "youthful") employees; and assumptions about older workers' knowledge or skills (for example, that they aren't tech-savvy or up-to-date on the latest trends).

Related terms: Age Discrimination in Employment Act; Older Workers Benefit Protection Act.

A

54 Is the New "Old Fuddy-Duddy": Google Sued for Age Discrimination

The California Supreme Court reinstated a fired manager's age discrimination lawsuit against the search-engine giant Google, finding that the trial court shouldn't have thrown the case out before a jury heard the facts. Brian Reid, who was fired at the grand old age of 54, claimed that he was demoted into a dead-end position and later fired because of his age.

- **Age-related comments.** He was referred to as an "old man," an "old guy," and an "old fuddy-duddy," told he was "slow," "fuzzy," "sluggish," and "lethargic," and told that his ideas were "obsolete" and "too old to matter." He was also told that he should replace the CD jewel case that served as his office placard with an LP. (Apparently, when only 2% of a company's workforce has celebrated a 41st birthday, as was true of Google at the time, those in their 50s start looking like visitors from the Stone Age.)

- **Email messages suggesting that Google's managers were trying to get their stories straight.** One message said that the company's decision to give Reid no bonus might not be "consistent with all similarly situated performers"; if that wasn't clear enough, the message also suggested giving Reid a bonus and severance package "to avoid a judge concluding we acted harshly." A company vice president asked for guidance on what to say if Reid asked for a position in another department, asking that the HR Director "make sure I am completely prepped" and "get me clear on this" before she had to talk to Reid. After much back and forth, the HR Director concluded, "We'll all agree on the job elimination angle."

- **Statistical evidence.** As a company that's perhaps best known for an algorithm, Google will need an answer for the claims of Reid's expert witness, a statistician who reported a statistically significant negative correlation between age and performance rating, as well as age and bonus amount, at Google. For every ten-year increase in age, the statistician found a corresponding decrease in performance rating and a 29% decrease in bonus.

Reid v. Google, 113 Cal. Rptr. 3d 327 (Cal. Supreme Court 2010).

Age Discrimination in Employment Act

The federal Age Discrimination in Employment Act (ADEA) was passed in 1967 to address the difficulties older employees face in the workplace, including mandatory retirement cutoffs and discrimination in hiring. The ADEA prohibits discrimination in every aspect of employment against employees and applicants who are at least 40 years old, with a few limited exceptions to recognize that advanced age may, in some circumstances, affect our ability to perform certain jobs effectively.

Congress amended the ADEA in 1990 when it passed the Older Workers Benefit Protection Act (OWBPA), which added detailed provisions on employment benefits (some of which may become more costly for employers to provide as employees age) and waivers. That law is covered in a separate entry.

Who the ADEA covers. The ADEA applies to federal and local governments, as well as private employers that have at least 20 employees. State government employees are also protected by the law, but they don't have the right to sue their employers to enforce those rights; only the Equal Employment Opportunity Commission may sue a state to protect state employees from age discrimination.

Discrimination prohibited by the ADEA. The ADEA protects employees who are at least 40 years old from harassment or discrimination based on their age. If an employee or applicant is denied a benefit (such as a job, promotion, or job-related perk) because of his or her age, it doesn't matter if the employee who received the benefit is also at least 40 years old.

> **EXAMPLE:** A company decides to promote a 45-year-old employee rather than a 65-year-old employee, based on age. Under the ADEA, that's age discrimination, even though the younger employee is old enough to be protected by the ADEA.

Employees may not claim "reverse" age discrimination even if they are 40 or older. For example, a 45-year-old employee may not claim age discrimination because older workers received better

A

benefits. If the older worker is treated better, the ADEA has not been violated.

Actually, you really *are* too old. Employers may use age as a basis for employment decisions in a few limited circumstances. If an employer who relies on one of these exceptions is sued for age discrimination, it will bear the burden of proving that its actions fell within the exception:

- **Bona fide seniority system.** An employer may rely on a bona fide seniority system (one that gives a preference to employees who have more tenure with the company) as a basis for employment decisions, even if that results in more favorable treatment of younger workers. Because older workers tend to have more seniority than younger workers, however, they are unlikely to be disadvantaged by an employer's reliance on its seniority system, which makes this a seldom-used exception.

- **Bona fide occupational qualification (BFOQ).** An employer may discriminate based on age in filling a position if the job, by its very nature, must be filled by an employee of a certain age. This typically comes up in regards to age limits for a job. To prove a BFOQ, the employer must show that the age limit is reasonably necessary to the essence of the employer's business, and that (1) all or substantially all people who are older than the age limit would be unable to perform the job, or (2) some people who are older than the age limit would be unable to perform the job and testing each person individually to determine whether he or she could perform the job would be impossible or highly impractical. If the employer's goal in using the BFOQ is public safety, the employer must show not only that the challenged age limit achieves that goal, but also that there is no acceptable alternative that is less discriminatory.

- **Bona fide employee benefit plan.** In some situations, an employer may reduce benefits paid to older workers if the employer acts in accordance with a benefit plan (see below).

- **Firefighters and peace officers.** State and local governments may adopt a mandatory retirement age of 55 or older for firefighters and law enforcement officers.
- **Bona fide executives and high policymakers.** Employers may require a high-ranking employee to retire or step down to a lesser position if all of the following are true:
  - The employee is at least 65 years old.
  - The employee has worked for at least the last two years in that position.
  - The employee is entitled to an immediate, nonforfeitable annual benefit of at least $44,000 from the employer. A benefit is "immediate" if payments start (or could have started, at the employee's election) within 60 days after retirement. A benefit is "nonforfeitable" if no plan provisions could cause payments to stop. For example, if the plan requires payments to be suspended if the employee files a lawsuit, that benefit is forfeitable.

Special rules for disparate impact claims. Employees claiming age discrimination may make a disparate impact claim, alleging that a facially neutral policy or practice had a disproportionate negative impact on older workers. To win a claim like this, the employee must point to a specific practice that led to the difference in treatment. If the employee identifies such a practice, the employer may escape liability by proving that the practice was based on a "reasonable factor other than age" (RFOA).

ADEA enforcement. Like Title VII, the federal law that prohibits discrimination on the basis of race, color, national origin, gender, and religion, the ADEA is enforced by the Equal Employment Opportunity Commission (EEOC). Employees who want to file an age discrimination lawsuit under the ADEA must first file a charge with the EEOC in order to preserve their right to sue.

ADEA damages. If a court finds that an employer has violated the ADEA, the employer may be ordered to do any or all of the following:

- Pay the employee all wages, benefits, and other forms of compensation lost as a result of the discrimination.
- Take action to remedy the results of the discrimination by, for example, reinstating or promoting the employee. If the court finds that such action is impractical (for example, if the employee's position has been eliminated or the work relationship is irrevocably poisoned), the court may require the employer to pay front pay—compensation for future lost earnings—instead.
- Pay a penalty (called "liquidated damages") equal to all of the wages, benefits, and other compensation owed the employee at the time of trial. This remedy is available only if the employer knew that its conduct was illegal or showed reckless disregard as to whether its conduct violated the ADEA.
- Pay the employee's court costs and attorney fees.

Related terms: age discrimination; bona fide seniority system; disparate treatment; disparate impact; Equal Employment Opportunity Commission: Older Workers Benefit Protection Act: reasonable factor other than age; Title VII.

agency shop

An agency shop is an establishment in which all workers must either be members of the union or pay fees to the union as a condition of getting or keeping a job. An agency shop is created through a union security agreement between the employer and the union, by which the employer agrees that it will fire any worker who does not either join or pay fees to the union. The union is obligated to represent everyone in the bargaining unit, regardless of their union membership. By requiring everyone to either join or financially support the union, these agreements prevent "free riders," employees who benefit from the union's work without having to pay for it.

Some states have passed laws, called "right to work" statutes, which prohibit union security agreements. In these states, every unionized workplace must be an "open shop": one in which employees are free to choose whether or not to join or support the union.

Related terms: bargaining unit; closed shop; open shop; right to work laws; union security agreement.

alternative base period

See base period.

alternative dispute resolution

The many ways people can work out their problems without going to court (or short of receiving a verdict) are referred to as alternative dispute resolution, or ADR.

Court-ordered ADR. Sometimes, ADR is required by a court. Many court systems require the parties to a lawsuit to try to resolve things through ADR before the trial begins. For example, some courts use an early neutral evaluation (ENE) program, in which an outside third party sits down with both sides, listens to their explanation of the issues, and tries to help them resolve the dispute, often by giving them a frank assessment of the strengths and weaknesses of their evidence.

Contractual ADR. ADR may also be required by contract. An employment agreement may provide that the parties will use particular types of ADR to resolve any disputes that arise under the contract, rather than going to court. Some employers require new employees to sign arbitration agreements, in which they agree to resolve any disputes over the employment relationship in arbitration. Typically, these agreements require employees to give up their right to sue.

Voluntary ADR. Parties to a dispute can also voluntarily choose ADR, whether or not a lawsuit has been filed. For example, a company might hire a mediator to help resolve some communication problems among members of the executive team. Or, an employee who has filed a lawsuit against an employer might propose that the two sides try to mediate the dispute before it goes to trial.

A

When most people refer to ADR, they are usually thinking of either mediation or arbitration.

Mediation. In mediation, a neutral third person helps the parties try to come to a mutual resolution of their dispute. The mediator has no power to order anyone to do anything; rather, the mediator facilitates discussions and negotiations between the parties, trying to help them identify areas of possible agreement and compromise. If the parties reach an agreement, they often memorialize it in a written settlement or contract.

Arbitration. Arbitration is more like a court proceeding, in that there is a decision maker (the arbitrator or panel of arbitrators), evidence is presented, and the arbitrator makes a final decision that both parties must abide by (if the arbitration is "binding").

ADR within a company. Some employers adopt ADR-type systems employees can use to raise complaints or concerns within the company. These systems might include:

- **Open-door policies.** These policies invite employees to bring their concerns and ideas to their immediate supervisor or to others within the company (such as any company officer or the human resource department).

- **Ombudsperson programs.** Some companies designate an ombudsperson to be available to employees who have complaints or concerns. Typically, the ombudsperson operates outside of the company's formal management structure, offering counseling, options for handling workplace problems, and the possibility of bringing in the employee's manager or coworkers to resolve issues. They are most common in large institutionalized settings (such as colleges and hospitals) and larger companies, where individuals can easily feel lost in the shuffle. Having a place to get help with their concerns can help diminish the feeling of being just another cog in the machine.

- **Peer review programs.** In a peer review program, employee complaints that cannot be resolved informally are heard by a group, typically composed of some employees and some managers, which decides how the issue should be handled. Companies often limit the issues a peer review panel can decide in order to reserve management's right to make policy and personnel decisions. For example, a peer review panel might have the authority to decree that an employee should report to a different supervisor, but not that the supervisor should be fired or demoted.

- **Step grievance procedures.** Modeled on union grievance programs, a step grievance procedure is a set of increasingly more formal options for handling complaints, each offered as a way to take a complaint further if the prior step doesn't resolve the issue to the employee's satisfaction. For example, the process might begin by asking the employee to discuss the issue with a manager. If the employee isn't satisfied, he or she might have the option of filing a formal complaint, to be heard by a peer review panel. After that, an appeal might be available, followed by mediation or arbitration.

Related terms: arbitration; mediation.

Americans with Disabilities Act

The Americans with Disabilities Act (ADA) is a landmark civil rights law, passed in 1990, which protects people with disabilities from discrimination in many contexts, including employment, government services, public accommodations, and telecommunications. The ADA's main employment provisions prohibit employers from discriminating against qualified people with disabilities. This prohibition applies to all terms, conditions, and privileges of employment, and protects both applicants and current employees. The ADA also requires employers to provide reasonable accommodations—modifications to the job or work environment—to enable qualified people with disabilities to perform their jobs.

The Americans with Disabilities Act Amendments Act (ADAAA). In 2008, President Bush signed the ADAAA, which makes a number of changes and clarifications to the ADA. The stated purpose of the ADAAA was to make clear that Congress intended for the term "disability" to be interpreted broadly, as a national mandate to end discrimination against people with disabilities. Several Supreme Court decisions had limited the scope of the ADA, and the ADAAA explicitly overturns those decisions.

Who has to follow the ADA? The following employers have to comply with the ADA's employment provisions:

- private employers with 15 or more employees
- employment agencies
- labor organizations
- joint labor/management committees, and
- local governments.

The ADA doesn't cover the federal government when it acts as an employer, but a similar law—the Rehabilitation Act of 1973—does.

State employers are required to follow the ADA, but unlike private employees, state employees may not sue their employer for money damages for violating the law. However, state employees may sue their employers for injunctive relief; that is, the employees may ask the court to require the state to take some action or refrain from taking some action. For example, a job applicant could sue the state to prohibit it from requiring all applicants to take a physical, or to require it to provide reasonable test-taking accommodations to applicants who must take civil service exams. State employees may also be able to sue their employers under state antidiscrimination laws. And, the Equal Employment Opportunity Commission (EEOC), the federal agency responsible for interpreting and enforcing federal antidiscrimination laws, may sue state employers on behalf of state employees whose ADA rights have been violated.

Who is protected by the ADA? The ADA protects all qualified people with disabilities who are either current or prospective employees of a covered employer, including part-time and probationary employees. To get the benefits of the ADA, a person must be qualified for the position and must have a disability as defined by the ADA.

Qualified for the position. A person is qualified for a position only if both of the following are true:

- The person satisfies the prerequisites for the position. For example, the person has the required educational degrees, employment experience, skills, licenses, and training.
- The person is able to perform the essential functions of the position, with or without a reasonable accommodation from the employer. Essential functions are the fundamental duties of a job; marginal or minor responsibilities don't count. A function is essential if, for example, the job exists to perform that function (as a pilot's essential function is to fly a plane), only a few employees can perform the function, or the function is so highly specialized that the employer hires people into the position because of their expertise in performing that function.

EXAMPLE 1: Rob has a disability that limits his use of his hands. He applies for a position as a legal secretary. Using a computer for word processing, data entry, and calendaring is an essential function of the job: It's the primary purpose of his position. Rob is physically unable to type, but he can do everything he needs to do using voice-activated software, a reasonable accommodation.

EXAMPLE 2: Rob applies for a job as an electrician. He worked as an electrician before his disability developed, and he has extensive knowledge of the field. Because he can no longer use his hands, Rob proposes that other employees should do all of the physical labor, while he plans projects, directs the work, and interacts with the clients. However, the company already has enough project managers; the job it's trying to fill is for an on-site electrician. Rob isn't qualified for the job because he can't perform its essential functions.

What is a disability? The ADA defines a disability as a physical or mental impairment that substantially limits a major life activity.

Major life activities are those functions that are of central importance to daily life, such as seeing, breathing, working, and caring for oneself. Major bodily functions are also major life activities: If a person's immune system, normal cell growth, or digestive, bowel, bladder, neurological, brain, respiratory, circulatory, endocrine, or reproductive functions are impaired, that constitutes a disability.

An impairment qualifies as a disability even if it is episodic or in remission, as long as it substantially limits a major life activity when it is active. This rule, added by the ADAAA, is intended to ensure that obviously serious conditions, like cancer and multiple sclerosis, are treated as disabilities, even if the degree to which they impair someone's day-to-day functioning waxes and wanes.

Another rule added by the ADAAA has to do with "mitigating" measures: drugs, prosthetic devices, implements (such as a cane, wheelchair, or hearing aid), and other items a person uses to counter-act the effects of an impairment. Other than ordinary prescription glasses and contact lenses, the ADAAA says that mitigating measures may not be considered when determining whether someone has a disability. Under previous Supreme Court cases, the employer could take mitigating measures into account when assessing someone's condition, which left many people with serious impairments outside of the ADA's protections. For example, someone whose diabetes or epilepsy was controlled with medication would not have been considered to have a disability before the ADAAA.

Alcohol and drug use. Someone who currently uses illegal drugs isn't protected by the ADA, even if the person is addicted. However, someone who no longer uses drugs illegally and is participating in or has completed a drug rehabilitation program is protected from discrimination. An employee who is an alcoholic is also protected by the ADA, but the employer may apply its usual standards of behavior and performance. For example, an employer may discipline an employee who misses work without notice, even if the employee is an alcoholic and was absent because of a binge-drinking episode. What the employer may not do is punish the employee simply for being an alcoholic (for example, because the employee attends

Alcoholics Anonymous meetings or takes prescription medication to curb the urge to drink).

Past and perceived impairments also count. The ADA doesn't just protect those who currently have a disability. It also protects those with a history of disability (for example, someone who had a stroke or suffered an episode of postpartum depression in the past). And, it protects those who are perceived, even incorrectly, as having a disability (these are referred to as "regarded as" claims). Although those who are incorrectly regarded as having a disability aren't entitled to a reasonable accommodation (because they don't actually have a disability), they are protected from discrimination.

> **EXAMPLE:** Jonas has a discernible stutter. He is able to speak clearly and be understood; he just occasionally gets stuck on a word. Jonas is up for a promotion that would require him to give a monthly report to a company's board of directors. His manager decides not to promote him, based on the incorrect belief that Jonas's stutter would prevent him from doing the presentations. Jonas isn't entitled to a reasonable accommodation because he doesn't need one: He is perfectly capable of giving a monthly report without any assistance. But Jonas is entitled to be protected from discrimination based on perceptions about his condition, which means he shouldn't be denied the promotion based on his stutter.

Rules for medical examinations and medical records. Under the ADA, an employer may require job applicants to take a medical exam only if all four of these requirements are met:
- The exam may be required only after the employer has made a conditional offer of employment.
- All applicants must be required to take the exam, whether or not they have a disability.
- The exam must be the final stage in the screening process.
- The results of the exam must be kept in separate, confidential medical files.

A

This final requirement applies to all records relating to an applicant's or employee's disability, not just records of medical exams. These records must be kept confidential, and may be revealed only under limited circumstances.

Related terms: Americans with Disabilities Act Amendments Act; disability; reasonable accommodation.

Americans with Disabilities Act Amendments Act

The Americans with Disabilities Act Amendments Act (ADAAA), signed by President Bush in 2008, makes a number of changes to the Americans with Disabilities Act (ADA). The ADAAA signaled Congress's frustration with the narrow way in which courts— particularly the U.S. Supreme Court—were interpreting the ADA, with the result that many people who should have been helped by the law were seeing their cases thrown out of court.

The ADAAA states that Congress intended for the term "disability" to be interpreted broadly, as a national mandate to end discrimination against people with disabilities. The law indicates that the courts have ignored this mandate, instead interpreting the term "disability" in such a limited way that very few people qualify for the ADA's protections. The law directs courts that their primary focus in ADA cases should be on whether the employer met its obligations under the law, and that determining whether the employee or applicant has a disability should not require extensive analysis.

To ensure that the ADA is interpreted more expansively, the ADAAA includes these changes:

- To ensure that more people are protected by the ADA, the EEOC is directed to change its interpretation of "substantially limits a major life activity" (the legal definition of a disability) to set a less restrictive standard for coverage.
- Major life activities include major bodily functions, such as the proper functioning of the immune system and normal cell growth.

The Case That Broke Congress's Back:
Toyota Motor Manufacturing v. Williams

Ella Williams worked on the Quality Control Inspections Operations (QCIO) team at Toyota, checking the shell and paint on cars passing on a conveyer. Williams was diagnosed with bilateral carpal tunnel syndrome and tendinitis while working on an engine assembly line. Initially, her work on the QCIO team included only two tasks, which she was able to perform.

But when additional tasks were added that required her to hold her hand and arms at shoulder height for several hours at a time, Williams developed additional problems, which caused her pain in the neck and shoulders. Williams asked Toyota to let her do only the two tasks that didn't cause her pain. Toyota refused, and Williams was eventually fired for poor attendance. Williams then sued Toyota for refusing to accommodate her disability.

Under the ADA, an employee has a disability if she has a physical or mental impairment that substantially limits one or more of her major life activities. Williams argued that her medical conditions substantially limited her ability to perform manual tasks. The Court of Appeals for the 6th Circuit agreed, finding that Williams's conditions substantially limited her ability to perform a class of manual activities related to her tasks at work. Toyota then appealed to the Supreme Court.

The Supreme Court found that it is not enough for an employee to show that she cannot perform the manual tasks her job requires: instead, she must show that her condition prevents or severely restricts her ability to do manual activities of central importance to most people's daily lives—like household chores, bathing, and brushing their teeth. The Court pointed out that some jobs require unique manual tasks that are not part of daily life and to say that people who can't perform these tasks are disabled would expand the reach of the ADA beyond what Congress intended when it passed the law.

Congress's response? Don't be so quick to tell us what we intended, Supreme Court. Congress mentions this case four times in the ADAAA, all with a strong tone of disapproval. In fact, one of the stated purposes of the ADAAA is to reject the standards of "substantially limits" and "major life activities" expressed in the *Toyota* case; another is to express the sense of Congress that the *Toyota* case "creates an inappropriately high level of limitation necessary to obtain coverage under the ADA." So there.

- Impairments can be disabilities even if they are in remission or episodic, as long as they substantially limit a major life activity when they are active.
- An employee may not make a "regarded as" claim of disability discrimination based on a minor and transitory impairment (one with an expected duration of six months or less). (In a "regarded as" claim, the employee argues that the employer discriminated against the employee not because the employee actually had a disability, but because the employer incorrectly regarded the employee as having a disability.)
- Mitigating measures, other than ordinary prescription glasses and contact lenses, may not be considered in determining whether an employee has a disability.
- Employees or applicants who qualify for the ADA's protection solely because their employer "regards" them as having a disability (in other words, employees who do not actually have a disability) are not entitled to reasonable accommodations.

Related terms: Americans with Disabilities Act; disability; major life activity; reasonable accommodation.

arbitration

Arbitration is an out-of-court procedure for resolving disputes in which one or more neutral third parties (called an arbitrator or arbitration panel) hears evidence and arguments from both sides, and then reaches a decision. (Because it's an alternative to litigation, arbitration is a form of alternative dispute resolution or ADR.) Arbitration has long been used to resolve commercial and labor disputes, but its popularity is growing as a means of resolving problems of all kinds.

Arbitration can be binding or nonbinding. In binding arbitration, the arbitrator or panel issues a decision that both parties are legally obligated to follow, just like a court order. Typically, it's difficult to appeal an arbitrator's ruling, except in cases where the arbitrator had a conflict of interest or was biased in some way. In nonbinding arbitration, either party is free to reject the arbitrator's decision and take the dispute to court, as if the arbitration had never taken place. Binding arbitration is far more common, particularly in employment disputes.

Although arbitration may be required by statute or court order, it's most often contractual. Sometimes, both parties agree ahead of time that it makes more sense to resolve their disputes outside of court. Sometimes, one side insists, as a condition of entering into an employment relationship, consumer agreement, or other contract, that the other side must give up its right to take disputes to court, and instead agree to resolve disagreements through arbitration. In the latter case, if the employee, consumer, or other person on the receiving end of the arbitration agreement later wants to sue, that person will have to prove that the arbitration provision is invalid.

Arbitration as a condition of employment. Contractual arbitration occurs only if both parties agree to it, and only according to their agreement. In employment disputes, however, arbitration usually works somewhat differently. Typically, an employee is asked to sign a standard arbitration agreement upon beginning employment, and there's no room for negotiation. The employee has the choice of signing the agreement as is, with terms of the employer's choosing, and keeping the job; or refusing to sign the agreement and looking for other work.

Because of the disparity in bargaining power between employers and employees, and because arbitration agreements require employees to give up a significant right—to take their disputes to court—these agreement are examined more closely when challenged in court than an arbitration agreement between equal parties (two businesses, for example). This is particularly so when an employer wants to compel an employee to give up the right to litigate claims over important statutory rights, such as the rights created by laws that prohibit discrimination and harassment.

Types of Arbitration

There are some hybrid forms of arbitration, including:

- **Med/arb** (pronounced "meed-arb"). The parties agree to try to resolve their dispute through mediation. However, they also agree that if the mediation doesn't result in a settlement, the mediator (or another neutral party) can act as an arbitrator and make a binding decision. Med/arb gives the assurance that the dispute will be resolved, one way or the other. The parties will either reach their own agreement or one will be imposed on them.

- **High-low arbitration.** Like most types of arbitration, high-low arbitration is binding on both parties. However, to reduce the risk of an unacceptable award, the parties agree in advance to high and low limits on the arbitrator's authority. For example, they might agree that the arbitrator can award no less than $300,000 and no more than $500,000 to the wining party.

- **Baseball arbitration.** Along with evidence and arguments, each side gives the arbitrator a figure for which he or she would be willing to settle the case. The arbitrator must then choose one party's figure or the other; no other award can be made.

- **Night baseball arbitration.** As in baseball arbitration, each side chooses a value for the case and exchanges it with the other side. However, these figures are not revealed to the arbitrator (the arbitrator is kept *in the dark*, get it?) The arbitrator makes a decision about the value of the case, and then the parties must accept whichever of their own figures is closer to the arbitrator's award.

The Supreme Court has held that employees may be required to arbitrate (rather than litigate) claims arising out of their employment if they have contractually agreed to do so. However, these arbitration agreements are enforceable only if they meet certain minimum standards, intended to make sure that the underlying rights at issue are preserved and enforced. No one factor or combination of factors is dispositive; instead, courts tend to evaluate all of the circumstances to decide whether the agreement is weighted so heavily in the employer's favor as to be unconscionable, given the disparity in bargaining power. The factors courts consider include:

- **Who pays the cost.** Agreements that require employees to pay more to arbitrate than they would have to pay to litigate a case are frowned upon.
- **How much discovery is allowed.** Giving the parties only limited rights to discovery—the process of exchanging documents, testimony, and evidence before the dispute is argued—tends to favor employers, who already have access to company records, employees, and managers.
- **What damages are allowed.** Agreements that limit the amount an employee can win to far less than the employee could be awarded in court might not be enforced.
- **Who has to arbitrate (and which claims).** Agreements that require employees to arbitrate all claims against the company but allow the company to take all or some claims to litigation might not pass legal muster. Some companies try to get around this requirement by not mentioning who must arbitrate, but only which claims must be arbitrated—and explicitly allowing litigation for claims typically brought only by employers (such as disputes over theft of trade secrets or violation of the duty of loyalty).

Related terms: alternative dispute resolution; mediation.

at-will employment

An employee who works at will may quit at any time, and can be fired at any time, for any reason that is not illegal. (Illegal reasons for firing include discrimination or retaliation, for example.) An at-will employee has no job security: The employee or the employer can end the employment relationship at any time, with or without cause, as long as neither breaks the law in doing so.

A

In every state but Montana, employees are legally presumed to work at will unless they can prove otherwise. Such proof usually takes the form of documents or oral statements by the employer. (In Montana, employees who have completed an initial probationary period—or have worked for the employer for at least six months, if the employer doesn't use a probationary period—may not be fired without cause.)

Employment documents. Many employers take pains to point out, in their written policies, applications, handbooks, job evaluations, or other employment-related documents, that their employees work at will. If an employee has signed a document agreeing that he or she is an at-will employee, that determines the issue. If the employee manual or other written workplace policies state that employees can be fired at any time or can be fired without cause, that's evidence of at-will status, even if the term "at will" isn't used. On the other hand, some employers have written policies that require good cause to fire, provide an exclusive list of reasons for which employees can be fired, or otherwise provide employees some job protections. If an employer has adopted these kinds of policies, they may undo the at-will presumption.

Similarly, an employee who has signed an employment contract that promises job security is not employed at will. For example, if an employee has a two-year contract that states the employee can be fired during the contract term only for committing a crime, then he is not an at-will employee. If the employee is fired for any reason not specified in the contract, he may well have a legal claim against the employer for breach of contract.

Statements by the employer. If an employer makes any statements, either during the hiring process or after, indicating that employees will be fired only for good cause, that may also undo the employee's at-will status. For example, an employer might say, "You'll always have a home here as long as you do a good job," or "We only fire employees who are unable to meet our performance standards, even after coaching and training." In this situation, especially if the comments have been made repeatedly or played a big role in the employee's decision to take the job, the employer may have restricted its ability to fire at will.

On the other hand, if an employee is told during the hiring process or afterwards that he or she will be an at-will employee, the employer will certainly rely on that statement as proof that it reserved the right to fire for any reason, if it later has to defend a wrongful termination lawsuit.

Related terms: employment contract; good cause; implied contract; wrongful termination.

back pay

An employee who wins a lawsuit against a current or former employer may be awarded damages for "back pay": what the employee would have earned, through the date of the judgment in the lawsuit, if the employer hadn't done something wrong. This might be the difference between what the employee earned and what she would have earned had she not been illegally denied a promotion or paid less than the minimum wage, or the amount an employee would have earned had he not been illegally fired.

> **EXAMPLE:** Bob is fired from his job on March 1, 2011. At the time, he was earning a monthly salary of $5,000. He files a wrongful termination lawsuit claiming that he was illegally fired for whistleblowing. He wins the lawsuit on June 1, 2012. Bob could be awarded back pay damages of $75,000 because he lost 15 months of his salary.

Employees have to look for work. Fired employees who sue for back pay have a legal obligation to "mitigate" their damages by looking for work. In other words, an employee can't simply sit idle for months, waiting to win a lawsuit. Instead, the employee must make diligent efforts to find another job. And, if those efforts pay off, the amount the employee actually earned is subtracted from the award. If the employee doesn't even try to find another job, the former employer might try to have the damages award reduced by the amount the employee would have earned had he or she really looked for another job.

B

EXAMPLE: Let's say Bob was previously employed as a finish carpenter. He tries for months to find a comparable position, but no one is hiring. After nine months, he accepts a position with a landscaping company, earning $2,500 a month. His back pay award would be $60,000: nine months of lost pay at $5,000 per month, plus six months of back pay at $2,500 per month (the $5,000 he used to earn minus the $2,500 he is earning now). Bob's former employer would have a tough time proving that he should have earned more, given Bob's diligent job search, recession-struck profession, and willingness to take a job that paid a lot less.

Now let's say that the market for finish carpenters in Bob's area is going gangbusters, but he sat around for nine months before looking for work. In the second week of his job search, he was offered a full-time position at about what he used to earn, but he decides to work part-time instead, so he can attend law school. In this situation, Bob's back pay award would be pretty small. Although he didn't actually earn much, he didn't look for work—and he didn't take a comparable position when it was offered. In this situation, Bob's former employer has a good argument that Bob's failure to earn more after he was fired is due to Bob's choices, not the employer's actions.

background check

When an employer runs a background check, it typically verifies that the information the applicant supplied is accurate and complete. For example, an employer might check an applicant's academic records and contact an applicant's former employers to make sure that the applicant has the degrees and experience claimed on his or her resume.

Background checks can also go beyond the information an applicant provides. For example, if the employer is hiring a delivery driver, it might check applicants' driving records. Some employers check applicant credit reports or criminal records, as well.

B

Employers that hire a third party (such as a private investigator or background checking firm) to conduct background checks must comply with the Fair Credit Reporting Act (FCRA). Among other things, this means the employer must get the applicant's consent in advance and provide certain information to the applicant. Even if the employer does the checking, it still must comply with the FCRA if it gets a report on the applicant from an outside business that compiles such reports regularly, such as a credit bureau.

Related term: Fair Credit Reporting Act.

bargaining unit

A bargaining unit is a group of employees whom a union represents (or seeks to represent) in collective bargaining with an employer. What constitutes an appropriate bargaining unit is often a source of dispute between labor and management, because a union may represent a group of employees only if it receives the support of a majority of employees in the bargaining unit.

To be part of the same bargaining unit, employees must have "a community of interests." In other words, their concerns and circumstances must be sufficiently common that it makes sense for one union to negotiate on behalf of all of the unit's members. Some of the factors a court or the National Labor Relations Board will consider when deciding whether a bargaining unit is appropriate include whether the employees are similar in respect to skills, job duties, supervision, working conditions, work site, and benefits. Usually professional and nonprofessional employees will not be combined in a single bargaining unit.

A single workplace may contain more than one bargaining unit (for example, the butchers, checkers, and janitors in a grocery store might all be members of different bargaining units). A bargaining unit can also include employees from different facilities (for example, all of the cashiers in a chain of retail stores). Employees of different employers may also be combined into one bargaining unit, if the

B

employers have formed an association or banded together for purposes of bargaining with the union.

Related terms: collective bargaining; manager; National Labor Relations Board.

base period

To determine whether an employee is entitled to unemployment insurance benefits, each state establishes a base period, typically a one-year stretch. Depending on the state's rules, an employee must have worked a certain number of weeks, earned a certain amount of compensation, or both, during the base period in order to be eligible for unemployment. In almost every state, the base period is the earliest four of the last five complete quarters of the calendar year immediately before the employee lost his or her job.

> **EXAMPLE:** Kwame is laid off in August 2011. The base period for his unemployment claim is April 1, 2010 through March 31, 2011. The last complete quarter of the calendar year before he was laid off was April 1, 2011 through June 30, 2011, so the base period is the four quarters preceding that one.

What about the last six months? As you can see, the way the base period is measured doesn't count the employee's most recent employment. Depending on when an out-of-work employee files a claim for unemployment, almost six months of work might not be included in the base period. Recognizing this, many states have created an exception for workers who don't have enough hours of work or earnings in the base period to qualify. In these states, employees don't have to skip the last complete calendar quarter. Instead, they can use an alternative base period that includes the last four calendar quarters. This measurement will include more of their most recent work history.

Employees on medical leave may get a longer base period. Some states also have an exception for those who have been out of work for a longer period, typically because of a job-related illness, injury, or disability. These former employees may be entitled to an extended base period, which looks at the worker's hours and earnings before the worker was injured, even if that work history falls outside of the usual base period.

Work and earnings requirements. Some states require employees to have worked a certain amount of time during the base period to be eligible for benefits. In almost every state that imposes this requirement, the employee must have done some work in at least two of the four calendar quarters that make up the base period.

Most states impose an earnings requirement for the base period—either instead of or in addition to the work requirement—before an employee will be eligible for unemployment compensation. States measure the minimum earnings requirement in a variety of ways. Here are the most common:

- **Flat dollar amount.** Some states require workers to earn a minimum amount of wages ($2,500, for example) during the base period.

- **High-quarter wages.** Some states require workers to earn a set minimum during their highest paid quarter of the base period. This requirement may stand alone (for example, the employee must have earned at least $1,300 during the highest paid quarter of the base period to qualify) or may be combined with an additional requirement for the entire base period. In some states, for instance, employees must not only earn a minimum amount during the highest paid quarter, but must also earn a multiple of that amount during the entire base period. This is another way of ensuring that the employee worked at least two quarters during the base period.

> **EXAMPLE:** In Washington, DC, employees must earn at least $1,300 during the highest paid quarter of the base period and at least 1½ times their wages for the highest paid quarter in the entire base period. If Claudette earns $2,200 in her highest paid quarter, she must earn a total of $3,300 during the entire base period to qualify for benefits.

B

- **Multiple of the weekly benefit amount.** In some states, a worker must earn at least a certain multiple of the weekly benefit he or she would receive in order to qualify. The multiple is generally between 30 and 40.

  > **EXAMPLE:** In Wisconsin, the weekly benefit is 4% of the employee's total wages in the highest paid quarter. If Russ earned $5,000 in this highest paid quarter, his weekly benefit would be $200. To be eligible to earn that benefit, Russ must have earned at least 35 times that amount, or $7,000, in the entire base period. Again, this type of requirement ensures that the employee has earnings in at least two quarters of the base period.

Related term: unemployment benefits.

benefits

Benefits are a type of compensation other than wages or salary. Benefits include things like:
- paid time off (vacation time, holidays, sick time, parental leave, and so on)
- insurance coverage (health insurance, dental coverage, vision insurance, disability insurance, and life insurance, for example)
- retirement plans (such as pensions or 401(k) plans)
- payment or subsidies for items or services the employee would otherwise have to buy (for instance, commuting costs, dry cleaning service, or meals in a company cafeteria), or
- items provided by the employer (including a company car, cell phone, or laptop).

Related terms: Consolidated Omnibus Reconciliation Act of 1985 (COBRA); EAP; health care reform; paid time off (PTO); sick leave; vacation.

Who Gets Benefits—And Who Pays for Them?

According to a March 2010 study by the Bureau of Labor Statistics (BLS), medical benefits are available to 71% of employees in the private sector. However, employers don't foot the whole bill for health care coverage: On average, the employer pays 80% of the premium for single coverage, and 70% of the premium for family coverage, with employees picking up the rest of the cost. (You can see the whole report at www.bls.gov.)

Almost two-thirds of employees in private industry have access to some type of retirement benefits, but that doesn't necessarily mean employers are paying the tab. These statistics could include, for example, companies that make a 401(k) plan available for employee contributions, but don't provide a match—as a growing number of companies have chosen to do in the current economic climate. According to a June 2010 study by the consulting firm Towers Watson, 18% of surveyed companies suspended or reduced their 401(k) match since September 2008, and about half of them hadn't restored their match by Spring of 2010.

bereavement leave

Bereavement leave is time off work to attend the funeral or deal with practical matters relating to someone's death. Employees in the United States have no legal right to bereavement leave, so employers that offer it are free to set limits as they see fit. Some employers that choose to offer bereavement leave provide it only for the death of an immediate family member or only to attend the funeral or memorial service, for example, while others are more generous.

BFOQ

See bona fide occupational qualification.

B

blacklisting

Blacklisting means trying to prevent someone from being hired or finding work (as in, "You'll never work in this town again!") More than half of the states have laws that prohibit employers from taking certain actions to prevent former employees from getting a new job. Some prohibit employers from actually creating or circulating a "blacklist" (made up, for example, of employees who are union organizers or supporters). Others are less literal, and prohibit a variety of actions a former employer might take to prevent employees from finding work or to get them fired from a new job. To violate this second type of law, the former employer typically has to make threats or false statements. An employer who is asked to give a reference and makes honest, good faith statements about the reasons an employee was fired isn't guilty of blacklisting.

The Hollywood Ten. A famous historical blacklist took effect in the entertainment industry after World War II. Actors, directors, screenwriters, and others who refused to testify before the House Un-American Activities Committee (HUAC) in 1947 regarding their current or former membership in the Communist party were the first names on the blacklist, the so-called "Hollywood Ten." Shortly after their refusal to testify before HUAC, a group of film industry executives announced that all ten would be fired and would not again be hired until they had sworn that they were not Communists. As HUAC continued its work, the blacklist grew to include others who refused to testify or who were accused of Communist tendencies.

Related terms: defamation; reference.

bona fide occupational qualification

A bona fide occupational qualification (or BFOQ for short) is a very narrow exception to Title VII, the primary federal law that prohibits employment discrimination. Title VII prohibits employers from making employment decisions (such as whom to hire, promote, or fire) on the basis of protected characteristics, including race, color, gender, religion, and national origin. The BFOQ exception allows employers to make decisions on the basis of gender, religion, or national origin (but not race or color) if that characteristic is "a bona fide occupational qualification reasonably necessary to the normal operation of that business or enterprise." In other words, if the nature of the job is such that it can be done only by a woman or a Catholic, the employer may use those criteria in filling the job.

What's a BFOQ? Here are some circumstances in which courts and agencies have found that an employer may rely on the BFOQ defense:

- When hiring prison guards who will perform intimate searches of inmates, an employer may choose employees of the same gender as the inmates.
- When conducting layoffs of nursing staff, a hospital may decide to keep a certain number of male nurses, to make sure they are available to assist with procedures in which male patients must be naked.
- A Jesuit university may reserve a certain number of teaching positions in its philosophy department for Jesuit professors.
- A director may consider only female actors to play a female role (such as Hamlet's mother) in a traditional stage production.

What isn't a BFOQ? Here are some BFOQ arguments that haven't worked:

- Customers prefer to see only women or only men in a particular job position. Courts haven't allowed this one. For example, airlines used to argue that it should be able to hire only female flight attendants, because that's what passengers wanted; courts disagreed.
- Gender stereotypes dictate that only men or women hold certain jobs—for example, that the waiters in high-class restaurants must be men or those working in the nursing profession must be women.

Related terms: religious discrimination; sex discrimination; Title VII.

B

Childbearing and the BFOQ: The *Johnson Controls* Case

The Johnson Controls Company, which manufactures batteries (among other things), prohibited women of child-bearing age from working in jobs that would or could expose them to lead. The company defined "women of child-bearing age" as all women except those whose infertility was medically documented. A group of women brought a class action challenging this fetal protection policy as illegal gender discrimination.

No one disputed that the intentions behind Johnson Controls' policy were good: The company wanted to prevent birth defects. However, the Supreme Court found that the policy was discriminatory. It excluded only women from these jobs, even though evidence shows that men's reproductive systems can also be harmed by lead exposure. Therefore, the policy was illegal unless Johnson Controls could prove a BFOQ defense.

The Supreme Court found that it could not. Johnson Controls argued that it was necessary to exclude women for their own safety (and the safety of their future children). However, the Court found that the BFOQ defense was available only if the protected characteristic in question (here, a woman's reproductive capacity) prevented those employees from doing the job. There was no dispute that women with the ability to bear children could make batteries just as well as anyone else.

The Court pointed out that decisions that could affect the welfare of future children had to be left to the parents, not their employer. The policy, which, as the Court put it, allowed the employer to fire a woman "because of her refusal to submit to sterilization" was illegal:

"It is no more appropriate for the courts than it is for individual employers to decide whether a woman's reproductive role is more important to herself and her family than her economic role. Congress has left this choice to the woman as hers to make."

International Union, UAW v. Johnson Controls, 499 U.S. 187 (1991).

bona fide seniority system

A bona fide seniority system is one that uses length of service with the employer as the primary criterion for deciding who will receive employment opportunities and benefits. For a system to be "bona fide," its essential terms and conditions must be communicated to employees and applied uniformly to everyone.

As a defense to discrimination claims. Under federal antidiscrimination law, an employer may make job decisions based on a bona fide seniority system even if there's an adverse impact on a protected class of employees, as long as the employer had no intent to discriminate.

> **EXAMPLE:** A manufacturing employer in Lewiston, Maine, has to lay off a large number of workers, and it selects employees for layoff strictly based on seniority. Lewiston has seen a huge influx of immigrants from Somalia in the last ten years, and many are employed with the company. Even if a disproportionately large number of employees of Somalian descent lose their jobs in the layoff, it will not be discriminatory as long as the selection was based on seniority, without intent to discriminate.

Related terms: Age Discrimination in Employment Act; Title VII.

boycott

When consumers refuse to patronize a company (or a person or country) because of its policies or practices, that's commonly known as a boycott. For example, many Californians boycotted table grapes grown in the state in the 1960s and '70s, to protest the treatment of farmworkers. Typically, the goal of a boycott is to create pressure for change.

B

That's Mr. Boycott to You

The term "boycott" comes from Captain Charles Cunningham Boycott, a farmer and a land agent for an English landlord in Ireland. After he refused to reduce tenant rents following a poor harvest (and evicted tenants who could not pay), he was subjected to the first recorded boycott. No one in the town, from laborers to merchants to the postman, would have anything to do with him.

Secondary boycotts. Under the National Labor Relations Act, unions may not engage in secondary boycotts. A secondary boycott is one in which the union tries to pressure another company to boycott the company with which it is having a dispute. For example, say the union is striking over wage cuts at a grocery store chain. If the union picketed a large dairy facility to try to get it to stop doing business with the chain, as a way to force the chain to give in to the union's demands, that would be an illegal secondary boycott.

Related term: unfair labor practice.

business necessity

Business necessity is a shorthand term for an employer's defense to a discrimination claim based on disparate impact. An employee who brings a disparate impact claim alleges that an employment policy or practice that appears to be nonbiased (or is "facially neutral") has a disproportionately negative effect on employees with a particular protected characteristic. For example, an employee might claim that requiring all applicants for promotion to achieve a minimum score on a written test had a disparate impact on African American and Latino candidates, or that requiring all applicants to be able to lift 50 pounds disqualified disproportionate numbers of women.

But what if the job requires it? Of course, job requirements like these may be perfectly legitimate. For example, a person who works loading and unloading heavy packages must have some strength to do the job, a police officer must be able to chase suspects, a litigator must have passed the state bar exam, and a public speaker must be fluent in the language(s) the audience speaks. Recognizing this, the law allows employers to defend against a disparate impact claim by showing that the policy or requirement is job related and consistent with business necessity.

How necessary is that necessity? Precisely what qualifies as a "business necessity" is in some dispute. The Supreme Court has said that, when the criteria for job selection are challenged as having a disparate impact, the employer must be able to show that the criteria are necessary to safe and efficient performance of the job. However, other courts have disagreed over whether it's enough for an employer to show that the challenged policy or practice is legitimately related to successful performance of the job or whether something more is required—for example, that meeting the criteria is essential to job performance or that the job itself is essential to the employer's business operations.

Even if the employer can prove business necessity, the employee can still win by showing that there is a less discriminatory alternative—another practice that would satisfy the employer's legitimate business interest with less disparate impact—which the employer is aware of and refuses to adopt.

The *Wards Cove* Case (Temporarily) Changes the Rules for Business Necessity

In the case of *Wards Cove Packing Co. v. Atonio*, the Supreme Court decided against a group of employees in a disparate impact case. The employees worked in Wards Cove's Alaskan salmon canneries. They claimed that the company's selection practices had resulted in a skewed workforce, in which most of the cannery line jobs were filled by nonwhite employees (primarily Alaska natives and Filipinos), while most of the higher paid cannery jobs that didn't involve actually working the line were filled by white employees. To add to the racial overtones, those who worked the line and those who did not were

B

The *Wards Cove* Case (Temporarily) Changes the Rules for Business Necessity (continued)

housed in separate dormitories and ate in separate cafeteria facilities, which led to segregation outside of work hours as well.

The Court decided a number of issues in the *Wards Cove* case, all of them controversial. For example, the Court found that, in order to prove a disparate impact, the employees had to prove that specific selection criteria caused the discrepancy; it wasn't enough to show a significant disparity in the ultimate outcome of who got hired for particular jobs.

The Court also took on the business necessity defense, finding that the employer had to present evidence that the challenged practice "serves, in a significant way, the legitimate employment goals of the employer." The Court went on to say that, once the employer presented some evidence in support of its business necessity defense, the employees bore the ultimate burden of disproving that defense. These controversial holdings were overturned by the Civil Rights Act of 1991, which explicitly stated that disparate impact and the business necessity defense were to be interpreted as they existed before the *Wards Cove* case.

Wards Cove Packing Co. v. Atonio, 490 U.S. 642 (1989).

Related terms: Civil Rights Act of 1991; disparate impact; Title VII.

Byrne v. Avon Products Inc.

See Family and Medical Leave Act.

charge

When someone files a formal claim of discrimination against an employer with the federal Equal Employment Opportunity Commission (EEOC), it's called a "charge" of discrimination. An employee may also file a charge of retaliation, alleging that the employer took some negative action against the employee (such as firing or demoting the employee) because the employee complained about harassment or discrimination. Filing a charge puts the employer on notice of the problem and gives the parties (and the agency, if it chooses to get involved) an opportunity to resolve the dispute without going to court.

An employee must file a charge of discrimination with either the EEOC or the state agency that handles discrimination complaints (called fair employment practices, or FEP, agencies) before bringing a discrimination lawsuit. (The same is true of harassment and retaliation lawsuits.) A charge or complaint filed with one agency is generally considered filed at the other, too, to protect the employee's rights under both federal and state law. Typically, the agency where the employee actually filed the charge will be responsible for handling it. If an employee files a lawsuit before filing a charge with the appropriate government agency, the lawsuit will be dismissed for failure to "exhaust" administrative remedies.

What happens when a charge is filed? Once an employee files a charge, the EEOC or state FEP agency will notify the employer, send it a copy of the charge, and explain how it can respond. Once the employer files its response to the charge, the agency might decide to investigate, offer to help the parties mediate or try to settle their dispute, issue a "right to sue" letter, which states that the employee has the right to file a lawsuit, or bring its own lawsuit against the employer.

Time limits for filing a charge. An employee must file a charge with the EEOC or state FEP agency within 180 calendar days of the discrimination or harassment. This deadline is extended to 300 days if a state or local agency enforces a law that prohibits discrimination on the same basis. For example, if an employee was sexually harassed and a state law prohibits sexual harassment, she has 300 days to file a charge with either the EEOC or the state FEP agency to protect her federal rights.

Some states provide longer time limits for filing a charge of discrimination. In these states, an employee who misses the 300-day deadline for filing an EEOC charge may still be able to file a timely charge of discrimination with the state FEP agency. However, that charge may allege only violations of state law, not federal law. In other words, if the employee blows the deadline to file under federal law, the employee can't bring a claim under Title VII or any of the other federal antidiscrimination laws.

> **EXAMPLE:** Deborah worked behind the counter at For Goodness Bakes!, a chain of pastry shops in California. The chain's owner and most of its management team attend the same evangelical church and often discuss their religious views at work. Deborah is fired on September 1, 2011, shortly after she turns down her manager's invitation to attend a church picnic and tells him she is not religious.
>
> Because both federal and California law prohibit discrimination on the basis of religion, Deborah has 300 days to file a charge of discrimination at either the EEOC or the Department of Fair Employment and Housing (DFEH), California's FEP agency. If Deborah doesn't file a charge within this time frame, she will have lost her opportunity to bring an EEOC charge and, if she wishes, a lawsuit based on violation of federal law. However, California gives employees one year to file discrimination complaints. If Deborah files a charge with the DFEH on

day 301, her state law claim will still be timely, and she will be able to file a lawsuit alleging that her employer discriminated against her on the basis of religion in violation of state law.

Discrimination Charges at an All-Time High

The EEOC collects statistics on how many discrimination charges are filed with the agency each year, and on what basis. More than 93,000 charges of discrimination were filed in fiscal year 2009 (which ended on September 30), a record high. As has been true in every year of the last decade, there were more charges alleging race discrimination than any other type, followed by sex discrimination. For what looks like the first time, however, the most frequently filed charge was not for any type of discrimination, but for retaliation.

Related terms: discrimination; Equal Employment Opportunity Commission; exhaustion (of remedies); FEP agency; retaliation; Title VII.

Chevron v. Echazabal

See direct threat.

child labor laws

Child labor laws protect children by limiting the type of work they may do and the number of hours they may work. The federal child labor laws are part of the Fair Labor Standards Act (FLSA), which also includes the minimum wage and rules for overtime. States also have their own child labor laws. The FLSA prohibits minors from working at hazardous jobs, limits the type of agricultural work children may do, and limits the hours children may work.

C

Hazardous work. According to the U.S. Department of Labor, which enforces the FLSA, workers younger than 18 may never perform the following types of hazardous jobs (some exceptions are made for apprentices and students):

- manufacturing or storing explosives
- driving a motor vehicle and being an outside helper on a motor vehicle (those who are at least 17 may do certain jobs that require incidental or occasional driving, provided that the teens are properly licensed, have no moving violations, and meet a number of other requirements)
- mining
- logging and sawmilling
- working with radioactive substances
- working with power-driven woodworking or paper products machines
- working with power-driven hoisting equipment
- working with power-driven metal-forming, punching, and shearing machines
- slaughtering, meat packing, or processing (including work involving power-driven meat slicing machines)
- working with power-driven bakery machines
- manufacturing brick, tile, and related products
- working with power-driven circular saws, band saws, or guillotine shears
- wrecking, demolition, or ship-breaking operations
- roofing and work performed on or near roofs, such as installing satellite dishes or working on gutters and downspouts, and
- excavation operations.

Meanwhile, back on the farm. The FLSA requires employers who own or operate a farm or other agricultural business to follow these rules for young workers:

- Children who are at least 16 may be hired to do any type of work, for unlimited hours.

C

- Children who are 14 or 15 may be hired to do any non-hazardous work, outside of school hours. (In the agriculture industry, hazardous jobs include operating a tractor that has more than 20 horsepower; working in a yard, pen, or stall occupied by a bull, a stud horse maintained for breeding purposes, or a sow with suckling pigs; felling timber with a diameter of more than six inches; working from a ladder or scaffold at a height of more than 20 feet; and handling or using blast agents).
- Children who are 12 or 13 may be hired to do any non-hazardous work outside of school hours, but only if the child's parents work on the same farm or have consented in writing to the arrangement.
- Children who are ten or 11 may be hired to harvest crops by hand for no more that eight weeks per calendar year, but only if the Department of Labor has granted the employer a waiver.
- Children of any age may be hired by their own parents or a person standing in the place of their parents to do any type of agricultural work, if the parents own or operate the business.

What about that kid at the video store? For work that is not agricultural and not hazardous, these rules apply:

- Children who are at least 16 may be hired for unlimited hours.
- Children who are 14 or 15 may be hired to do certain retail, food service, and service station jobs. However, they may not work more than three hours on a school day or eight hours on a nonschool day, nor more than a total of 18 hours per school week or 40 hours per nonschool week. They may not be required to start work before 7 a.m. or end after 7 p.m. (except during summer vacation, when they can work until 9 p.m.).

And what about those Olsen twins in *Full House*? Child actors or performers are exempt from the general child labor rules, as are newspaper carriers, children under the age of 16 who are in certain training and apprenticeship programs, or children under the age of 16 who work for their own parents in fields other than mining, manufacturing, or other hazardous jobs.

C

City of Ontario, California v. Quon

See privacy.

Civil Rights Act of 1866

See Section 1981.

Civil Rights Act of 1964

This landmark piece of federal legislation outlawed many forms of discrimination, including by governmental bodies and in voting, public accommodations, and employment. The prohibitions on discrimination appear in Title VII of the law, which is how they are generally referred to.

See Title VII.

Civil Rights Act of 1991

In the Civil Rights Act of 1991, Congress responded to a series of Supreme Court decisions on employment discrimination issues— essentially, by overturning them. The law also added some new provisions, most significantly one that allowed employees who won Title VII discrimination cases to collect punitive and compensatory damages, as explained below.

Oh no you didn't! One of the controversial decisions addressed by the law was *Patterson v. McLean Credit Union*, 491 U.S. 164 (1989). In that case, the Court found that racial harassment on the job was not prohibited by the Civil Rights Act of 1866 (commonly referred to as "Section 1981"). Section 1981 prohibits racial discrimination in a number of things, including the right to "make and enforce contracts." The Court found that the law applied only to the process of contracting: Anything that happened after a contract was in place was not covered by the law.

This limitation was a major blow to employees, even though Title VII also prohibits racial discrimination and harassment.

Section 1981 often is the better remedy for employees, because they have a longer time to sue and no statutory limits on the damages available to them. Also, Title VII plaintiffs must bring charges with the EEOC or a similar state agency before they can file a lawsuit. Section 1981 plaintiffs are not subject to this "exhaustion" requirement, so it gives employees who missed their Title VII deadline another opportunity to sue.

Although *Patterson* was widely decried by civil rights advocates as unjust, it could have been a whole lot worse. While it was considering the case, the Supreme Court asked the parties to submit briefs on whether it should revisit a 1976 decision (called *Runyon v. McRary*) that found the Civil Rights Act of 1866 prohibited discrimination by private actors as well as the government. Ultimately, the Court decided to uphold *Runyon* and continue to allow private entities to be sued under the law. *Patterson* limited the applicability of Section 1981 to the employment relationship, but didn't eliminate private employees' right to sue under the law entirely.

Adding insult to injury. *Patterson* wasn't the only Supreme Court case stuck in Congress's craw. A few other cases had also changed the law in ways that Congress didn't like—and were overturned by the Civil Rights Act of 1991—including:

- *Wards Cove Packing Co. v. Atonio.* In this disparate impact discrimination case, the Court made a number of controversial rulings. It found that the employees bringing this type of case had to pinpoint the employment practice that caused the alleged disparate impact. The Court also made it easier for employers to make out a defense of business necessity (in part, by deciding that employees had the burden of proving that the defense didn't apply, rather than employers having the burden of proving the defense). Congress overturned the case in its entirety.
- *Martin v. Wilks.* In this reverse discrimination case, a group of white firefighters sued the city of Birmingham, claiming that a consent decree the city entered into with African American

C

firefighters resulted in discrimination in promotions. The consent decree came about as a result of a lawsuit the African American firefighters brought, and the white firefighters did not intervene in that lawsuit. The Supreme Court decided that the white firefighters could challenge the consent decree even though they knew about the earlier lawsuit and could have gotten involved then. Congress rescued employers from the resulting possibility of endless rounds of lawsuits by finding that a party may not challenge employment actions taken to comply with a consent decree or court judgment if they had actual notice of the decree or judgment and a reasonable opportunity to object to its terms earlier, or their interests were adequately represented by someone else who had already challenged the decree or judgment.

- *Price Waterhouse v. Hopkins.* In this sex discrimination case, the plaintiff proved that she was denied partnership, in part, because of her gender, and the perception that she did not conform to traditional female stereotypes. However, the employer presented evidence that she was also denied partnership because of her lack of interpersonal skills and her abrasiveness with subordinates. In this type of "mixed motives" case, the court found that the employer could prevail by showing that, even if it was motivated partly by bias, it would have made the same decision for wholly legitimate reasons. Congress overturned this ruling, finding that an employee in a case in which discrimination played a part in the employer's decision is entitled to injunctive relief and attorney fees and court costs, even if the employee might not be entitled to back pay or reinstatement.

And while we're amending things ... Although much of the Civil Rights Act of 1991 is about Congress taking the Supreme Court to the woodshed, the law also adds some new provisions to employment discrimination laws. Perhaps the two most important additions give plaintiffs in Title VII and Americans with Disabilities Act cases the right to a jury trial, and give winning plaintiffs the right to collect not only their out-of-pocket losses, but also damages for pain and suffering and punitive damages. These damages, combined, are capped at $50,000 to $300,000, depending on the size of the employer.

Related terms: affirmative action; Americans with Disabilities Act; business necessity; disparate impact; disparate treatment; Section 1981; Title VII.

class action

A class action is a lawsuit in which a group of people sue over the same legal issue. In a class action, a representative group brings the lawsuit on behalf of everyone who's in the same position. For example, a group of clerks in a convenience store chain might sue the company on behalf of all of its clerks, arguing that they were illegally denied their right to a lunch break or were required to work overtime for which they weren't paid. Or, a group of female employees might sue on behalf of all female employees who have been denied a promotion to management, claiming that the company's selection standards unfairly discriminate against women.

Class actions are intended to promote efficiency and fairness by allowing everyone's claims to be decided at the same time, according to the same standards, rather than through a number of separate lawsuits that could result in contradictory outcomes. Because class actions adjudicate the rights of people who aren't playing an active role in the lawsuit, and because they subject defendants to costly, time-consuming litigation, they are allowed only if certain requirements are met. These requirements are intended to make sure that it's fair and appropriate for the case to proceed en masse. Under the Federal Rules of Civil Procedure and similar state laws, these requirements include:

- **Numerosity.** There must be enough members of the proposed class to make it impractical for all of them to be actual parties to the lawsuit. Although courts have to look at each case on its own facts, this requirement is typically satisfied if there are at least 40 or 50 proposed class members.

C

- **Common issues of law or fact.** A class action makes sense only if class members share legal or factual claims against the employer, and those claims can be decided based on evidence that applies to the whole class, not just a few members. Differences in the amount of damages each class member claims won't defeat a class action, but different facts and legal theories will.

  EXAMPLE: A group of employees at a grocery store chain brings a class action, claiming that company policy required employees to work an extra half hour each day for which they were not paid. Employees on the morning shift were required to show up half an hour early to stock shelves; evening shift workers had to stay half an hour late to count out the registers and clean the store. This case has sufficient commonality to go forward as a class action: All the employees are complaining about the same company policy. And their legal claim—that they were not paid for hours worked—is also common to the class. That the employees' damages will be different depending on how long they've worked at the store and how many shifts they work doesn't defeat their class action. If the employees win the liability portion of the case, the court can use a simple formula to decide how much money each employee should be awarded in damages, based on the employee's tenure and schedule.

- **Typicality.** In addition to the whole class having common legal and factual claims, the class representatives—the people who are actually named as the parties suing in the lawsuit and will participate actively in it—must have claims that are typical of the rest of the class. Otherwise, the class as a whole won't be properly represented in the lawsuit.

  EXAMPLE 1: Three older employees of a bank bring a class action lawsuit, claiming that they and other employees over the age of 55 were fired for discriminatory reasons. They want to represent all bank employees who have lost their jobs in the past six months and are older than 55. All three work at the same branch of the bank, and two of the three had serious performance problems, which the company claims was the reason they were let go. The company also says that personnel decisions are entirely up to each branch's manager. This class action probably won't get off the ground, in part because of lack of typicality. Because they all work in the same branch, they can only speak to what happened there, and the decisions their own manager made. Employees in other branches may have had entirely different experiences. What's more, the company's defense is likely to differ for each named class member, which means that each employee's situation will have to be judged individually.

EXAMPLE 2: Three older employees who work at different branches of a bank bring a class action lawsuit claiming that the bank discriminated against older workers in conducting layoffs. The employees claim that the bank's written guidelines to branch managers who chose the employees for layoff stated that the bank was seeking a "more energetic, hip image, designed to appeal to younger urban customers," and that managers should consider which employees are best able to project this image when making layoff selections. Now, the class action looks like a better bet. The named class representatives are claiming that everyone was subjected to the same policy, and they worked in different branches, under different managers. Their claims are now more representative of the whole class.

- **Adequacy of representation.** The named plaintiffs who will represent the class must be up to the challenge. They must be ready, willing, and able to participate actively in the lawsuit, and they must not have any conflicts of interest with the rest of the class.

Other requirements must be met as well, depending on the type of case and the type of remedies the plaintiffs are seeking.

C

closed shop

A closed shop is a company that has entered into an agreement with a union to hire only union members and to require union membership as a condition of continuing employment. Closed shops were outlawed after World War II by the Labor Management Relations Act (more commonly known as the Taft-Hartley Act).

Related terms: agency shop; open shop; Taft-Hartley Act; union security agreement.

COBRA

COBRA, short for the Consolidated Omnibus Budget Reconciliation Act of 1985, is a federal law that enables employees and their families to continue receiving health care coverage under an employer's group health plan, even after an event—such as a layoff, cut in hours, or termination—that would end their coverage under ordinary circumstances. Employees must pay the full premium for this coverage, even if the employer picked up part or all of the tab while the employee was employed.

Who is eligible for COBRA. COBRA covers private employers with at least 20 employees. Employees, their spouses, and their children are eligible for coverage in these circumstances:

- **Employees** who are covered by an employer's group health plan are eligible to continue coverage under COBRA if they quit, are laid off, are fired for reasons other than gross misconduct, or become ineligible for coverage because of a cut in hours.
- **An employee's spouse** who receives benefits through the employer's plan is eligible for COBRA if the employee loses coverage for any of these reasons. The spouse is also eligible if the employee becomes entitled to Medicare, the employee and the spouse divorce or legally separate, or the employee dies.
- **Dependent children** who receive coverage through a parent are eligible for all of the reasons listed for spouses and employees above. They are also eligible if they lose dependent status

C

under the employer's plan. If, for example, the employer's plan covers dependent children only until they turn 18, COBRA kicks in on the child's 18th birthday.

How COBRA works. Employers must provide several notices to employees of their eligibility for health care coverage and COBRA continuation coverage. Once employees or covered family members become eligible through one of the events described above, the employer must send an election notice, informing them of their right to continue coverage and their responsibility to give notice if they choose to exercise that right.

What About That Subsidy?

As part of the stimulus package in 2008, Congress provided some help to employees who lost their jobs in the recession. Those who were involuntarily terminated from September 1, 2008 through December 31, 2009 were eligible for a subsidy of 65% of the premium for up to nine months. (Employers initially had to pay the remaining 35%, for which they could claim a credit on their payroll taxes.) The subsidy was later expanded to cover employees who were terminated through the end of May 2010, as well as employees who initially lost coverage due to a cut in hours, then were terminated. The subsidy was also extended to last up to 15 months.

As we go to press, however, this subsidy has not been reauthorized or extended beyond May 31, 2010 As a result, employees who lost their jobs on or after June 1, 2010 must pay the full premium if they want to continue their health insurance coverage.

Length of coverage. How long COBRA continuation coverage lasts depends on who is using it and the event that made the beneficiary eligible, as shown in the chart below. In some circumstances, the coverage periods may be lengthened if certain events occur while the employee is on COBRA.

C

Coverage Periods		
Qualifying Event	**Qualified Beneficiary**	**Coverage Period**
Voluntary termination Involuntary termination Reduction of hours	Employee Spouse Dependent child	18 months
Divorce Legal separation Employee's death Employee on Medicare	Spouse Dependent child	36 months
Loss of dependent child status	Dependent child	36 months

Related terms: benefits; health insurance reform.

collective bargaining

Collective bargaining is the negotiation process between a union (on behalf of the bargaining unit it represents) and the company to work out an agreement that will govern the terms and conditions of the workers' employment. The contract that results from the negotiation is called a collective bargaining agreement (CBA).

The National Labor Relations Act (NLRA) requires a duly elected union and an employer to meet and negotiate over wages, hours, and other employment terms, as well as to negotiate over issues that may arise under an existing CBA. The two sides don't have to reach an agreement, but they always have to bargain in good faith. Although neither side is required to make a particular concession, a party that refuses to bend on a single issue or put any offer on the table might be acting in bad faith.

Employers must provide information. Employers have a clear bargaining advantage over the union in one important respect: Employers have access to more information. Although the union can poll its members to find out what they know, the employer

C

will always be better informed about a variety of issues, especially the company's financial situation. To level the playing field a bit, employers are legally required to make certain types of information available to the union during the collective bargaining process. For example, if an employer claims that financial problems make a requested wage increase impossible, the union has the right to request and review documents that support the company's claims. Similarly, employers may have to give the union current employee salary and benefit data so the union can base its demands on accurate information.

Mandatory subjects of bargaining. An employer doesn't have to bargain over every conceivable employment issue. However, employers must bargain with the union over issues that are central to the employment relationship, such as wages, hours, and layoff procedures. Employers must give the union advance notice of any proposed workplace changes that involve these issues—but only if the union requests it. An employer who refuses to bargain or takes unilateral action in one of these mandatory bargaining areas commits an unfair labor practice. At that point, the National Labor Relations Board (NLRB) can step in to remedy the situation, but the union may also take certain actions against the employer, including a strike.

Given these dire consequences, you'd think there would be a list of mandatory bargaining topics included in the labor laws, but that's not the case. Although there is general agreement that wages, hours, layoff procedures, production quotas, and other substantial work rules are mandatory bargaining topics, many other issues fall into a gray area.

Part of the problem is that whether a topic qualifies as a mandatory subject of bargaining may depend on the employer's reasons for taking action. For example, if the employer decides to close a plant in order to avoid paying union wages, that's likely a mandatory bargaining topic. But if the employer bases its decision on concerns unrelated to the union—for example, the employer's customer base in the area has dried up or the employer can reap significant tax advantages by relocating—bargaining may not be required.

C

Mandatory Bargaining Is Required
Even if the CBA Has Expired

When the CBA between the union and the Frontier Hotel & Casino in Law Vegas expired, the two sides were unable to negotiate a new agreement. Which is when things got ugly: A member of Frontier's management started eavesdropping on conversations between workers and their union representative. When Frontier didn't like what it heard, it kicked the union rep out of the workplace. Then, Frontier instituted 63 new work rules and stopped making contributions to the employees' pension fund.

The union filed a charge against Frontier with the National Labor Relations Board (NLRB). Both the NLRB and the Ninth Circuit Court of Appeals decided that Frontier's actions were illegal. The eavesdropping was an obvious no-no, but the court also decided that ejecting the union rep from the premises interfered with the workers' right to discuss union issues.

The court also found that Frontier's decision to issue major changes in work rules—including a requirement that workers suspected of being drunk or high on illegal drugs had to agree to undergo a medical exam or risk immediate termination—violated its duty to bargain with the union. Even though the first CBA had expired, Frontier was legally required to negotiate these mandatory bargaining issues, as well as its decision to stop paying into the pension fund, before taking action. Its failure to do so—and its insistence on filing legal appeals on issues that were such clear losers—convinced the court to slap the company and its attorney with a hefty fine for wasting everyone's time.

NLRB v. Unbelievable, Inc., 71 F.3d 1434 (9th Cir. 1995).

Please ask before giving us a raise. Before changing a workplace rule or policy that clearly requires bargaining (such as revamping a seniority system or adjusting pay scales), a company must ask the union to negotiate. Mandatory bargaining applies whether the changes will benefit or harm the workers. In other words, a company may not offer an across-the-board pay raise or offer more generous paid leave on its own initiative without consulting the union. If this sounds silly, consider that some employers make positive changes like these on their own to convince workers that they don't need a union. And, some employers might try to disguise a controversial change as a "benefit" (for example, by linking a wage increase to higher production quotas).

Related terms: bargaining unit; collective bargaining agreement; National Labor Relations Act; National Labor Relations Board; unfair labor practice.

collective bargaining agreement

A collective bargaining agreement (CBA) is the contract reached through negotiations between a union and an employer. Typically, a CBA addresses wages, hours, benefits, grievance procedures, selection procedures for deciding which employees will be promoted or laid off, and other terms and conditions of employment. Once in place, a CBA contract governs the relationship between the employer and the employees covered by the agreement. Workers are entitled to the rights set forth in the agreement, even if they go beyond what the employer would otherwise have to provide.

Related terms: bargaining unit; collective bargaining.

company union

The National Labor Relations Act (NLRA) prohibits employers from establishing, dominating, or interfering with any labor organization. This rule effectively outlaws company unions: groups that appear to represent employees in their dealings with the employer, but are in fact controlled by the company, not the workers.

Before the NLRA prohibited company unions, some employers created their own groups within the company, which workers could use to raise grievances and concerns. These groups allowed employers to effectively bypass recognition of, or negotiations with,

C

independent labor organizations. The logic behind the ban on company unions is to make sure employee interests are represented: If an employer "negotiates" with a union of its own creation, the employees' chair at the bargaining table is empty.

What puts the "company" in a company union? Courts and the National Labor Relations Board (the federal administrative body that hears labor disputes) look at all of the relevant circumstances in deciding whether an employer unfairly controls a particular union, including:

- whether the employer started the group
- whether the employer played a role in the group's organization and function
- whether management actually attends the group's meetings or otherwise tries to set its agenda, and
- what the group's purpose is.

The more influence the employer has over the group and the more traditional union concerns the group takes on, the more likely it will be classified as an illegal company union.

Employee committee or company union? Many companies have established committees or work groups: informal teams of workers and management that meet to resolve workplace problems. Common examples include committees on safety, policy review, or productivity. But even if these groups are not unions, they may still constitute illegal employer-dominated labor organizations. If management supports or dominates the group (for example, by choosing employee representatives or setting the committee's agenda) and the group deals with the employer on traditional topics of collective bargaining, like working conditions or wages and hours, it might be an illegal company union.

EXAMPLE: Crown Cork & Seal, a company that manufactures aluminum cans, adopted a decision-making structure at its Texas plant that it called "the Socio-Tech System." Employees serve on one of four production teams, each having significant authority to make and carry out workplace decisions, including decisions about safety, training, discipline, production, and more.

One level above the production teams are three more committees, which recommend changes in policies, terms and conditions of employment, safety procedures, and pay. Those recommendations go to the plant manager, who has always adopted them without question.

Illegal company unions? Not in the opinion of the National Labor Relations Board. These groups were doing more than "dealing with" the employer on traditional bargaining topics: They had the power to make important decisions, about disciplining employees, shutting down the production line, or stopping delivery of products, that are traditionally made by managers. In effect, the committees were managing the plant. Even though the plant manager had the right to disapprove some of these decisions, he never did, which meant that the committees and teams were actually managing the plant. *In re. Crown Cork & Seal Company Inc.*, 334 NLRB No. 92 (2001).

Related terms: collective bargaining; National Labor Relations Act; National Labor Relations Board; unfair labor practice.

comparable worth

Comparable worth refers to the theory that men and women should be paid equally for doing jobs that are of similar value to the employer, even if those jobs are quite different. The comparable worth theory advocates determining how important various jobs are to an employer, and paying people who do them according to that value. For example, social workers might be as valuable as parole officers to a government employer; dining hall workers may be as valuable as gardeners on a college campus; nurses and lab technicians may do equally valuable work for a hospital. According to comparable worth theory, they should be paid the same for their equally valuable contributions.

C

Current law: The Equal Pay Act. Comparable worth theory stands in contrast to the existing law on gender discrimination in pay, set forth in the Equal Pay Act, which requires that men and women be paid equally only if they are doing equal work. Jobs don't have to be absolutely identical to qualify as "equal," but they must be quite similar: The jobs must require substantially equal skill, effort, and responsibility, and be performed under similar working conditions in the same work establishment. As a practical matter, these strict definitions have made it tough for women to win equal pay claims unless they really are doing exactly the same job as men.

Comparable worth theory seeks to expand beyond equal jobs to jobs of equal value. Advocates argue that this is necessary to address the ongoing effects of gender discrimination both past and present, including sex segregation in employment, wage discrimination against women, stereotyped notions that working women are not primary breadwinners and therefore do not need to earn as much as men, and the devaluation of jobs that have historically been filled by women. Advocates point to the wage gap, which currently shows that women earn 77 cents for every dollar earned by men, as proof that more must be done to address the problem.

The Fair Pay Act. Congress periodically considers legislation to ease the strict requirements of the Equal Pay Act and introduce some elements of comparable worth. The most recent incarnation is the Fair Pay Act, which would amend the Equal Pay Act to require equal pay for "equivalent" jobs, defined as positions with an overall combination of skill, effort, responsibility, and working conditions that are equivalent in value, even if the jobs are dissimilar. The Fair Pay Act would also extend the prohibition on discrimination in pay to race and national origin.

Related Terms: Equal Pay Act; sex discrimination.

compensation

Compensation refers to all payment an employee receives for doing work. It might include hourly pay or salary, overtime, bonuses, commissions, benefits, job perquisites, and so on.

compensatory time (comp time)

See overtime.

Consolidated Omnibus Reconciliation Act of 1985

See COBRA.

constructive discharge

Under the legal theory of constructive discharge, an employee who quits can still bring a claim of wrongful termination, even though the employee was never technically fired. Employees in this situation must show that their work conditions were so intolerable that they were essentially forced to quit—and that any reasonable employee would have done so. Constructive discharge isn't a stand-alone legal claim; instead, it allows an employee to bring a wrongful termination case that would otherwise not be allowed.

Related term: wrongful termination.

consumer report

Under the federal Fair Credit Reporting Act (FCRA), a consumer report is any written or oral communication of information about an employee's or applicant's:
- creditworthiness
- credit standing
- credit capacity
- general reputation
- personal characteristics, or
- lifestyle.

C

This type of information qualifies as a consumer report only if the employer will use it for employment purposes—that is, to decide whether to hire, promote, reassign, or terminate someone—and it comes from a consumer reporting agency (rather than the employer's own inquiries, such as calling former employers or contacting a state board to make sure an applicant is properly licensed).

Examples of consumer reports include background checks, credit reports, and criminal records checks. An employer that wants to obtain a consumer report on an employee, applicant, or independent contractor must follow the rules set out in the FCRA, which include providing notice to the subject of the report and getting written consent in advance. An employer that wants an "investigative consumer report"—one that goes beyond checking the basic facts provided by the employee or applicant—must follow stricter FCRA rules.

Related terms: background check; consumer reporting agency; credit report; Fair Credit Reporting Act; investigative consumer report.

consumer reporting agency

A consumer reporting agency is a person or entity that regularly provides consumer reports—that is, information about someone's creditworthiness, credit standing, credit capacity, general reputation, personal characteristics, or lifestyle—to third parties. Examples of consumer reporting agencies include credit bureaus, private investigators, records search firms, law firms that conduct background checks, and criminal records search firms. When an employer plans to get a consumer report on an employee or applicant from a consumer reporting agency, the employer must follow the requirements in the Fair Credit Reporting Act (FCRA), which include getting the employee's or applicant's consent and providing certain notices.

Employers are not themselves consumer reporting agencies. They don't have to follow the FCRA rules if they gather information by talking directly to primary sources, such as former employers or colleges that applicants claim to have attended. State entities that are required to keep certain information as a matter of public record, such as licensing boards, are also not considered consumer reporting agencies.

Related terms: background check; consumer report; Fair Credit Reporting Act; investigative consumer report.

contingent workforce

Temporary workers, leased workers, and independent contractors are all part of the contingent workforce, so called because they don't have the same open-ended attachment to an employer that typically accompanies full-time employment. Instead, their work usually lasts for one season or one project. For example, an office supply chain may bring on some temps to help with the back-to-school shopping crunch, or a company may hire an independent contractor to help it design a new website.

Related term: independent contractor.

continuing violation

A continuing violation is an illegal employment practice that is ongoing. If a continuing violation exists, an employee may be able to include actions that occurred well in the past in a charge of discrimination.

The continuing violation rule creates an exception to the general time limits for filing claim. Usually, an employee has to file a charge with the Equal Employment Opportunity Commission within 180 days of an alleged incident of harassment, discrimination, or retaliation (or within 300 days, if the state where the employee works also has an antidiscrimination law). If the employee misses this deadline, the employee may not bring a charge—and, because filing a charge is a prerequisite to filing a lawsuit, the employee therefore loses any right to challenge the employer's actions.

But if a continuing violation exists, the rule is different. An employee can challenge a series of actions, including some that occurred outside of the time limit, if they are part of a continuing violation.

Although it might sound like the continuing violation exception pretty much does away with the time limit for filing a claim, it has been interpreted quite narrowly. The Supreme Court has held that discrete acts—such as demotions, pay cuts, disciplinary actions, or failures to promote—are actionable only if challenged within the applicable time limit. Although these earlier acts may be relevant evidence, the employee cannot recover damages for them.

> **EXAMPLE:** Sarah has applied for a promotion several times, but has been denied each time. The first decision was made in January 2008, the next in June 2010, and the final decision in March 2012. Sarah files a charge of discrimination in April 2012, alleging that she was not promoted because she has a disability that requires her to use a wheelchair. Only the most recent promotion decision is actionable, because it's the only one that falls within the time limit. Although Sarah could present evidence about the earlier promotion decisions, she cannot collect damages for these actions.

However, in hostile environment harassment cases, in which the employee alleges an ongoing pattern of inappropriate behavior, the employee can recover for actions that took place more than 180 or 300 days before the employee filed a charge. In this situation, it often takes a while for the employee to realize that ongoing offensive behavior might in fact be illegal harassment.

> **EXAMPLE:** Sarah was transferred to a different department in January 2010, and her new manager made jokes and teased her about using a wheelchair. Sarah went along with the jokes for a while, but began feeling uncomfortable about them. Over time, the teasing became more pointed and unkind. When her manager made a cruel statement about Sarah's disability to a

client in June of 2011, it was the last straw: Sarah immediately filed a charge of harassment with the EEOC. Although the jokes began more than 300 days before Sarah filed her charge, she can present evidence of all of the teasing—and, if she prevails, she can collect damages for all of the harassment she faced.

Related terms: Equal Employment Opportunity Commission; exhaustion (of remedies); discrimination; harassment.

course and scope of employment

The course and scope of employment refers to the range of activities or actions an employee might reasonably undertake as part of his or her job. Employees who are working, doing business for the company, or acting on the employer's behalf are acting within the course and scope of employment.

Respondeat superior. If an employee is acting within the course and scope of employment, the employer is legally responsible for the employee's actions under a legal theory called "respondeat superior" (let the superior answer). The purpose of this rule is fairly simple: to hold employers responsible for the costs of doing business, including the cost of employee carelessness and misconduct. If an employee injures someone or causes property damage while acting within the course and scope, it's considered one of the risks of doing business, for which the employer is liable. But if the employee acted independently or purely out of personal motives, the employer might not be liable.

> **EXAMPLE 1:** A restaurant promises deliver in 30 minutes "or your next order is free." If a delivery person hits a pedestrian while trying frantically to beat the deadline, the company may be liable to the pedestrian.

> **EXAMPLE 2:** A company gives its sales staff company cars to call on customers. If a salesperson hits a pedestrian while running

personal errands after work hours, the company probably is not liable to the pedestrian.

Good intentions don't count. If a company is sued for damages caused by an employee under the respondeat superior theory, the victim generally won't have to show that the company should have known the employee might cause harm or even that the company did anything demonstrably wrong. If the employee caused harm while acting within the course and scope of employment, the company will have to answer to the victim.

Workers' compensation cases. Many states also use the "course and scope" concept to determine whether an employee's injury is covered by workers' compensation. An employee who suffers an accident, injury, or illness in the course and scope of employment is eligible for workers' comp benefits. If an employee is hurt outside the course and scope of employment, however, workers' comp isn't implicated.

Related term: workers' compensation.

covenant not to compete

A covenant not to compete (also called a noncompete agreement) is a contract, usually between an employee and an employer, in which the employee agrees not to work for a competitor or start a competing company for a stated period of time after the employment relationship ends. (A covenant not to compete might also be created among business partners or between the original owner and the purchaser of a company.)

Some states don't enforce employee noncompete agreements (California, for example) or put limits on how restrictive they may be. Generally, a noncompete agreement is more likely to be enforced if the employee receives something valuable (such as a bonus) in exchange for signing the agreement, and the agreement is drawn narrowly. For example, an agreement that prohibits the employee from working for only a short list of direct competitors, applies to a limited geographical area, and lasts for a relatively short period of time is more likely to be enforced than one that is more restrictive. The broader the agreement, the more likely a court is to find that it unfairly restricts the employee's right to earn a living.

Related terms: nondisclosure agreement; nonsolicitation agreement; trade secret.

Crawford v. Nashville

See investigation.

credit report

A credit report is a collection of information about a person's bill paying history, debts and loans (such as mortgages, student loans, or car loans), credit cards, current and former addresses, bankruptcy filings, lawsuits, and criminal records. Credit reports are put together by credit reporting agencies (also called credit bureaus); the three big national credit reporting agencies are Equifax, Experian, and TransUnion. These agencies then sell the reports to creditors, insurance companies, banks, employers, landlords, and others who will use it to decide whether to do business with (including whether to hire or rent a home to) the subject of the report.

A credit report qualifies as a consumer report under the Fair Credit Reporting Act (FCRA). Before an employer can pull a credit report on an applicant or employee, it must follow the rules set out in the FCRA, which include providing notice to, and getting consent from, the subject of the report.

Related terms: consumer report; consumer reporting agency; Fair Credit Reporting Act.

damages

Damages are the monetary compensation awarded to the winner of a lawsuit. The winner may be entitled to other compensation (for example, the other side may have to pay his or her attorney fees and court costs) and nonmonetary remedies as well (such as an order that the employer change its policy, implement harassment training, provide a reasonable accommodation for an employee with a disability, or reinstate an employee who was wrongfully discharged).

The type (and amount) of damages available in employment cases depend on the basis for the lawsuit.

Compensatory damages. A plaintiff/employee who wins a lawsuit is entitled to compensation for losses suffered as a result of the employer's misconduct. The purpose of these damages is to put the employee in the same position he or she would have been in had the employer acted properly. These damages might include:

- **Back pay.** Back pay compensates the employee for money already lost. For example, an employee who was wrongfully terminated is entitled to recover wages, benefits, bonuses, and other compensation lost as a result of the termination. An employee who is denied a promotion is entitled to the difference between his or her earnings and what those earnings would have been if the promotion were awarded. Back pay is measure from the date of the employer's illegal action(s) until the date of the judgment in the trial.

- **Front pay.** Front pay compensates the employee for lost wages going forward after the judgment, if the employee is not reinstated. Front pay awards are usually limited in time, based on the expectation that the employee will get another job in

D

the future. A court might also award damages for lost future earnings if, for example, the employee's reputation or career has been damaged by the employer's actions, and that harm will affect the employee's earning power going forward.

- **Emotional distress.** Damages for emotional distress are intended to compensate the employee for mental pain and suffering caused by the employer's actions. These damages are available only in some employment cases, and there may be a limit on the size of this type of award. For example, under Title VII, an employee's entire award for emotional distress damages and punitive damages (see below) is capped at an amount from $50,000 to $300,000, depending on the size of the employer.

Punitive damages. Punitive damages are damages intended to punish the employer for particularly egregious behavior. They are not compensatory damages, because they aren't intended to make the employee whole; instead, they are intended as a penalty to the employer that committed the misconduct and a deterrent to other employers, to discourage them from engaging in similar behavior. Punitive damages are not allowed in every type of employment lawsuit, and may be capped as noted above.

Related terms: back pay; front pay.

decertification

When a union that has been certified as the representative of a bargaining unit is removed from that position, it's called decertification. Decertification requires a vote of the bargaining unit employees, conducted by the National Labor Relations Board (NLRB). To put the process in motion, an employee must file a decertification petition with the NLRB, supported by the signatures of at least 30% of the employees in the bargaining unit. If the NLRB holds an election, and a majority of those voting opt for decertification, the union will be removed.

Time limits on decertification. The NLRB will not hold an election to decertify the union within one year after the union is certified. Once the union and the employer enter into a valid collective bargaining agreement, no decertification petition may be filed while the agreement is in effect or for three years, whichever period is longer. There is an exception to this rule, however: A petition may be filed during the 30-day period 60 to 90 days before the collective bargaining agreement expires.

Related terms: bargaining unit; collective bargaining agreement; National Labor Relations Board; unfair labor practice.

defamation

Defamation is committed when someone makes an intentional false statement that causes another person injury. Typically, this injury is to the person's reputation or standing in the community. When the statement is made orally, it's called slander; a written statement is called libel. Either way, defamation is a tort: a personal injury for which the person harmed may sue.

Defamation in the employment context. In employment law, defamation claims are most often made by employees claiming that an employer or former employer made a false statement, in a reference or otherwise, that damaged the employee's reputation and/or harmed his or her changes of getting another job. Typically, the alleged defamatory statement is about the reasons why the employee was fired or the quality of the employee's performance. The statement might be made in a reference, performance review, or announcement within the company as to why an employee was fired, for example.

Elements of a defamation claim. To prove defamation, the plaintiff must show:

- **The defendant made a false statement of fact about the plaintiff.** Statements of opinion ("I think John had an attitude problem") cannot form the basis of a defamation claim. Nor can true statements: If the defendant's statement is true, no

D

matter how damaging or private ("John was caught stealing his coworkers' wallets"), it isn't defamation, although it might lead to a claim for invasion of privacy.

- **The defendant published the statement.** In this context, "publication" simply means making the statement to someone, whether orally or in writing. In some states, making the statement only to the plaintiff may satisfy this element, if the plaintiff has to repeat the statement to others. This theory is called "compelled self-publication."

    EXAMPLE: Gary is fired. His boss tells him that he's being fired for stealing money from his register. In fact, Gary never stole money, but he is fired despite his protests that the company has its facts wrong.

    When Gary applies for a new job, the application asks him to list his last three positions and the reasons why he left each. It also states that lying on the application will be grounds for termination if he gets the job. If Gary answers the question truthfully and doesn't get the job as a result, he might have a defamation claim in a state that recognizes the theory of compelled self-publication. The application form requires him to repeat his boss's false statement, even if Gary's former employer has a strict policy of giving out only the names, position, and salaries of former employees when called for a reference.

- **The defendant knew or had reason to know the statement was false.** Defamation occurs only if the defendant knew the statement was false or acted with reckless disregard as to its truth or falsity. For example, if a manager who is asked to give a reference for a former employee repeats the rumor going around the office that the employee was fired for having child pornography on his computer, without any first-hand knowledge of what really happened, that shows reckless disregard. On the other hand, if the defendant has a

Failing to Tell the Whole Truth

Many employers, fearing defamation claims, take a "name, rank, and serial number" approach to reference requests, giving out only very basic facts about, for example, the employee's job title, salary, and dates of employment. Some employers go even further to avoid liability to former employees by providing only positive information to prospective employers, even if the truth about the employee is not so pleasant. If the employee's conduct was dangerous, however, employers who go this route can get into a different kind of legal trouble for failing to warn prospective employers of the danger. Here's a real-life example:

Randi was a student at a California middle school when she was called into the vice principal's office one day in 1992. Later, she claimed that the vice principal, Robert Gadams, sexually molested her while she was in his office.

The school had hired Gadams after receiving positive recommendations from another school district where he had worked. Even though supervisors in his former school district knew that Gadams had been accused of sexual misconduct and impropriety with students, it failed to mention these claims when the new middle school asked for a reference. In fact, the former district gave letters of recommendation for Gadams filled with unconditional praise. One letter recommended Gadams "for an assistant principalship or equivalent position without reservation."

When Randi sued Gadams's previous school district, the district claimed that she had no legal grounds for a personal injury lawsuit. After all, it argued, it didn't have any sort of obligation to her, a student in a different district. The California Supreme Court disagreed. It said that Randi could sue because the school district had a duty not to misrepresent the facts when describing the character and qualifications of an employee to a prospective employer—in this case, the middle school that Randi attended. The school district could have chosen to say nothing. Because it said something substantive about Gadams, however, it had to tell the whole truth.

Randi W. v. Muroc Joint Unified School District, et al., 14 Cal.4th 1066 (1997).

D

reasonable, good faith belief in the truth of the statement, that could defeat a defamation claim.

- **The statement was not privileged.** Many states recognize that in certain contexts, public policy should encourage candor and open communication. Statements made in these contexts are privileged, which means that the speaker is protected from liability. For example, most states provide an absolute privilege—which protects the speaker from lawsuits, even if the statement was made with malice—for statements made in court or in administrative proceedings (for example, to the state's unemployment or labor department). Many states also recognize a qualified privilege—which protects the speaker as long as he or she acted without malice—for statements made in the context of employment references.

- **The plaintiff suffered harm as a result of the statement.** Certain types of statements are considered "defamatory per se," which means that the plaintiff doesn't have to prove that the statement caused harm, because the law presumes that it did. For example, statements that the plaintiff committed a crime or lacks the skills for his or her chosen trade, office, or profession, are considered defamatory per se in most states. For statements that don't make the list, the plaintiff must show an actual injury caused by the statement. In employment cases, this injury typically involves another company's refusal to hire the plaintiff because of the statement.

Related terms: reference; tort.

Department of Labor

The Department of Labor (DOL) is a federal government agency that interprets and enforces most laws that protect employees and sets workplace standards (other than the federal laws prohibiting discrimination, which are handled by the Equal Employment Opportunity Commission). Among the laws enforced by the DOL are:

D

- the Fair Labor Standards Act (FLSA), which sets the minimum wage, gives employees the right to overtime, and sets the rules for child labor
- the Family and Medical Leave Act (FMLA), which gives employees the right to take time off to care for an ailing family member, care for a new child, recuperate from a serious health condition, handle practical matters arising from a family member's military deployment or call to active duty, or care for a family member who is seriously injured while serving in the Armed Forces
- the Occupational Safety and Health Act (OSHA), which sets the standards for workplace safety and gives employees the right to work in an environment free of recognized hazards
- the Uniformed Services Employment and Reemployment Rights Act (USERRA), which gives those who take leave to serve in the military the right to reinstatement and some protection from job loss after returning to work
- the Employment Polygraph Protection Act (EPPA), which prohibits employers from requiring employees to take lie detector tests (with a few exceptions), and
- the Worker Adjustment and Retraining Notification Act (WARN), which gives employees the right to 60 days' advance notice if they will lose their jobs in a mass layoff or plant losing.

Every state also has its own department of labor (although these agencies go by many different names), which enforces similar state laws. You can find the federal DOL online at www.dol.gov; the site also includes contact information for every state's labor department.

Related terms: child labor laws; Employee Polygraph Protection Act; Fair Labor Standards Act; Family and Medical Leave Act; minimum wage; Occupational Safety and Health Act; overtime; Uniformed Services Employment and Reemployment Rights Act; Worker Adjustment and Retraining Notification Act (WARN).

direct threat

An employer can defend against a claim of disability discrimination under the Americans with Disabilities Act (ADA) by showing that the employee posed a direct threat: a significant risk of substantial harm to the health or safety of that employee or others, which cannot be eliminated or reduced by a reasonable accommodation. An employee who presents a direct threat is not protected by the ADA. In other words, the employer can fire or refuse to hire an employee who poses a direct threat, even if the threat is due to the employee's disability.

An employer's determination that an employee poses a direct threat cannot be based on fears, misconceptions, or stereotypes about the employee's disability. For example, an employer could not refuse to hire an employee who is HIV positive based on the incorrect assumption that HIV can be spread through casual contact. Instead, the employee must look at all of the evidence objectively, taking into consideration:

- the duration of the risk
- the nature and severity of the potential harm
- how likely it is that the potential harm will occur, and
- how imminent the potential harm is.

EXAMPLE: Joe has epilepsy. If his epilepsy is largely controlled by medication, he has seizures very infrequently, and he works at a desk job, his employer would be hard-pressed to show that Joe presents a direct threat. On the other hand, if he has frequent seizures and he spends most of his workday operating heavy, dangerous machinery, his employer would have a better direct threat argument.

Related terms: Americans with Disabilities Act; Americans with Disabilities Act Amendments Act; disability; reasonable accommodation.

Posing a Direct Threat to Yourself

For almost 25 years, Mario Echazabal worked for independent contractors at a Chevron oil refinery. Echazabal applied for a job with Chevon twice, but was turned down both times because he could not pass the company's physical. Echazabal's exam showed that he suffered from liver problems, later identified as Hepatitis C, which Chevron said would be worsened by continued exposure to the toxins at the refinery. The second time Echazabal failed the physical, Chevron asked the contractors who employed him to either fire him or move him to another facility, to get him out of the refinery. The contractors fired him.

Echazabal sued Chevron under the ADA, claiming that the company discriminated against him by refusing to hire him or let him work in the refinery because of his Hepatitis C. Chevron's defense was that Echazabal's disability posed a direct threat to himself because working in the refinery would be harmful to his health. Echazabal countered that only direct threats to "other individuals in the workplace" were covered by the law, and that an EEOC regulation expanding this defense to direct threats to the employee him- or herself went beyond what Congress intended and encouraged employer "paternalism" toward employees with disabilities.

The U.S. Supreme Court found in favor of Chevron. It decided that the EEOC's interpretation of the statute to cover threatened harm to the employee with a disability was reasonable. The Court found that the regulation did not reflect a paternalistic attitude, but instead allowed employers to make decisions based on "specific and documented risks to the employee himself, even if the employee would take his chances for the sake of getting a job."

Chevron USA Inc. v. Echazabal, 536 U.S. 73 (2002).

disability

D

Under the Americans with Disabilities Act (ADA), a disability is a physical or mental impairment that substantially limits a major life activity. Major life activities are functions that are of central importance to daily life, such as seeing, breathing, working, and caring for oneself. Major bodily functions are also major life activities: If a person's immune system, normal cell growth, or digestive, bowel, bladder, neurological, brain, respiratory, circulatory, endocrine, or reproductive functions are impaired, that constitutes a disability.

Disability is defined differently under other laws and programs. For example, under many state workers' compensation programs, a temporary disability is a work-related injury or illness that prevents an employee from doing his or her usual job while recovering. The Social Security program uses a five-part test to determine whether someone has a disability that qualifies for benefits:

- The person must not be working.
- The person's condition must be severe, in that it interferes with basic, work-related activities.
- The person's condition must either appear on the department's list of disabilities or must be equally severe to the conditions on that list.
- The person's condition must prevent him or her from doing the work he or she did previously.
- The condition must also prevent the person from adjusting to new work, considering the person's age, education, experience, and skills.

Related terms: Americans with Disabilities Act; Americans with Disabilities Act Amendments Act; impairment; major life activity; qualified individual with a disability; reasonable accommodation; temporary disability insurance.

discovery

Discovery refers to the legal process by which the parties to a lawsuit gather evidence from each other and from witnesses before trial. The general rule is that any evidence that is admissible at trial or is reasonably calculated to lead to the discovery of admissible evidence can be requested in discovery, unless it is protected from discovery because it is private, privileged (for example, it was a statement made to an attorney or a spouse), or otherwise off limits.

Types of discovery. There are a number of different types of discovery (called "discovery devices") that the plaintiff (the person bringing the lawsuit, who is almost always the employee in employment cases) and defendant (the person or entity defending the lawsuit, typically the employer and perhaps individual managers or officers) can use. They include:

- **Requests for production of documents:** written requests from one party to the other to hand over specified documents. In an employment case, for example, the plaintiff often asks the employer to hand over the employee handbook, the plaintiff's entire personnel file, all written policies that pertain to the plaintiff's employment, and all documents—including email messages—relating to the plaintiff's firing (or other job action). When a party wants to request documents from someone who isn't a party to the lawsuit, it serves a subpoena "duces tecum" instead. For example, a defendant might serve such a subpoena on the plaintiff's current employer, seeking any documents regarding the plaintiff's salary, credentials, and stated reasons for leaving the previous job.
- **Depositions:** question and answer sessions, conducted under oath. One party (or much more likely, the party's lawyer) questions the witness or opposing party, and a stenographer makes a transcript of all of the questions and answers. In an employment lawsuit, depositions are typically taken of the plaintiff (employee), key decision makers working for the employer (such as the employee's manager, the human

D

resources director, and perhaps higher-level executives, such as an officer who approved the manager's decision to fire the employee), witnesses (for example, coworkers who saw a manager harass the plaintiff), and perhaps expert witnesses (such as an economist who has calculated how much money the plaintiff will lose as a result of being fired or a psychiatrist who can testify about the plaintiff's emotional distress caused by workplace bullying).

- **Interrogatories:** written questions sent by one party to the other, which must be answered under oath. In an employment case, the plaintiff is often asked to give the names of every person who might have witnessed the alleged mistreatment, to provide every fact underlying his or her claims, and to provide every fact supporting his or her claim for damages. The employer might be asked to provide every reason why the plaintiff was fired, to name every person who participated in the decision to fire the plaintiff, to name all other employees who have been disciplined or fired for the same behavior in the past few years, and to provide financial and insurance information.

- **Requests for admission:** written requests in which one party asks the other to agree that stated facts are true. Sometimes, requests for admission are simply time-savers: If both parties agree on a fact, they can submit that agreement to the judge and avoid having to prove it at trial. For example, a plaintiff might ask the defendant to admit that it is a Delaware corporation, or the defendant might ask the plaintiff to admit that she does not have a bachelor's degree.

- **Requests for medical examination:** requests that a party be examined by a doctor. In an employment case, the employer might ask the plaintiff to submit to a medical examination (often called an independent medical examination or IME) if, for example, the plaintiff claims to have a disability or to have suffered extreme emotional distress as a result of the employer's actions.

discrimination

In lay terms, discrimination means simply making distinctions. In the context of employment law, discrimination means making job decisions based on illegitimate criteria, such as race, gender, and so on. Discrimination is illegal only if the basis for the distinction is prohibited by law.

> EXAMPLE: Roger owns a bookstore. He likes to surround himself with creative types, so he looks for employees who are artists, musicians, writers, and so on. He always asks applicants about their outside interests, and he hires only those who have some kind of creative gig on the side. Roger's choices may not make a lot of business sense, but they aren't discriminatory. Neither Congress nor any state or local legislature protects those who lack artistic skill from job discrimination.

Even if an employer's basis for decisions isn't itself discriminatory, the employer might still be acting illegally if there's a disparate impact—that is, if the employer's decisions have the effect of disproportionately screening out members of a protected class.

> EXAMPLE: Now let's say that Roger is an avid baseball fan, and hires applicants only if they share his interest in the San Francisco Giants. No law prohibits employers from discriminating based on sports team affiliation. However, it's possible that Roger's criteria could screen out disproportionate numbers of female candidates. If so, that might give rise to a discrimination claim, even though that isn't Roger's intent.

Related terms: age discrimination; disparate impact; disparate treatment; marital status discrimination; protected characteristic; protected class; race discrimination; religious discrimination; reverse discrimination; sex discrimination; sexual orientation discrimination; Title VII; weight discrimination.

disparate impact

Disparate impact is a way to prove employment discrimination based on the effect of an employment policy or practice rather than the intent behind it. Laws that prohibit employment discrimination apply not only to intentional discrimination, but also to apparently neutral policies and practices that have a disproportionate adverse affect on members of a protected class. For example, a strength requirement might screen out disproportionate numbers of female applicants for a job, and requiring all applicants for promotion to receive a certain score on a standardized test could adversely affect candidates of color.

Proving disparate impact. To get a disparate impact case off the ground, the employee must present evidence that an employer's neutral policy, rule, or practice has a disproportionate negative impact on members of a protected class. Objective criteria, such as tests, degree requirements, and physical requirements (for lifting or stamina, for example), may be challenged under a disparate impact theory. Subjective criteria, such as performance, collegiality, or impressions made during an interview, may also be the subject of a disparate impact case.

Once the employee makes this showing, the employer may defend itself either by challenging the employee's evidence (usually by attacking the statistics used to demonstrate the disparate impact) or by proving that the policy or rule in question is job-related and consistent with business necessity. If the employer proves the business necessity defense, the employee can still win by proving that the employer refuses to adopt an alternative practice with a less discriminatory effect.

Different rules for age discrimination cases. Until the Supreme Court decided the case of *Smith v. City of Jackson*, 544 U.S. 228 (2005), it wasn't clear whether employees could sue for age discrimination based on disparate impact. The Court in *Smith* decided that these claims were allowed, but what the employer and employee have to prove is a bit different than for other types of discrimination.

D

Disparate Impact Is Recognized for the First Time: The *Griggs* Case

Before Title VII went into effect in 1965, the Duke Power Company's plant in North Carolina openly discriminated against African Americans. African Americans could be employed only in the labor department, where the highest paying jobs paid less than the lowest paying jobs in the plant's four other departments.

After Title VII became law, the company dropped the overt segregation, but adopted a requirement that applicants for hire or transfer to any but the labor department had to have a high school diploma or receive a satisfactory score on two IQ tests. Thirteen African American employees sued, claiming that these requirements were discriminatory.

The Supreme Court agreed, finding that "practices, procedures, or tests neutral on their face, and even neutral in terms of intent, cannot be maintained if they operate to 'freeze' the status quo of prior discriminatory employment practices." Because of the nation's long history of providing inferior educational opportunities to African Americans in segregated schools, the company's requirements for hire or transfer did not offer equal opportunity. The Court adopted the rule of business necessity, holding that an employment practice that has a discriminatory effect must be related to job performance. Here, the IQ tests did not measure any job-related skill, and were therefore illegal.

Griggs v. Duke Power Co., 401 U.S. 424 (1971).

In an age discrimination case, the employee must point to a specific employment practice (such as a policy, screening test, or job requirement) that led to the disparate impact. And, the employer can escape liability if it can show that its practice was based on a reasonable factor other than age (RFOA), even a factor that often correlates largely with age, such as seniority. The Supreme Court more recently clarified that the RFOA is an affirmative defense, which means that the employer bears the ultimate burden of proving it; the employee doesn't have to show that the employer's practice was unreasonable. *Meacham v. Knolls Atomic Power Laboratory*, 128 S.Ct. 2395 (2008).

Related terms: Age Discrimination in Employment Act; business necessity; discrimination; disparate treatment; race discrimination; reverse discrimination; Title VII.

disparate treatment

Disparate treatment is a way to prove illegal employment discrimination. An employee who makes a disparate treatment claim alleges that he or she was treated differently than other employees who were similarly situated, and that the difference was based on a protected characteristic. In other words, the employee alleges that the employer treated the employee worse because of his or her race, gender, age, or other protected trait.

In disparate treatment discrimination claims, the arguments are usually over how similarly situated the other employees were and whether the employer's decision was made because of the employee's protected characteristic or for other reasons.

> **EXAMPLE:** Horacio worked in a call center for a software developer, and claims that he was fired because he is Latino. The employer claims that he was fired because he received three customer complaints in the previous quarter. If Horacio can show that other employees who received three or more complaints in a quarter were not fired, and that those employees were not Latino, his argument looks better. On the other hand, if the employer can show that every employee who gets three complaints in a quarter is fired, and that employees of all races have been subjected to this rule, the employer's defense looks stronger. Similarly, if Horacio can show that his supervisor made derogatory comments about Latino employees or culture, his case is strengthened. On the other hand, if no such comments

were made, and the employer can show that it has a strong record of hiring and promoting Latino employees, Horacio will have a tougher time.

Proving a disparate treatment claim. To prove a disparate treatment claim, an employee must first present enough evidence to allow the judge or jury to infer that discrimination took place. This is called presenting a "prima facie" case, because it seems at first appearance to be discrimination; what this evidence consists of depends on the facts, as explained below. If the employee can present a prima facie case, then the employer must state a legitimate, nondiscriminatory reason for the decision. Once the employer presents such a reason, the employee must prove pretext: that the employer's stated reason is false, a mere pretext for its true motive, which is discrimination.

What's a prima facie case? The type of evidence an employee has to present to prove a prima facie case of disparate treatment discrimination depends on the facts. If there is direct evidence of discrimination, that's enough. For example, if an employer hires only female bartenders or has said it will not promote African Americans to management positions, that's prima facie evidence of discrimination.

Absent this type of smoking gun, an employee has to make a prima facie case through circumstantial evidence. The Supreme Court has laid out a four-part test for the employee's prima facie case of disparate treatment discrimination. What each part consists of depends on the type of employment decision at issue, but the basic parts of the test are these:

- The employee is a member of a protected class (for example, the employee is African American, female, or over the age of 40).
- The employee was qualified for a job benefit. For example, the employee applied—and was qualified—for an open position, or the employee held a position that he or she was performing adequately.

D

- The employee was denied the job benefit. In other words, the employee was fired, not hired, or not promoted.
- The benefit remains available or was given to someone who is not in the employee's protected class. For example, if an Asian American employee claims that he was not hired because of his race, he can pass this part of the test by showing either that he was rejected for the position and the employer continued its job search or that the job was filled with an employee of a different race.

The employer's legitimate, nondiscriminatory reason. If the employee can prove a prima facie case, the employer must "produce" a legitimate, nondiscriminatory reason for its decision. The verb is important: The Supreme Court has held that the employee has the burden of proving discrimination; the employer need not prove that it didn't discriminate. Therefore, the employer merely has to present some evidence to support its stated reason.

Typically, the employer's reason has to do with the employee's qualifications (for example, that the employee wasn't qualified for a job, had performance or conduct problems that justified termination, or lacked the necessary skills or credentials for a promotion). The employer might also rely on factors unrelated to the employee, such as an economic slowdown that necessitated layoffs, a decision to take a job in a different direction (for which the employee was unqualified), and so on.

Proving pretext. Once the employer states a legitimate reason for the decision, the employee must prove that it's a pretext for discrimination. This doesn't mean the employee has to come up with absolute proof of an illegitimate motive. Instead, the employee has to present some evidence that calls the employer's stated reason into question and allows the jury to conclude that the employer was really motivated by discrimination. Here are some examples:

- **Shifting justifications.** If an employer gives different reasons at different times for its decision, that might be enough to prove pretext. For example, an employer tells an employee that her job is being eliminated in a company-wide restructuring, but then claims at trial that she was fired for poor performance.

- **Applying the rules differently.** If an employer doesn't consistently follow its own legitimate, nondiscriminatory reason for making job decisions, that might demonstrate pretext. For instance, an employee is denied a promotion, and the employer claims that it was because the employee lacked an MBA. If the employee who was promoted also didn't have an MBA, the employer's decision looks suspect.
- **Remarks by decision makers.** Part of the employee's pretext argument could be other evidence of a discriminatory motive. For example, if an employee's manager made sexist comments and told dirty jokes, then presided over a layoff in which a high percentage of women lost their jobs, that could undermine the employer's stated reason for the action.

Related terms: age discrimination; discrimination; disparate impact; marital status discrimination; pretext; protected characteristic; protected class; race discrimination; religious discrimination; reverse discrimination; sex discrimination; sexual orientation discrimination; Title VII; weight discrimination.

domestic violence leave

Laws that provide for domestic violence leave give victims of domestic violence the right to take time off from work. The federal Family and Medical Leave Act (FMLA) may allow domestic violence victims to take time off in certain circumstances, and some states have passed laws that specifically require employers to provide domestic violence leave: time off to handle the medical, legal, psychological, and practical ramifications of domestic violence.

Domestic violence—mental or physical abuse at the hands of an intimate partner—often affects the victims' ability to work. According to Legal Momentum, an advocacy group, victims of domestic violence lose an average of 137 hours of work a year. Some need time off to seek medical attention, seek a restraining

D

order, or relocate to a safe place. Others are prevented from getting to work when an abuser disables or takes the car, sabotages child care arrangements, or leaves the victim without cash to use public transportation.

These problems have led a number of states to pass domestic violence leave laws, which give victims of domestic violence the right to take time off for certain reasons. Some states allow those who are victims of, or witnesses to, any crime to take time off to attend court proceedings; these laws protect victims of domestic violence, although they also apply more generally. And, the federal Family and Medical Leave Act (FMLA) may also provide a right to leave for some domestic violence victims.

State domestic violence leave laws. Almost a dozen states—including California, Florida, Illinois, and Washington—and the District of Columbia have passed laws giving victims of domestic violence the right to take some time off work. These laws vary significantly in the details, including:

- **How much time off.** Some states allow employees to take up to a set amount of days or weeks off; others allow employees to take a "reasonable" amount of leave or simply prohibit employers from disciplining or firing employees who take time off for reasons related to domestic violence.

- **Reasons for leave.** The list of covered activities varies by state, but most allow time off for medical care and psychological counseling, relocation or other safety planning, and seeking a restraining order or participating in legal proceedings relating to domestic violence.

- **Notice and paperwork requirements.** Most states require employees to give reasonable advance notice that they will need leave, although these laws also recognize that the employee may be facing an emergency and be unable to give notice. State law may also require employees to provide some written proof that they took leave for reasons related to domestic violence.

D

- **Use of paid leave.** Currently, no state requires employers to pay employees for this time off; only the District of Columbia does. Some states allow employees to use their paid leave (such as sick or vacation days) while taking time off for domestic violence; others require employees to use up all of their paid leave before taking domestic violence leave.

You can find information on each state's domestic violence leave laws at www.legalmomentum.org (look for the article titled "Employment Rights for Victims of Domestic or Sexual Violence").

State crime victim laws. In addition to laws that require employers to provide domestic violence leave, most states have laws that protect employees who must take time off for legal matters relating to a criminal case in which they are a victim or witness. These laws differ in the legal matters they cover: Some states protect only employees who have been subpoenaed to appear in court and testify; others cover more activities, such as seeking a restraining order, attending court hearings, or preparing to testify.

Family and Medical Leave Act (FMLA). The FMLA is a federal law that allows certain employees to take up to 12 weeks off every 12 months for their own serious health condition, to care for a family member with a serious health condition, or to care for a new child (among other things). An employee who is physically injured or develops psychological trauma as a result of domestic violence might be entitled to FMLA leave. An employee might also be able to take time off to care for a parent or child who has been a victim of domestic violence.

FMLA leave is unpaid, although employees may use their accrued paid sick or vacation leave while on FMLA leave. The FMLA applies only to employers that have at least 50 employees working within 75 miles of each other, and employees who have worked for at least a year, and at least 1,250 hours in the past year, for the employer.

Related terms: Family and Medical Leave Act; restraining order (for employer); workplace violence.

dooced

Have you been fired for what you wrote in a personal blog or other online post? Then consider yourself "dooced." The term comes from the name of a blog kept by Heather Armstrong, www.dooce.com. Armstrong was fired by her employer (whom she never identified on her blog) for humorous posts about the annoying habits of her coworkers and what she actually did when she was supposed to be working at home. Armstrong now gives this hard-won advice to others, in the "About" section of her blog:

> Never write about work on the internet unless your boss knows and sanctions the fact that YOU ARE WRITING ABOUT WORK ON THE INTERNET. If you are the boss, however, you should be aware that when you order Prada online and then talk about it out loud that you are making it very hard for those around you to take you seriously.

She's also enjoying a very hearty last laugh, however: Her blog is so popular that it's now her full-time job; she's the author of two books; and she made Forbes's list of the top 25 "Web Celebs."

downsizing

A company that is reducing the size of its workforce is said to be downsizing. Downsizing is almost always achieved through layoffs, although it may include other strategies to make the company smaller, such as attrition (not replacing employees who leave the company), hiring freezes, and retirement incentives.

Would you like to rightsize that? How does downsizing differ from layoffs? Not much at all in practice, although some commentators have pointed out that the term "downsizing" implies an intent to streamline a company and make its operations more efficient, and might happen even when there's no economic need to trim payroll costs. Layoffs, on the other hand, are usually seen as a more direct response to economic pressures on the company. Perhaps this explains the brief popularity of the term "rightsizing," an effort to make putting people on the unemployment line sound more strategic and less desperate.

You Can Thank Detroit

According to a study by Matissa Hollister, a professor at Dartmouth, the term "downsizing" was first used during the oil crisis in the 1970s, to refer to the American automobile industry's effort to make cars smaller and more gas efficient. Shortly thereafter, the term was used to refer to any physical shrinking or scaling down of an object, from downsizing one's home (that is, moving to a smaller one) after the kids go to college to reducing the size of consumer products, such as candy bars.

Companies began using the term in the early 1980s in its modern context, hoping to capitalize on the term's positive connotations of efficiency and competitiveness. By playing on the metaphor of the company as a machine (like an automobile), using the term downsizing drew attention away from the very real human costs of workers losing jobs, as well as the fact that a company engaging in downsizing is usually having economic problems.

"Speaking of Downsizing: The use of the term 'downsizing' in American news media 1975-2007," by Matissa Hollister, available at www.dartmouth.edu/~socy/pdfs/HollisterSpeakingDownsizing.pdf.

Related terms: layoff; mass layoff; plant closing; Worker Adjustment and Retraining Notification Act (WARN).

dress codes

Many employers impose dress codes that regulate employee appearance. Some employers simply require employees to maintain a neat, clean appearance at all times. Other employers are more specific. Among the more common requirements are rules that:

D

- require employees to wear or refrain from wearing certain clothing (for example, a requirement that men wear a sport coat and tie or a prohibition on jeans or shorts at work)
- prohibit certain types of jewelry (for instance, no dangling earrings or no facial piercings)
- require or prohibit certain grooming (such as a rule that prohibits long hair for men or requires women to wear makeup)
- require employees not to have tattoos or to cover tattoos completely while working
- require employees to wear safety gear, such as steel-toed boots, hairnets, hardhats, or gloves, and
- require employees to wear uniforms.

Different requirements for men and women. Employees have challenged gender-based dress codes (those that impose different standards for men and women) as illegal sex discrimination. For the most part, however, courts have found that these differing standards are legal as long as they are in line with societal norms and don't impose a greater burden on employees of one sex.

Other types of discrimination claims. Dress code requirements might also discriminate on the basis of race, national origin, religion, and disability. Here are some examples:

- An employer requires all male employees to be clean-shaven. Such a policy might have a disparate impact on African American men, who are more likely to suffer from Pseudofolliculitis barbae (a painful skin condition caused and exacerbated by shaving).
- An employer disciplines an employee for wearing traditional Indian clothing at work. Its dress code requires only that employees be neat and clean, and it has never enforced the dress code before. The employee might have a claim of national origin discrimination.
- An employer requires all male employees to have hair no longer than their collars. An employee asks for an accommodation, because his Native American religion requires him not to cut

Yes, That Makeup Is a Job Requirement

Darlene Jespersen was a bartender at Harrah's casino for 20 years, and had an excellent performance record. All bartenders, male and female, were required to wear the same uniform: black pants and vest, a white shirt, and a black bow tie. Throughout Jespersen's employment, women were also "encouraged," but not required, to wear makeup.

In 2000, Harrah's adopted grooming requirements that imposed different standards on men and women. The rules were fairly detailed: Among other things, they prohibited men from having ponytails, wearing make-up, or wearing colored nail polish; and required women to tease, curl, or style their hair every day (and wear it down), and to refrain from exotic nail art or length. Jespersen objected to only one of the rules, which required women to wear makeup. (Specifically, the rules required women to wear face powder, blush, and mascara "in complementary colors" and to wear lip color at all times.) Jespersen never wore makeup, felt that doing so conflicted with her self-image, and found having to wear it so demeaning and degrading that it interfered with her ability to do her job. Because she wouldn't comply with the requirement and didn't qualify for any positions at the casino with comparable pay, she had to leave her job.

Jespersen sued, claiming that these requirements amounted to illegal sex stereotyping, whose purpose was to exploit female bartenders. The federal Court of Appeals for the Ninth Circuit disagreed, however. The Court found that grooming standards and dress codes that differentiate between men and women are acceptable unless they impose an unequal burden on one gender. Jespersen didn't show that the policy was more onerous for women, and there was no proof that Harrah's purpose was to require female employees to conform to a stereotypical image of how women should look (especially in light of the fact that the uniform requirement was largely unisex).

Jespersen v. Harrah's Operating Co., Inc., 444 F.3d 1104 (9th Cir. 2006).

D

his hair. If the employer fails to grant the accommodation, it might be subject to a religious discrimination lawsuit.

- An employee who uses a wheelchair complains that the stiff polyester uniform he must wear bunches up and irritates his skin. To avoid a disability discrimination lawsuit, the employer should work with the employee to come up with an alternative outfit that approximates the uniform without causing the employee discomfort.

Religious tattoos and piercings. In a recent twist, some employees have claimed that their religious beliefs require them to have tattoos or piercings, and that covering or removing them for work is unacceptable. For example, a server at Red Robin claimed that the tattoos on his wrists were part of his Kemetic religion (an ancient Egyptian faith), and that covering the tattoos for work, as Red Robin asked him to do, was a sin. The EEOC sued Red Robin, which settled the case after the company lost its motion for summary judgment. A Costco employee didn't fare so well: She refused to remove or cover her facial piercings for work, claiming that her membership in the Church of Body Modification required her to display her piercings at all times. She lost her lawsuit after the court found that Costco was entitled to require its employees to have a professional appearance, and had offered a number of accommodations that allowed her to cover her piercings.

Related terms: religious discrimination; sex discrimination.

drug testing

Many employers require drug testing: screening of the urine, saliva, breath, blood, or hair of employees or applicants to determine whether they use specified drugs. Contrary to popular belief, drug testing is legally required only for certain employees in the transportation industry and other safety-sensitive positions (for example, working with pipelines, national security, or aviation). Otherwise, employers are not required to test for drugs, although many do.

D

Which Employers Test—and When?

Despite the legal hurdles, many employers test for drugs or alcohol. According to the National Survey on Drug Use and Health, nearly half of all full-time employees reported that their employers tested for illegal drug use, and more than 35% reported that their employers tested for alcohol use. Testing was most likely to happen during the hiring process: About 43% of employees reported that their employers tested applicants, but only about 30% reported random drug or alcohol testing of current employees.

Employees in the transportation, moving, and protective services industries are much more likely to face random alcohol and drug testing: Almost two-thirds of employees in these industries reported that their employers conducted random testing. Employees engaged in manufacturing, installation, maintenance, and repair also reported high rates of random testing. At the other end of the spectrum, employees working in legal occupations, entertainment industries (including media and sports), and education and libraries reported the lowest levels of random testing.

Legal limits on drug testing. Except for the testing required of transit and other safety-sensitive employees, federal law neither requires nor prohibits drug testing. However, some states encourage testing by offering employers discounts on their premiums for workers' compensation insurance if they adopt a drug-free workplace program, which may include drug testing for employees or applicants.

At the same time, many states limit an employer's ability to test. For example, some states allow random drug testing; others allow testing only if the employer has some reason to suspect drug use (following an accident or based on the employee's appearance or behavior, for example). States that allow testing often impose notice and policy requirements, and some states give employees the right to contest a positive result, ask for a retest, or receive a copy of the test results.

After you, boss. Fair is fair in Utah, a state that allows employers to drug test applicants, but only if management also submits to periodic testing.

Even in states that don't limit drug testing, employees might have a legal claim against their employer based on the way the test was conducted, the reasons for the test, or what the employer did with the test results. Here are some of the legal challenges that might be made:

- **Discrimination claims.** If a company singles out certain groups of employees—by race or disability, for example—for testing, it could face a discrimination claim. Similarly, a company that tests only union members or supporters could face an unfair labor practices charge.

- **Invasion of privacy.** Even if a company has a legal right to test, the way the testing is conducted could lead to invasion of privacy claims. For example, an employee who is required to provide a urine sample while others are watching might have a valid legal claim.

- **Disability-based claims.** An employee who is taking medication for a disability is protected from discrimination by the Americans with Disabilities Act (ADA). Some prescribed medications turn up on drug tests, and some drugs that would otherwise be illegal are legitimately prescribed for certain conditions. Someone who is fired or not hired because of a positive drug test might have a valid claim of disability discrimination under these circumstances.

- **Defamation.** An employee might have a valid defamation claim against an employer who publicizes that the employee tested positive, if the employer has reason to know that the test result might not be accurate. For example, if a retest showed that the first test was a false positive or the employee has appealed the first test, the employer may be liable for revealing the results of the positive test beyond those with a need to know.

Related terms: Americans with Disabilities Act; defamation; medical marijuana; privacy; reasonable accommodation; workers' compensation.

duty of fair representation

A union has a duty of fair representation—an obligation to act equitably and in good faith toward the employees in the bargaining unit. This means that the union may not discriminate (for example, on the basis of race or of whether the employee supports or is a member of the union) among bargaining unit employees in deciding how to handle employee grievances or how to enforce the collective bargaining agreement. Although the union has broad discretion to decide how best to handle individual cases, it must always act fairly and in good faith toward the employees it represents.

Related terms: bargaining unit; collective bargaining agreement.

duty of loyalty

Employees have a duty of loyalty toward their employer, which generally means they may not act in ways that conflict or compete with the employer's interests while employed. Although states define and interpret the duty of loyalty in different ways, it typically prohibits employees from, for example, starting a competing business while working for the employer, giving (or selling) the employer's trade secrets or other confidential information to a competitor, or acting in ways that benefit the employee or another company at the employer's expense (such as using a high-priced vendor that gives the employee a kickback).

The duty ends with the job. An employee's duty of loyalty to an employer lasts only as long as the employee is working there. However, other laws or contractual agreements may limit an employee's actions after leaving the job. For example, state laws prohibit employees from disclosing a previous employer's trade secrets to a new employer. Similarly, if the employee has signed a valid noncompete agreement, the employee may be prohibited from working for a competitor for a period of time after the job ends.

Related terms: covenant not to compete; trade secret.

D

EAP

EAP is the acronym for an "employee assistance program." Some
companies offer an EAP as an employee benefit to help employees
deal with personal or family issues, such as financial problems,
divorce, substance abuse, elder care, or estate planning. An EAP
might provide written materials, counselors, access to information
(through a website, for example), and treatment programs. An
employee might be referred to the company's EAP for problems that
are interfering with work, such as anger management or substance
abuse. Or, the employee might seek help independently for a
personal issue, such as learning about options for caring for an aging
parent or finding out how to make a budget and control spending.

EEOC

See Equal Employment Opportunity Commission.

email monitoring

Email monitoring is the practice of reviewing the content of email
messages. Among the practitioners are concerned parents, suspicious
spouses, and plenty of employers. According to a 2007 survey
by the American Management Association, 43% of companies
monitor employee email. Almost three-quarters of employers who
monitor use technology to automatically review messages (typically
for keywords that could indicate inappropriate content, offensive
language, or company trade secrets); 40% have an actual human
being read employee email.

E

Who's Monitoring the Monitors?

One-third of IT administrators admit snooping through employee email, files, and other confidential information, according to a 2007 survey. (Manek Dubash, "Study: IT Admins Read Private Email," *PC World*, May 29, 2007). The employees apparently had very little "need to know," but the technology was in place—and the opportunity to spy on their coworkers was just too tempting.

Monitoring versus privacy. Almost every court to consider the issue has found that an employer has the right to monitor email messages stored, sent, and received on the company's email system. The employer's legitimate interest in keeping track of how employees spend their work hours, preventing electronic harassment and other misconduct, and protecting company trade secrets has been found to outweigh any privacy interest the employee may have in the content of email messages. Employers that monitor employee email often take precautions to diminish employees' expectations of privacy, such as adopting a written policy explaining that the company monitors email, requiring employees to sign an acknowledgment of the company's right to read employee email, and restricting use of the company's email system to business purposes only.

What about personal email accounts? Some employers monitor not only messages sent and received on the company's email system, but messages sent and received from employees' personal Web-based email accounts, if those communications take place using the employer's equipment. However, a company's legal right to actually read messages sent to and from an employee's personal email account, even if those messages are sent using company equipment, is unsettled. A few courts have held that an employer may not read personal messages (and particularly not messages exchanged with an attorney) in an employee's personal email account. This is especially so if the employer accesses the messages using the employee's password, as captured by monitoring software.

Related term: privacy.

employee

An employee is someone who does work for another person or company in exchange for pay, and is not an independent contractor.

Related term: independent contractor.

employee assistance program

See EAP.

Employee Polygraph Protection Act

The Employment Polygraph Protection Act (EPPA) is a federal law that strictly limits the circumstances in which an employer can require employees or applicants to take a polygraph test. Most private employers are prohibited from requiring employees or applicants to take a polygraph (very limited exceptions apply to employers that manufacture, distribute, or dispense certain controlled substances and employers that provide certain security services).

The ongoing investigation exception. There is one exception that applies to *all* private employers. An employer may ask an employee to take a polygraph test during an ongoing investigation of wrongdoing if all of these conditions are met:

- The test is administered in connection with an ongoing investigation of economic loss or injury to the employer's business.
- The employee had access to the property that is the subject of the investigation.
- The employer has a reasonable suspicion that the employee was involved in the incident or activity under investigation.
- The employer provides the employee with certain information about the incident, the loss, and the reasons for its suspicion, in writing.

E

Procedural requirements. Even if an exception applies, the employer must follow a long list of technical requirements before it can use the results of the test to make a disciplinary decision about the employee. For example, the employee must receive a variety of written notices, must receive the test questions in advance, cannot be asked certain types of questions, and must receive a copy of the test results, among other things. In addition, the employer may only use a polygraph examiner who meets certain qualifications and reports the results of the test in a particular form.

Employee Retirement Income Security Act

The Employee Retirement Income Security Act (ERISA) is a federal law that regulates the benefit and pension plans offered by private employers. ERISA doesn't require employers to adopt these plans; instead, it regulates plans that are voluntarily adopted. Among other things, ERISA requires employers to provide certain information about the plans to employees and imposes fiduciary duties on those responsible for managing the plans.

employer

At the most basic level, an employer is a person or company that employs workers. Because different laws define the term "employer" differently, however, a company might qualify as an employer under one law but not under another. For example, a person or company must have at least 15 employees to be an employer under Title VII, but must have at least 20 employees to be an employer under the Age Discrimination in Employment Act. Some laws define "employer" in a way that includes individual managers, supervisors, and human resources personnel. For example, the Family and Medical Leave Act (FMLA) defines an employer to include any person who acts in the interests of an employer toward its employees, whether directly or indirectly; courts have found that managers and HR professionals may be named personally as defendants in FMLA lawsuits because they are "employers" under this provision.

employment contract

An employment contract is an agreement between an employer and an employee regarding the terms of employment. An employment contract can range from a simple handshake agreement ("The job is yours if you want it; can you start tomorrow?") to a lengthy written contract filled with legalese.

At-will employment contracts. As explained previously (see the entry for "at-will employment," above), most employees in the U.S. are presumed to work at will, which means they can quit at any time, and can be fired at any time, for any reason that isn't illegal. (Illegal reasons for firing include discrimination and retaliation.) An employment contract doesn't necessarily change an employee's at-will status: An employer and employee can agree on important details about the job without agreeing that the employee will have job security. In fact, many employers ask employees to sign written employment agreements explicitly acknowledging that they will be employed at will.

> **EXAMPLE:** When FunCo hires a new employee, the human resources director sends the new hire a letter formally offering the job, which includes information about the employee's position, salary, reporting relationships, job duties, and work hours. The letter also clearly states that the employee will work at will. The director signs and sends two copies of the offer letter and asks the employee to sign and return one copy of the letter to indicate his acceptance of the position on the terms offered. Once signed by employer and employee, the offer letter becomes a written contract for at-will employment.

Even though an at-will employee can be fired at any time for any legal reason, that employee still has a right to enforce the terms of an employment contract. For example, let's say an employee signs a written employment agreement that includes an at-will provision and a formula that will be used to calculate commissions the employee earns. After a year, the employee is fired. The employee may not rely on the contract to challenge his firing; it says he can be fired at will. However, if the company paid him only half of the promised commission amount, he can sue for breach of that contractual provision.

Types of contracts. An employment contract may be written, oral, or implied from the circumstances.

- **Written contracts.** A written contract is a document that sets forth the terms of employment. As noted above, some written contracts are for at-will employment. Others limit the employer's right to fire. For example, it's not unusual for high-level executives to be hired pursuant to a written contract that obligates them to stay with the company for a set period of time (for example, two or three years), and obligates the company to retain the executive for the same period unless he or she does something specified in the contract as grounds for termination (such as committing a felony, embezzling from the company, or engaging in financial malfeasance).

- **Oral contracts.** An oral contract is simply an agreement that's spoken rather than written down. For example, an employer might call a successful applicant on the phone, offer her the job, and settle on a starting date, salary, and schedule. Once the employee says, "that sounds great; I accept," there is an oral contract of employment. Oral contracts are just as enforceable as written contracts, but much harder to prove. If there's a dispute, it will be the employee's word against the employer's. Like a written contract, an oral contract might be for at-will employment or it might limit the employer's right to fire. If, for example, an employer says, "I need a two-year commitment from you; during that time, the company won't fire you as long as you make your numbers," and the employee agrees, the employee can hold the employer to that promise. If the employee is fired for any other reason, that's a breach of the oral contract.

- **Implied contracts.** An implied contract is one that has not been reduced to a formal document or even stated explicitly, but is instead implied from a combination of the employer's oral and written statements and actions. Whether there's an implied contract typically comes up after an employee has been fired. The employer argues that the employee was at will, and so can't sue for breach of contract; the employee counters that the employer's actions and statements led the employee to believe that the employee would be fired only for good cause, and were sufficient to create a contract to that effect. Here are some of the factors courts consider in deciding whether an implied employment contract was created (different states apply different standards when considering implied contract claims):

- **Whether the employer gave the employee assurances of job security.** For example, if the employer says that the employee will be fired only for good cause or will have a job as long as he or she performed well, that might lead a court to find that an implied contract exists.

- **Whether the employer's policies limit its right to fire at will.** For example, progressive discipline policies that don't give the employer leeway to depart from the stated procedures, policies providing that new employees become "permanent" after completing a probationary period, policies promising regular promotions and raises if performance meets a certain standard, and policies requiring good cause to fire might be used as evidence that the employer had given up the right to fire at will.

- **The employee's tenure.** A long-term employee who has received regular promotions, raises, and positive performance evaluations has a better shot at making an implied contract claim than a short-term employee.

If the employee has signed an at-will agreement, a court will not allow the employee to argue that there was a contradictory implied contract.

Related terms: at-will employment; good cause; implied contract; permanent employee; progressive discipline.

Employment Division, Dept. of Human Resources of Oregon v. Smith

See Religious Freedom Restoration Act.

Employment Eligibility Verification Form (I-9)

USCIS Form I-9, *Employment Eligibility Verification Form,* is a form employers and employees must complete when a new employee starts work, showing that the employee is authorized to work in the United States. Employees must provide basic identifying information and swear under penalty of perjury that they are authorized to work in the U.S. The employer must review documents presented by the employee proving identify and work authorization, then swear under penalty of perjury that the documents were reviewed and appeared to be genuine. Form I-9 need not be submitted to the federal government, but must be kept on file and available for review in the event of an audit.

Related term: Immigration Reform and Control Act.

employment practices liability insurance (EPLI)

Employment practices liability insurance (EPLI) is a type of insurance policy that protects a company if employees bring legal claims against it arising out of the employment relationship, such as discrimination, harassment, wrongful discharge, breach of employment contract, and so on. This type of policy typically covers the cost of defending a lawsuit, including attorney fees and the amount of any judgment entered against the company. However, these policies might not cover awards of punitive damages: damages intended to punish the employer for misconduct rather than to compensate the employee for harm suffered as a result of the employer's actions.

Related terms: damages; discrimination; employment contract; harassment; wrongful discharge.

English-only rules

English-only rules are workplace policies that prohibit employees from speaking any language other than English on the job, or at certain times and places (for example, while serving customers). Many employers have legitimate reasons for requiring employees to speak English, including the ability to communicate with coworkers and customers. At the same time, however, the language people speak is often closely associated with their national origin: their ancestry, birthplace, and ethnicity. Because federal law and the laws of many states prohibit discrimination based on national origin, courts carefully scrutinize English-only rules to make sure they aren't discriminatory.

Generally, English-only rules are legal if they are necessary for business reasons and don't evidence intentional discrimination. The rule must not have been adopted for discriminatory reasons or be applied in discriminatory ways. For example, an employer may not adopt an English-only rule as a subterfuge to get rid of Latino workers. Similarly, an employer may not selectively enforce an English-only rule (against workers who speak Farsi but not workers who speak Spanish, for example).

As long as the English-only rule isn't motivated by discriminatory intent, it will pass legal muster if it is necessary for the safe or efficient operation of the business. For example, if most customers or coworkers speak English and aren't fluent in other languages, then an English-only rule might be necessary to promote communication and ensure safety, in case of an emergency. If employees work closely together and some speak only English, an English-only rule might be necessary to allow them to do their jobs.

Even if there are valid reasons for adopting an English-only rule, the rule must be narrowly tailored to address the actual needs of the workplace. For example, it is reasonable to require employees who deal with English-speaking customers to communicate in English. However, a rule that forbids workers from ever speaking another language, even during breaks or when a customer who also speaks that language is present, may be too broad to survive a legal challenge.

Before an employer adopts an English-only rule, it must notify employees and tell them of the consequences of breaking the rule.

Related term: national origin discrimination.

EPA

See Equal Pay Act.

EPPA

See Employment Polygraph Protection Act.

Equal Employment Opportunity Commission

The Equal Employment Opportunity Commission (EEOC) is the federal government agency that administers, interprets, and enforces the federal laws that prohibit employment discrimination. Created by the Civil Rights Act of 1964, the EEOC is a large government agency with hundreds of employees and numerous field offices throughout the United States. The actual "commission" for which it is named has five members, appointed by the President, who set policy for the agency and oversee its litigation, among other things.

Laws enforced by the EEOC. The EEOC enforces these federal antidiscrimination laws:

- Title VII (part of the Civil Rights Act of 1964), which prohibits discrimination on the basis of race, color, national origin, religion, and sex
- The Equal Pay Act, which requires employers to pay men and women equally for doing equal work
- The Age Discrimination in Employment Act, which prohibits age discrimination against those who are at least 40 years old
- The Americans with Disabilities Act, which prohibits discrimination on the basis of disability

- The Genetic Information Nondiscrimination Act, which prohibits discrimination based on genetic information.

What the EEOC does. The EEOC has a number of functions, including:

- accepting, investigating, and settling charges of discrimination from employees and applicants
- filing lawsuits on behalf of employees and applicants who have been discriminated against or harassed
- providing education, outreach, and training on discrimination issues
- issuing regulations interpreting the laws the agency enforces, and
- enforcing the laws that prohibit discrimination against federal employees.

Related terms: Age Discrimination in Employment Act; Americans with Disabilities Act; Equal Pay Act; Genetic Information Nondiscrimination Act; Title VII.

Equal Pay Act

The Equal Pay Act (EPA) requires employers to give men and women equal pay for equal work. Congress passed the EPA to combat "the ancient but outmoded belief that a man, because of his role in society, should be paid more than a woman." (*Corning Glass Works v. Brennan*, 417 U.S. 188, 195 (1974).) Despite its gender-specific origins, however, the EPA protects both men and women from wage discrimination based on sex.

Who's covered by the EPA. Most government and private employers must comply with the EPA. Unlike other antidiscrimination laws, the EPA applies regardless of how many employees work for an employer. Businesses that generate at least $500,000 in annual sales are covered. Businesses that generate lower sales are also covered if they are involved in interstate commerce (because of the way courts and Congress have defined interstate commerce, most employers are covered).

E

Defining equal work. Although jobs need not be identical to qualify as equal, they must be pretty darn close. They must require substantially equal skills, effort, and responsibility, and be performed under similar working conditions within the same establishment. Job titles don't determine whether jobs are equal: Courts look at the actual tasks an employee has to perform rather than the job designation. For example, an employer may not pay a male "administrative assistant" more than a female "secretary" if they have essentially the same duties.

Defining equal pay. The EPA requires only that workers performing equal work be paid at the same pay rate, not that workers receive the same total amount of pay. If an employer pays a commission or by the piece, for example, the employer must use the same formula— such as 10% of the company's gross profit per sale or $1 per unit produced—to calculate pay for men and women. If one worker earns more than another because of higher productivity, that does not violate the EPA. Financial incentives for good performance work the same way. An employer may not offer men the opportunity to earn a bonus for high sales volume or productivity while denying the same opportunity to women. However, if a bonus is offered on the same terms to all employees and the only workers who meet the criteria for the bonus are men, an employer may legally pay the bonus to those men only.

With a few exceptions. There are four exceptions to the EPA, which allow an employer to pay employees of one sex at a higher rate than workers of the opposite sex without violating the law:

- **Seniority.** An employer may pay more to employees who have been with the company longer, even if this results in workers of one sex getting paid more to do the same job.
- **Merit.** An employer may pay higher rates (larger bonuses or raises, for example) to employees whose performance is better, regardless of gender.
- **Quantity or quality of production.** An employer may pay a higher rate for better quality work or pay workers based on productivity (on commission, for example), as long as both men and women have the opportunity to earn the higher rate.

- **Any factor other than sex.** This catchall exception is intended to encompass any legitimate reason why an employer might pay one worker more than another to do the same job, as long as the discrepancy isn't based on gender. It would not violate the EPA, for example, to pay a shift premium to all employees on the night shift.

What about Title VII? Title VII, the primary federal law that prohibits discrimination in employment, also outlaws wage discrimination. However, there are some important differences between Title VII and the EPA:

- **Exhaustion requirements.** To bring a Title VII lawsuit, an employee must first file a charge of discrimination with the Equal Employment Opportunity Commission (EEOC) and receive a right to sue letter. (This is called "exhausting" administrative remedies.) Employees who want to sue under the EPA may go straight to court. They may also file a charge of discrimination at the EEOC, but aren't required to do so.

- **Available damages.** An employee who wins an EPA claim is entitled to back pay (what the employee should have earned less what the employee actually earned). The employee may also be awarded an additional penalty, called liquidated damages, equal to the entire back pay award, unless the employer can demonstrate that it acted in good faith and had reasonable grounds to believe that its conduct did not violate the law. Under Title VII, liquidated damages aren't available, but employees can be awarded damages for pain and suffering and punitive damages, which aren't available under the EPA.

- **Time limits.** An employee must file a Title VII claim within 300 days of the discriminatory act (the time limit is shorter if the state where the employee files doesn't have its own law prohibiting gender discrimination in pay). Under the EPA, an employee has two years to file a lawsuit, or three years if the employer committed a willful violation of the law.

Related terms: comparable worth; exhaustion (of remedies); sex discrimination; Title VII.

ergonomics

Ergonomics is the study of fitting the conditions, equipment, tools, and demands of a job to the human beings who perform that job, with the intent of avoiding injury and strain. For an employee who enters data on a keyboard, for example, ergonomics may address the proper height and tilt of the employee's chair; height of the desktop; placement and shape of the keyboard and mouse; height, tilt, brightness, and glare protection of the screen, and so on.

The Fight Over an Ergonomic Standard

The Occupational Safety and Health Administration (OSHA), the federal agency that enforces workplace safety laws, announced in 1992 that it intended to propose regulations on ergonomics. Almost immediately, a pitched battle arose between supporters and opponents of such a rule, with unions and employee rights advocates lining up in favor and business and employer advocacy groups lining up against. Congress even got into the act when it passed a 1995 bill that prohibited OSHA from issuing ergonomics regulations (President Clinton vetoed this effort). After years of battles, both within Congress and without, OSHA finally released a proposed ergonomics standard in 1999, which was finalized in 2000.

But the standard was in effect for only a couple of months. Congress passed a resolution to repeal it, which President Bush signed in March 2001. The measure also prohibits OSHA from issuing subsequent regulations that are substantially similar to the ones that were repealed.

OSHA has issued guidelines that address ergonomics issues in particular work environments, such as nursing homes and poultry processing plants. The agency has also said that the OSH Act's "general duty" clause, which requires employers to provide a place of employment free from recognized hazards that are likely to cause death or serious physical harm to employees, encompasses serious ergonomic hazards. To date, however, it has not issued new regulations on ergonomics.

Related terms: Occupational Safety and Health Act; Occupational Safety and Health Administration.

ERISA

See Employee Retirement Income Security Act.

escalator position

The escalator position is the position an employee would have attained, had he or she not taken time off to serve in the military. The Uniformed Services Employment and Reemployment Rights Act (USERRA) guarantees certain employment rights to workers who are in the uniformed services: the Army, Navy, Marine Corps, Air Force, Coast Guard, Reserves, Army or Air National Guard, and Commissioned Corps of the Public Health Service. Among other things, USERRA gives employees who take up to five years of leave to serve in the uniformed services the right to be reinstated not to the position they previously held, but to the escalator position: the position the employee would have held if not for taking leave.

The escalator position includes any promotions, pay raises, increased responsibilities, and other benefits the employee ordinarily would have attained. However, the escalator doesn't just go up: The escalator position could also reflect a demotion, transfer, or even layoff, if those events would have occurred if the employee had not taken leave. If the employee isn't qualified for the escalator position, the employer must make reasonable efforts to help the employee qualify. If these efforts fail, the employer may reinstate the employee to the position he or she held prior to taking leave for military service.

Related term: Uniformed Services Employment and Reemployment Rights Act.

essential job functions

Essential job functions are the fundamental duties of a position: the things a person holding the job absolutely must be able to

E

do. Essential job functions are used to determine the rights of an employee with a disability under the Americans with Disabilities Act (ADA). An employee who is otherwise qualified (for example, because the employee has the degrees and experience required for the position) and can perform the essential functions of a job, with or without a reasonable accommodation from the employer, is protected from discrimination on the basis of disability. However, an employee who can't perform the essential functions, even with a reasonable accommodation, is not protected.

If a function is truly essential, and an applicant or employee cannot perform it even with a reasonable accommodation, then that person is not "qualified" for the job as a legal matter. The person cannot bring a disability discrimination lawsuit against the employer, even if the person couldn't perform the essential job functions because of a disability. On the other hand, if a function is not truly essential, the employer cannot exclude a person with a disability from consideration for the position just because that person can't perform the function. Legally, it may not play a role in the employer's decision-making process.

Which job duties are essential. The Equal Employment Opportunity Commission, the federal agency that enforces the ADA and other antidiscrimination laws, looks at these factors in determining whether a function is essential:

- the employer's assessment of which functions are essential, as demonstrated by job descriptions written before the employer posts or advertises for the position
- whether the position exists to perform that function (if the entire job consists of one function, such as loading and unloading boxes or entering information into a database, then that function is essential)
- the experience of employees who actually hold that position
- the time spent performing the function
- the consequences of not performing the function
- whether other employees are available to perform that function, and

- the degree of expertise or skill required to perform the function.

Related terms: Americans with Disabilities Act; disability; Equal Employment Opportunity Commission; qualified individual with a disability; reasonable accommodation.

exempt employee

An exempt employee is one who isn't entitled to overtime under the Fair Labor Standards Act (FLSA).

Exempt from overtime and minimum wage requirements. Some employees are exempt from both the minimum wage and the overtime rules set in the FLSA (although they are still protected by the rest of the law's provisions):

- executive, administrative, and professional employees who are paid on a salary basis
- independent contractors
- volunteer workers
- outside salespeople
- computer systems analysts, programmers, and software engineers who earn at least $27.63 an hour or $455 a week
- employees of seasonal amusement or recreational businesses, like ski resorts or county fairs
- employees of organized camps or religious and nonprofit educational conference centers that operate fewer than seven months a year
- newspaper deliverers and employees of certain small newspapers
- workers engaged in fishing operations
- seamen on international vessels
- employees who work on small farms
- certain switchboard operators, and
- casual domestic babysitters and people who provide companionship to those who are unable to care for themselves (this exception does not apply to those who provide nursing

care or personal and home care aides who perform a variety of domestic services).

Exempt from overtime requirements only. In addition, these employees are exempt from only the overtime provisions of the FLSA:

- rail, air, and motor carrier employees
- employees who buy poultry, eggs, cream, or milk in their unprocessed state
- those who sell cars, trucks, farm implements, trailers, boats, or aircraft
- mechanics or parts persons who service cars, trucks, or farm implements
- announcers, news editors, and chief engineers of certain broadcasting stations
- local delivery drivers or drivers' helpers who are compensated on a trip rate plan
- agricultural workers
- taxi drivers
- domestic service workers who live in the employer's home, and
- movie theater employees.

Related terms: administrative employee; Fair Labor Standards Act; independent contractor; manager; minimum wage; outside salesperson; overtime; pay docking; professional employee; salary basis; volunteer.

exhaustion (of remedies)

Before filing a lawsuit based on certain types of legal claims, the plaintiff may be required to "exhaust" other options for resolving the dispute. In employment law, employees may be required to raise their claims before an administrative agency before filing a lawsuit. For example, an employee who wishes to file a discrimination lawsuit must exhaust remedies by first filing a charge of discrimination with either the Equal Employment Opportunity Commission (EEOC) or the state agency that handles discrimination complaints (called fair employment practices, or FEP, agencies). If an employee files a lawsuit before filing a charge with the appropriate government agency, the lawsuit will be dismissed for failure to exhaust administrative remedies.

Related terms: charge; Equal Employment Opportunity Commission; FEP laws.

exit interview

An exit interview is a discussion or question-and-answer session an employer holds with an employee who is leaving the company. Exit interviews are not legally required, and not all employers use them. Some employers use exit interviews for routine housekeeping matters. For example, the employer might collect company property from the employee, review paperwork (such as health insurance continuation, severance agreements, or ongoing contractual obligations, such as a noncompete agreement or confidentiality agreement), and distribute the employee's final paycheck. Some employers use exit interviews to gather information about the employee's experience at the company. For example, if a star performer quits, the employer might want to find out what led to the decision, so it can take steps to prevent similar incidents in the future.

Related terms: Consolidated Omnibus Budget Reconciliation Act (COBRA); covenant not to compete; final paycheck; severance agreement.

extended base period

See base period.

FAA

See Federal Arbitration Act.

Fair Employment Practices Laws

See FEP laws.

Fair Credit Reporting Act

The Fair Credit Reporting Act (FCRA) is a federal law that regulates the collection and use of consumer credit information. The FCRA has two purposes:

- to protect the privacy of consumer credit information by restricting access to those who have both a legitimate need for the information and the consent of the person whose records are sought, and
- to ensure the accuracy of that information by giving people the right to see their credit reports (and other records, in some circumstances), the right to know whether someone has decided not to offer them credit, employment, housing, or other benefits based on that information, and the right to dispute information that is incorrect or incomplete.

To serve these goals, the FCRA imposes a number of legal obligations on consumer reporting agencies (such as credit bureaus) and on those who use credit information and other information gathered by third parties to make important decisions. This includes employers who pull credit reports, run criminal records checks, or conduct detailed background checks on applicants, current employees, or independent contractors.

F

Special Rules for Investigation of Workplace Misconduct

Once upon a time, employers had to follow the FCRA's notice and adverse action procedures when they hired an outside investigator to look into allegations of workplace misconduct. Before the investigation could take place, the employer had to tell the accused employee that an investigation would be conducted, get the employee's written consent to the investigation ahead of time, give a copy of the investigation report to the employee, and wait a "reasonable time" before taking any adverse action based on its contents. Needless to say, these requirements had the potential to completely derail an investigation.

After much protest and controversy, the rules for investigations were changed in 2003. Now, employers who hire an outside investigator are no longer required to notify the accused employee or get written consent. If the employer decides to take action against the employee based on the investigation report, the employer has to give the employee only a summary of the nature and substance of the report, which need not identify the employees who were interviewed as part of the investigation.

When the FCRA applies. The FCRA covers all employers, but it applies only when the employer gathers information in a way that is covered by the FCRA. The FCRA applies only when an employer requests a consumer report from a consumer reporting agency. A consumer report is any written or oral information to be used for employment purposes, relating to someone's creditworthiness, credit standing, credit capacity, general reputation, personal characteristics, or lifestyle. A consumer reporting agency is a person or entity that regularly provides consumer reports to third parties, such as credit bureaus, private investigators, records search firms, and background checking services. Governmental agencies that are required to keep certain information as a matter of public record are not considered consumer reporting agencies. Employers who gather information for their own purposes (such as running background checks) also don't qualify as consumer reporting agencies, because they aren't providing that information to a third party.

> **EXAMPLE:** Lynette is in charge of hiring delivery drivers for her company. She asks all applicants to submit a copy of their driving record from the DMV and she contacts former employers for references. Lynette doesn't have to comply with the FCRA because she gathered this information herself and from a governmental agency, not through a consumer reporting agency. If Lynette had hired a firm to conduct background checks on applicants or pulled credit reports on applicants, she would have had to follow the FCRA.

What the FCRA requires of employers. The FCRA has four main provisions that apply to employers who use consumer reports:

- **Notice, authorization, and certification procedures.** Before seeking a consumer report or an investigative consumer report (a report based in part on personal interviews that go beyond simply verifying facts the applicant supplies to the employer), employers must notify the subject of the report, in writing, that they want a report. Employers must obtain written authorization from the subject before actually requesting the report, and then verify to the consumer reporting agency that they have given notice and requested authorization.
- **Address-checking procedures.** To protect applicants from identity theft, an employer that requests a report and receives a notice of address discrepancy must take steps to make sure that the report actually relates to the person about whom it requested the report.
- **Adverse action procedures.** If an employer decides not to hire an applicant or to take some other adverse action based in any part on the information in the consumer report, the employer must provide the subject of the report with a copy of the report and information about how the applicant can dispute its accuracy or completeness, among other things.

- **Disposal rules.** Employers that gather or use consumer reports or information must limit access to that information. They must also follow specified methods of destroying the information, to prevent identify theft and other unauthorized uses of that information.

Related terms: background check; consumer report; consumer reporting agency; investigative consumer report; Vail letter.

Fair Labor Standards Act

The Fair Labor Standards Act (FLSA) is the primary federal law governing wages and hours of employment. It includes the federal minimum wage, rules on what counts as an hour worked, overtime provisions, and child labor laws. (Each of these topics is covered in a separate entry in this book.)

When the FLSA Was Passed
The FLSA was enacted in 1938 as part of President Franklin D. Roosevelt's New Deal. One purpose of the law was to create an incentive for employers to spread their work among more employees (by requiring employers to pay an overtime premium once an employee had worked 40 hours in a week). Lawmakers thought this would help the country recover from the Great Depression.
The minimum wage today stands at $7.25 an hour. When the FLSA was enacted, there was nothing to the left of the decimal point: The minimum wage was a quarter an hour.
Under the National Industrial Recovery Act, which preceded the FLSA, businesses that voluntarily agreed to abolish child labor, pay a minimum wage, and limit work hours were allowed to display a "Blue Eagle" poster with the motto, "We Do Our Part."

Who is covered by the FLSA. The FLSA applies to public employers, private employers with gross sales of at least $500,000, and private employers who engage in interstate commerce or the production of goods for interstate commerce. Although this might sound limited, courts have interpreted it to apply to almost all employers because it includes any business whose employees handle, sell, produce, or otherwise work on goods or materials that have come from, or will go to, another state, or employee who use the mail, telephone, cable, or other equipment to communicate across state lines.

How the FLSA is enforced. The FLSA is interpreted and enforced by the federal Department of Labor (DOL). Although employees may file a complaint with the DOL if their rights have been violated, they don't have to do so: They can also go straight to court and file a lawsuit. (In other words, there is no requirement that employees "exhaust" their administrative remedies.)

An employee who wins an FLSA lawsuit may be awarded back pay, equal to the difference between what the employee actually earned and what the employee should have earned if the employer had followed the law (for example, by paying required overtime), plus interest. An employee can collect up to two years' worth of back pay (or three years' worth, if the employer committed a willful violation of the statute). Employees may also be awarded an additional sum as liquidated damages, equal to the entire back pay award, if the employer's violation was willful.

Related terms: child labor; Department of Labor; exhaustion (of remedies); hour worked; minimum wage; overtime.

false imprisonment

False imprisonment is a personal injury (tort) claim for restraining someone against his or her will. In the employment context, false imprisonment claims often arise out of an employer's investigation or questioning of an employee, particularly in a situation when misconduct has just occurred and the employer feels a need to get to the bottom of things right away. For example, an employee thought to have taken a valuable piece of jewelry might be locked in a room until she gives it back, or a few employees who got into a fight might be restrained until they admit what happened and who started it.

To make out a claim of false imprisonment, the employee must show that there was an actual or implied threat that force would be used to make the employee stay. An employer doesn't have to actually use force against an employee—for example, by handcuffing the employee, locking the employee in a room, or physically pushing the employee into a room or chair—to commit false imprisonment. If an employee is herded into an office, told that he will not be allowed to leave until he admits stealing from the company, and left in the room with a guard blocking the door, that could be enough to prove false imprisonment, even if the employee never tries to leave.

Related term: tort.

Family and Medical Leave Act

The federal Family and Medical Leave Act (FMLA) requires employers to allow employees to take time off for certain caregiving, medical, and family needs. As originally passed in 1993, the law allowed eligible employees to take leave to care for a new child, recuperate from a serious health condition, or care for a seriously ill family member. The law was amended in 2008 to create additional leave rights when an employee's family member was called to active military duty or returned home from duty with a serious illness or injury.

Who's covered by the FMLA. The FMLA applies to federal, state, and local governments, as well as private employers with at least 50 employees. Not all employees of a covered employer are eligible for leave, however. To qualify, employees must:

- have worked for a covered employer for at least 12 months
- have worked at least 1,250 hours for the employer in the 12 months just before the employee takes leave, and
- work at a location with 50 or more employees within a 75-mile radius.

The basic leave entitlement. Eligible employees may take unpaid time off for specified reasons; certain types of leave may be taken intermittently (a little at a time, as needed). Employees must be reinstated when their leave ends. (An employer may refuse to reinstate key employees—those in the highest paid 10% of the employer's workforce within a 75-mile radius—if the employee's return would cause "substantial and grievous" economic injury to the employer.) Employees may substitute accrued paid leave during FMLA leave, if the employee meets the criteria and follows the procedures of the employer's paid leave plan. During leave, employees are entitled to continue their health benefits, and the employer must continue to pay whatever premiums it would pay if the employee were not on leave. If the employee voluntarily chooses not to return from leave, however, the employer may require the employee to reimburse the premiums it paid while the employee was out.

12-week leave provisions. An employee is entitled to 12 weeks of FMLA leave in a 12-month period for the following reasons:

- to bond with a newborn child, newly adopted child, or a child placed with the employee for foster care
- to care for a family member (parent, spouse, or child only) with a serious health condition
- for the employee's own serious health condition that makes the employee unable to work, or
- for a qualifying exigency relating to a family member's active duty or call to active duty. (Qualifying exigencies include things like attending military events or briefings, helping arrange child care and school transfers, and spending time with the family member on rest and recuperation leave.)

26-week military caregiver leave. Eligible employees are entitled to up to 26 weeks of leave in a single 12-month period to care for a covered service member (or a veteran) with a serious illness or injury suffered in the line of duty. The service member must be undergoing medical treatment, recuperation, or therapy; otherwise in outpatient status; or otherwise on the temporary disability retired list. The

Giving Notice by Falling Asleep

Although the FMLA requires employees to give notice, some courts have found that no notice is required if the employee's behavior changes so drastically that the employer should have known the employee had a serious health condition. Case in point: John Byrne, who worked for four years as stationary engineer on the night shift at Avon Products. By all accounts, Byrne was a model employee until November 1998, when a coworker reported finding him asleep in a break room. The company checked its security logs and found that Byrne had been spending a lot of time in the break room lately. So the company installed a camera, which filmed Byrne sleeping for three hours one night and six hours the next.

Byrne's managers planned to talk to him about the problem on November 16, but Byrne left work early. He told a coworker that he wasn't feeling well and would be out the rest of the week. A manager called Byrne's house, where his sister answered the phone and said that he was "very sick." When Byrne came to the phone, he mumbled some odd phrases and agreed to come to a meeting at work the following day. When he didn't show up for the meeting, he was fired.

It turns out that Byrne was unable to attend the meeting because he had been hospitalized for severe depression, after relatives convinced him to come out of a room in which he had barricaded himself. Byrne had begun hallucinating and having panic attacks, and required two months of treatment. When Byrne felt better, he asked Avon for his job back. The company refused, and Byrne sued for violation of the FMLA.

Avon argued that Byrne never gave adequate notice that he needed FMLA leave. The court didn't see it that way, however. Although Byrne never mentioned the FMLA or said that he needed medical leave, the court found that his marked change in behavior might have been sufficient to put Avon on notice that he needed FMLA leave. The court also found that Byrne might have been unable, because of his mental state, to give notice that he needed leave. Either way, the court found that Byrne should be able to present his claims to a jury.

Byrne v. Avon Products Inc., 328 F.3d 379 (7th Cir. 2003).

rules are different for veterans, who must have been members of the military within the past five years and be suffering from a service-related serious illness or injury. The employee must be the covered service member's or veteran's spouse, child, parent, or next of kin. Unlike regular FMLA leave, this entitlement doesn't renew every year: It is a per service member, per injury entitlement.

Employer procedural requirements. The FMLA has a number of paperwork and other requirements. An employer must provide basic information about the FMLA, on a workplace poster and with their other written materials explaining employee benefits or information distributed to new employees. When an employee requests leave, an employer must provide several additional notices regarding the employee's eligibility, rights and responsibilities, and amount of leave designated as FMLA leave.

Employee procedural requirements. Employees must provide notice of their need for FMLA leave. Generally, 30 days' notice is required if the need for leave is foreseeable. If not, the employee must give notice as soon as is practicable. An employer may require employees to provide a medical certification of the need for leave, as well as certification of a family relationship or need for qualifying exigency leave. An employer may also require employees to check in periodically on their status and intent to return to work from leave, and may require returning employees to provide a fitness-for-duty certification.

Faragher-Ellerth defense

The *Faragher-Ellerth* defense is a claim employers can make when defending against a harassment lawsuit brought under Title VII. (Some states also recognize this defense in cases brought under state laws prohibiting harassment; others don't.) The defense is named after two Supreme Court cases that determine when an employer can be held liable for harassment by a supervisor: *Faragher v. City of Boca Raton*, 524 U.S. 775 (1998), and *Burlington Industries v. Ellerth*, 524 U.S. 742 (1998).

Generally, an employer has a legal duty to take effective action to stop harassment as soon as management learns of it. In some cases, however, an employer will be legally responsible for harassment committed by a supervisor, even if no one else in the company knew what was going on. The employer's legal liability depends on the results of the harassment and the steps the company has taken to prevent and respond to harassment.

Harassment resulting in a tangible employment action. If a supervisor's harassment results in a "tangible employment action"—a significant change in the harassed employee's job status, like getting fired, demoted, or reassigned—then the company is legally liable to the victim. Even if no one else but the supervisor knew about the harassment and the company had procedures in place for dealing with harassment complaints, the employer is liable. The logic behind this liability is that the employer may take job actions like these only through its supervisors. When supervisors make these types of decisions, they are acting for the company, and the company is responsible.

Harassment that doesn't result in a tangible employment action. An employer is not necessarily responsible for harassment by a supervisor that doesn't have any of these repercussions—for example, a supervisor who tells racist jokes or repeatedly asks an employee out on dates. In these cases, an employer can use the *Faragher-Ellerth* defense if it can show these two things:

- The employer exercised reasonable care to prevent and promptly correct any harassment. To meet this requirement, the employer must prove that it made efforts to create a harassment-free work environment by, for example, training employees and managers to recognize and report harassment, adopting a policy prohibiting harassment, creating a complaint procedure that encourages employees to come forward, and investigating harassment complaints quickly and fairly.
- The employee unreasonably failed to take advantage of opportunities the employer offered to prevent or correct the harassment (for example, by failing to make a complaint).

Who's a Supervisor?

These rules—which make employers liable for harassment resulting in a tangible employment action, even if the employer isn't aware of it—apply only to harassment by supervisors. So which employees qualify as supervisors? According to the Equal Employment Opportunity Commission (EEOC), a supervisor is someone who either has the authority to make or recommend decisions affecting the employee or has the authority to direct the employee's daily work activities.

However, certain employees occupy such a lofty position on the corporate ladder that they are something more than supervisors. These employees—which might include corporate officers, the president, the CEO, an owner, or a partner, depending on how the company is organized—generally have the authority to act on the company's behalf in all matters. Therefore, if they harass employees, the law will presume that the company knows about it, even if the harassment doesn't result in a negative job action. The company will always be liable for harassment by these high-ranking employees.

If the employer can prove both parts of the defense, it is not liable for a supervisor's harassment. However, the employer's efforts must be genuine: If an employee can show that previous harassment complaints weren't taken seriously, for example, the defense won't apply. And, the employer is always liable for harassment it is aware of, whether it learns about the harassment through an employee complaint or in any other way.

EXAMPLE 1: Sheila's boss, Roger, has asked her out several times. She has turned him down each time, explaining that she has no romantic interest in him and would prefer to keep their relationship professional. Roger refuses to approve Sheila's scheduled raise (a tangible employment action) because she won't go out with him. Roger's employer is legally responsible for Roger's harassment and cannot rely on the *Faragher-Ellerth* defense, even if Sheila never complains about the harassment. Because Sheila has suffered a tangible employment action, the defense doesn't apply.

EXAMPLE 2: Katherine works on the production line in a food manufacturing plant. Her coworkers and supervisor, mostly men, constantly tell sexual jokes and refer to women in crude terms. The top executives in the company visit the plant. Although the men are on their best behavior during the official tour, several executives remain in the building afterwards to review paperwork, and they overhear the men's crude remarks. The company cannot rely on the *Faragher-Ellerth* defense and will be liable for any harassment Katherine suffers after the visit. Although Katherine has not made a complaint or suffered a negative job action, the company now knows about the harassment and has a duty to take action.

EXAMPLE 3: Same as Example 2, except the executives never visit the plant. If Katherine wants to hold the company responsible for her harassment, she will have to make a complaint to put the company on notice of the problem. If Katherine fails to make a complaint, the company can successfully rely on the *Faragher-Ellerth* defense unless Katherine can show that (1) the company had no policy against harassment, or (2) the company did not take complaints seriously, failed to investigate, or failed to act on reported problems. For example, if Katherine can show that several women from her plant had complained in the past few years and nothing was done about the problem, the employer will be liable despite her failure to complain.

Related terms: harassment; sexual harassment; tangible employment action; Title VII.

FCRA

See Fair Credit Reporting Act.

featherbedding

Featherbedding occurs when an employer is required to hire more workers than are necessary to do a job, to pay for work that is not done or intended to be done, or to adopt unnecessary extra steps or "make work" so as to require the employment of more workers. It is an unfair labor practice under the National Labor Relations Act for a union to require an employer to pay employees for work that isn't performed.

Related terms: National Labor Relations Act; unfair labor practice.

Federal Arbitration Act

The Federal Arbitration Act (FAA) is a federal law that sets forth the rules for enforcing private arbitration agreements. The purpose of the law, passed in 1925, is to encourage the use of arbitration as an alternative to litigation, and to require courts to recognize and enforce arbitration agreements as binding contracts. The FAA also sets forth procedures for one party to an arbitration agreement to compel arbitration and standards for the judicial review of arbitration awards.

Preemption of state laws that disfavor arbitration. Courts have interpreted the FAA to preempt state laws that are less favorable toward arbitration. For example, the Supreme Court held that a franchisee had to arbitrate its claims against the franchisor subject to an arbitration clause in the franchise agreement, despite a California law that prohibited the waiver of certain franchisee rights. The Court stated that, in passing the FAA, "Congress intended to foreclose state legislative attempts to undercut the enforceability of arbitration agreements." *Southland Corp. v. Keating*, 465 U.S. 1 (1984).

Unconscionability may defeat an arbitration agreement. Under the FAA, arbitration agreements must be enforced, except "upon such grounds as exist in law or in equity for the revocation of any contract." An employee who wants to bring a claim in court may try to invalidate an arbitration provision by claiming that it is unconscionable: drafted by the party with superior bargaining power (the employer), presented on a take-it-or-leave-it basis, and heavily weighted in favor of the drafting party. (For a discussion of the types of terms that might lead a court to conclude that an arbitration agreement is unconscionable, see the entry for "arbitration.")

The dispute over "contracts of employment." Section 1 of the FAA excludes certain arbitration agreements from its purview, including those contained in maritime transactions and in "contracts of employment of seamen, railroad employees, or any other class of workers engaged in foreign or interstate commerce." For a number of years, plaintiffs' lawyers argued that this exclusion meant arbitration clauses in employment agreements were not enforceable. This argument relies on Congress's broad interpretation of "interstate commerce" to include not just employees who actually carry goods from state to state, but all employees at companies that have out-of-state customers, vendors, suppliers, goods, and so on (which is to say, almost all employees, period).

The Supreme Court resolved this dispute in favor of arbitration in 2001. The Court found that the FAA's exclusion was intended to apply only to the employment contracts of transportation employees, not to all employment contracts. *Circuit City, Inc. v. Adams*, 532 U.S. 105 (2001).

Related terms: alternative dispute resolution; arbitration.

FEP laws

State laws that prohibit employment discrimination are often referred to as FEP laws (short for "fair employment practices"). Virtually every state (and the District of Columbia) prohibits at least some types of discrimination. Some state laws are very limited; for example, Alabama prohibits only age discrimination, while Mississippi outlaws discrimination only on the basis of military status, unless the employer receives public funding. Other states have expansive laws that go well beyond what federal law requires by, for example, creating additional protected characteristics (such as weight, marital status, or sexual orientation) and applying to smaller employers.

An employer that is subject to more than one antidiscrimination law must follow the law that provides the most protections to employees in all circumstances. In other words, employees are entitled to every protection of every applicable law.

> **EXAMPLE:** The Corner Store opens in Fresno, California; it has six employees. The store is too small for federal antidiscrimination laws to apply: Title VII and the Americans with Disabilities Act cover only employers with at least 15 employees, and the Age Discrimination in Employment Act kicks in only when an employer has at least 20 employees. However, California has its own antidiscrimination law, which prohibits discrimination by employers with at least five employees. It also prohibits several types of discrimination that aren't covered by federal law, including discrimination based on sexual orientation, marital status, and political activities or affiliations. Although the Corner Store is too small to be subject to federal law, it is covered by the state's law.

Related terms: Age Discrimination in Employment Act; Americans with Disabilities Act; discrimination; protected characteristic; Title VII.

final paycheck

A final paycheck is the last paycheck a departing employee receives. Departing employees are entitled to be paid all wages they have earned, and a number of states also require employers to include accrued but unused vacation time in an employee's final paycheck.

State laws control when an employee is entitled to receive the final paycheck. Some states require employers to provide a final paycheck more quickly when an employee is fired or laid off than when an employee quits. In California, for example, an employer must provide a fired employee's paycheck immediately, but may wait a few days to pay an employee who quits.

Related term: vacation.

first responder

First responders are the safety and medical personnel who are first to arrive at the scene of an emergency, such as an accident, fire, crime, and so on. Firefighters, emergency medical technicians, paramedics, HazMat teams, search and rescue personnel, and law enforcement officers all qualify as first responders. Under the Fair Labor Standards Act (FLSA), first responders are categorically excluded from any exemption categories: In other words, they are entitled to earn overtime, even if they would otherwise fit into one of the exceptions to the overtime laws.

Related terms: exempt employee; Fair Labor Standards Act; overtime.

fitness-for-duty exam

A fitness-for-duty exam is a medical examination of a current employee to determine whether the employee is physically or psychologically able to perform the job. Sometimes, fitness-for-duty exams are required when an employee is ready to return to work after taking time off for a serious illness or injury. For example, an employee with a serious back injury might have to take a fitness-for-duty exam before coming back to work, to make sure the employee is capable of meeting the physical requirements of his job. A fitness-for-duty exam might also be required of an employee whose conduct on the job gives the employer reason to believe that the employee is not able to perform the job safely.

> EXAMPLE: A police officer suffered a head injury, for which he had to take time off work. Several years later, he began acting erratically, responding emotionally and angrily during

conversations with coworkers, losing control during a traffic stop, being accused of a domestic altercation with his wife, and making comments about his situation such as "It doesn't matter how this ends" and "I'm not sure if it's worth it." The employer required the officer to take a fitness-for-duty exam in order to stay on the job. The federal Court of Appeals for the Ninth Circuit upheld the employer's decision. The Court cautioned that although preemptive psychological exams (exams required while the employee was still on the job) could be abused by employers seeking to harass employees or force them off the job, it was justified in this case by the officer's volatile behavior and the stress and danger inherent in his job. Because the employer had reasonable cause to question the officer's ability to do his job, the exam did not constitute disability discrimination under the ADA. *Brownfield v. City of Yakima*, 612 F.3d 1140 (9th Cir. 2010).

Fitness-for-duty and the Americans with Disabilities Act (ADA). Because fitness-for-duty exams may reveal information about an employee's disability, they are regulated under the ADA. An employer may require a fitness-for-duty exam of an employee with a disability only if the exam is job related and consistent with business necessity. This standard will generally be met if:

- the employer has a reasonable belief that the employee's condition may prevent the employee from performing the job's essential functions, or
- the employee poses a direct threat to his or her own safety or the safety of others.

The exam must be limited to the employee's ability to return to work; the employer may not take advantage of the opportunity to request far-reaching information or medical testing about the employee's condition.

Related terms: Americans with Disabilities Act; direct threat; essential job functions; medical records.

FLSA

See Fair Labor Standards Act.

FMLA

See Family and Medical Leave Act.

F

foreseeable leave

Under the Family and Medical Leave Act (FMLA), foreseeable leave is leave that the employee knows will be necessary in advance. For example, an employee who has a medical procedure scheduled in six weeks or is due to give birth in a few months knows that time off will be necessary. When an employee's need for leave is foreseeable, the employee must give the employer notice at least 30 days in advance. If the employee's need for leave is foreseeable less than 30 days in advance (for instance, if the employee's parent is scheduled for surgery the following week or the employee is informed of a foster child placement with only a couple of weeks' lead time), then the employee must give as much notice as is practicable. When it is practicable for an employee to give notice depends on the facts, but ordinarily employees are expected to give notice the same day or the following day after learning of the need for leave.

If an employee doesn't give the required notice. If an employee could have given notice of the need for foreseeable leave 30 days in advance and failed to do so, the employer may deny the employee's leave request or delay the start of the employee's leave until 30 days have passed since the employee gave notice.

Related terms: Family and Medical Leave Act; unforeseeable leave.

fraud

Fraud is a personal injury claim that can be made when someone takes action in reliance on another's false statement and suffers harm as a result. In the employment law context, fraud claims are typically made by employees who are induced to come work for a company based on knowingly false statements, then learn that the situation is very different than advertised.

F

> **EXAMPLE:** Rykoff-Sexton intensely recruited Andrew Lazar to leave his lucrative job in New York City, his home of 40 years. Rykoff promised Lazar job security, significant pay increases, an eventual executive position, and a bright future with a company that was financially strong. Lazar quit his job and moved himself and his family to California to work for Rykoff, in reliance on these promises. Although Lazar excelled in his new job, the raises and bonuses never came, and he was eventually fired in a "reorganization."
>
> Lazar sued for fraud and won. He argued to the California Supreme Court that Rykoff should have to keep the promises it made to recruit him, and the court agreed. The court found that Rykoff's broken promises amounted to fraud because the company knew the promises where untrue when they were made. *Lazar v. Rykoff-Sexton, Inc.,* 12 Cal.4th 631 (1996).

Elements of a fraud claim. To win a fraud claim, an employee generally has to prove all of the following:

- The employer knowingly made false statements or concealed the truth.
- The statements or concealed facts were material—that is, they played a role in the employee's decision to accept the job, leave another job, or otherwise take action.
- The employer intended for the employee to rely on the false statements.
- The employee justifiably relied on the statements (in other words, the employee took action, such as quitting another job, that was reasonable under the circumstances).
- The employee suffered damages as a result of the reliance.

False promises. Some states allow employees to sue if the employer made false promises to induce the employee to leave another job.

However, it isn't enough that the employer's promises don't come true or can't be kept for some reason. For example, an employee couldn't bring a successful fraud claim if an employer promises—and has every intention of giving—employees a bonus, but is financially unable to do so when the time comes. The employee must show that the promises were false when they were made. In other words, the employee must prove that the employer made them to deceive the employee and never intended to make good on the promises.

Related term: tort.

freelancer

See independent contractor.

frolic and detour

Frolic and detour refer to employee activities that are undertaken for the employee's own purposes, rather than to serve the employer. The employer's liability often depends on whether the employee was on a frolic, a detour, or neither.

Under the legal theory of respondeat superior, the employer is legally responsible for the actions its employees take within the course and scope of employment. This rule holds employers liable for the costs of doing business, including the expenses associated with their employees injuring people or damaging property while performing their jobs. If, for example, an employee is driving his regular delivery route and hits a pedestrian, the employer would be liable for the pedestrian's injuries.

This rule of liability doesn't apply if the employee is acting solely for personal purposes and is no longer engaged in activities that fall within the scope of employment, however. In this situation, the employer's liability depends on whether the employee is on a "frolic" or a "detour." An employer will not be legally liable for damage caused by an employee on a frolic, but may be liable if the employee is on a detour.

Frolic versus detour. Generally, a frolic is behavior that is pretty far afield of the employee's duties, while a detour represents only a slight deviation from the employee's usual activities. Courts look at issues such as the employee's intent, how long the extracurricular activities took, where the activities took place, the job for which the employee was hired, and how much freedom the employee enjoys on the job to decide whether an employee's activities are fairly attributable to the employer or should be the sole responsibility of the employee.

EXAMPLE 1: A delivery driver makes a quick stop to pick up his dry cleaning. The employer's policies allow employees to take care of personal errands on their routes, as long as they make all of their deliveries on time. If the driver rear ends another driver pulling out of the parking lot, the employer is likely liable. Because the employer allows employees to run errands, the errand didn't take the employee far from his regular route and responsibilities, and the employee's job requires him to drive safely, this looks more like a detour than a frolic.

EXAMPLE 2: A delivery driver spends a few hours at the racetrack when he should be working. After having several drinks, he gets in a fistfight with another spectator, who suffers a broken jaw. His employer may not be liable for this injury: The driver's actions are so far beyond his usual job duties that they likely constitute a frolic.

Related terms: course and scope of employment; respondeat superior.

front pay

Front pay is a type of damages that may be awarded in discrimination and other employment cases. Front pay compensates the employee for lost wages going forward from the date judgment is entered at trial until the employee is reinstated or finds a new job, if the employee is not reinstated. For example, if the employer is ordered to reinstate the employee but there will be a delay before

F

Front Pay Isn't Capped Under Title VII

When Congress amended Title VII in the Civil Rights Act of 1991, it added provisions allowing victorious plaintiffs to be awarded compensatory and punitive damages (in addition to the economic damages—such as back pay and lost benefits—to which they were already entitled). Compensatory damages are for emotional pain and suffering, mental anguish, loss of enjoyment of life, and future economic losses; punitive damages are intended to punish the employer for its misconduct and deter other employers from acting similarly.

These damages provisions were controversial, so a compromise was struck in order to get the votes needed in Congress: Compensatory and punitive damages are allowed, but only up to a cap of $50,000 to $300,000, depending on the size of the employer. When lower courts began applying the new damages provisions, they reached different conclusions as to front pay awards. Some courts found that these awards were intended to compensate for "future economic losses," and so should be subject to the cap; other courts found that front pay awards should not be capped.

The Supreme Court decided the issue in 2001. The Court found that front pay awards were not subject to the cap. Even though they could arguably fall into the category of "future economic losses" (and therefore, be treated as compensatory damages), the Court found that it made more sense to treat front pay as an alternative to reinstatement, a remedy that has always been available to Title VII plaintiffs. Therefore, the new damages provisions—and their caps—didn't apply to front pay awards.

Pollard v. E.I. du Pont de Nemours & Co., 532 U.S. 843 (2001).

an appropriate position opens up, an award of front pay would compensate the employee for that time. Or, if the work environment has become so poisoned or the employee has suffered such extreme hostility that reinstatement isn't workable, the employer may be required to pay the employee what he or she would have earned until the employee finds new work.

Related terms: back pay; Civil Rights Act of 1991; damages; reinstatement.

F

G

gender identity

Gender identity refers to the gender with which a person identifies, as distinguished from the person's current biological gender or biological gender at birth. A person may identify as male, female, intersex, or transgender, for example.

Some states prohibit discrimination. Federal law does not currently prohibit employment discrimination on the basis of gender identity, but a handful of states do. In these states, it is illegal to discriminate based not only on an employee's or applicant's gender (for example, to refuse to promote women to jobs that require travel or to pay men more based on the stereotypical assumption that they are more likely to have families to support), but also on the gender with which an employee identifies, even if that is different from the employee's biological gender. For example, an employer may not discriminate against an employee who is anatomically male but is undergoing female hormone therapy, dressing in a feminine style, and otherwise living as a woman in preparation for sex reassignment surgery.

Related terms: discrimination; sex discrimination.

General Electric Co. v. Gilbert

See Pregnancy Discrimination Act.

Genetic Information Nondiscrimination Act

The Genetic Information Nondiscrimination Act (GINA), was signed in May 2008. GINA prohibits health insurers from using genetic information to deny insurance coverage or determine premiums. It also prohibits covered employers from making employment decisions based on an applicant's or employee's genetic information, and requires employers to keep employee genetic information confidential. GINA applies to federal and state governments, as well as to private employers with at least 15 employees.

Discrimination is prohibited. Employers may not make employment decisions based on genetic information about an employee, an applicant, or a family member of an employee or applicant. (Strangely, given that the name of the law includes the word "genetic," family members are not limited to biological relatives.) However, disparate impact claims—in which an employee alleges that a seemingly neutral employment practice has a disproportionately negative effect on a protected group—are not allowed under GINA. An employer also may not retaliate against an employee or applicant who complains about a violation of GINA or participates in a hearing or investigation of such a violation.

Acquisition of genetic information. GINA prohibits employers from requiring or asking workers to provide genetic information about themselves or a family member. Employers also may not purchase genetic information about employees or their family members. There are a handful of exceptions to these rules (set out below), but even if an exception applies, employers must keep the information confidential and may not use it as the basis for employment decisions.

Exceptions. It isn't illegal for an employer to obtain genetic information on an employee or family member if one of these exceptions applies:

- The employer inadvertently requests or requires family medical history from an employee or family member.
- The employer offers health or genetic services (as part of a workplace wellness program, for example) and all three of the following are true:
    - The employee provides prior, knowing, voluntary, and written authorization.
    - Only the employee or family member receiving services, along with the health care professional or genetic counselor

involved in providing the services, receive individually identifiable information about the results.

- Any individually identifiable genetic information resulting from such services is available only for the purpose of those services and is not disclosed to the employer except in aggregate terms that don't reveal the identity of any individual employee.

- The employer requires family medical history from the employee to comply with the certification requirements of the Family and Medical Leave Act (FMLA) or a similar requirement under a state leave law.

- The employer purchases documents that are commercially and publicly available and include family medical history. This exception applies to newspapers, magazines and books, for example, but not to medical databases or court records.

- The information acquired is to be used for genetic monitoring of the biological effects of toxic substances in the workplace (only if a number of safeguards are met).

- The employer conducts DNA analysis for law enforcement purposes as a forensic laboratory or to identity human remains, and requests or requires genetic information from its employees only for analysis of DNA identification markers as a means of detecting sample contamination.

Confidentiality of genetic information. Employers that have genetic information about an employee must keep it on separate forms, in separate files, and treat it as a confidential medical record. It may be revealed only in these circumstances:

- to the employee or family member, upon written request
- to an occupational or health researcher, for research conducted in compliance with part 46 of Title 45 of the Code of Federal Regulations (the Department of Health and Human Services' rules for the protection of human research subjects)
- in response to a court order, the employer may disclose only the genetic information expressly authorized by that order (if the court order was obtained without the family member's or

employee's knowledge, the employer must notify the employee or family member of the order and of any genetic information disclosed as a result)

- to government officials investigating compliance with GINA, if the information is relevant to the investigation
- in connection with the employee's compliance with the certification requirements of the FMLA or a similar state law, or
- to a federal, state, or local public health agency, an employer may disclose only information about the manifestation of a disease or disorder in an employee's family member if that information concerns a contagious disease that presents an imminent hazard of death or life-threatening illness. The employer must notify the employee of the disclosure.

How GINA is enforced. The Equal Employment Opportunity Commission (EEOC) interprets and enforces GINA, using the same enforcement procedures and damages allowances that apply to Title VII cases.

The First Reported GINA Charge

In April 2010, Pamela Fink filed a charge with the EEOC, alleging that she was fired from her job after telling her employer that she carried the BRCA2 gene (linked to some forms of breast cancer) and had undergone a voluntary double mastectomy after her two sisters had both been diagnosed with the disease. According to news reports, this is the first publicized case under GINA, and one of the first EEOC charges to allege wrongful termination rather than improper disclosure of medical information.

In this case, Fink told her supervisors about the genetic test results and her surgery. She said that she felt comfortable doing so because she had received positive reviews, merit increases, and bonuses. Once she returned from surgery, she claims that her job duties were taken away, she was demoted, and was soon fired. The company has denied the allegations and said that its actions were warranted.

GINA

See Genetic Information Nondiscrimination Act.

good cause

Good cause (sometimes called "just cause" or simply "cause") is a legitimate, good faith, business-related reason to fire an employee. For example, an employee might be fired for good cause because of a pattern of unexcused absences, poor performance, or serious misconduct.

Most employees work at will, which means that they can be fired at any time, for any reason that is not illegal. An employer doesn't need good cause to fire an at-will employee; the basis for firing can even be arbitrary (for example, because the employer doesn't like the employee). If, however, an employee has an employment contract stating that the employee may be fired only for good cause, then the employee may have a breach of contract claim if the employer lacked good cause to fire. For example, an employee who is fired so the owner can give some work to his daughter's husband might have a breach of contract claim; an employee who is fired for stealing from the company would not.

Related terms: at-will employment; employment contract; implied contract.

Griggs v. Duke Power Co.

See disparate impact.

H-1B visa

An H-1B visa is a visa issued to foreign nationals who want to come to the United States temporarily to fill a particular job for a particular employer. To qualify, the job must be a "specialty occupation" (a job that requires specialized knowledge and a higher education, such as in medicine, architecture, engineering, or the arts); certain services relating to Department of Defense projects; or work as a fashion model of distinguished merit or ability.

The employer must file an application with the U.S. Citizenship and Immigration Services (USCIS). The employee must meet certain educational or licensing requirements, and the job must meet certain criteria as well.

An H-1B visa allows a worker to stay in the U.S. for three years; it may be extended for up to a total of six years. Only 65,000 H-1B visas may be issued each fiscal year, but certain types of workers aren't subject to the cap.

harassment

Harassment is offensive, unwelcome conduct—whether words, actions, gestures, or visual displays—that is so severe or pervasive that it affects the terms and conditions of the victim's employment. Legally, harassment is a form of discrimination: It is illegal only if based on a person's race, gender, age, disability, or other protected characteristic. Sexual harassment gets the most publicity, but harassment can be based on other characteristics, too.

Types of harassment. Sometimes, harassment directly affects the victim's job opportunities (for example, when a supervisor tells an employee, "I'm not going to give you that promotion unless you agree to go on a date with me" or subjects an employee to harsher rules because of her religion or disability). In sexual harassment cases, when the harasser conditions job benefits on the victim's complying with sexual demands, it's often referred to as "quid pro quo" (this for that) harassment. Sometimes, harassment doesn't result in discipline or lost job opportunities but does make it difficult for the victim to work because of constant ridicule, belittling comments, teasing, or sexual come-ons. This second type of harassment is called "hostile environment" harassment.

Unwelcome conduct. To constitute illegal harassment, the conduct or statements must be unwelcome to the victim. In many harassment cases, this isn't a disputed issue. Someone who is referred to in offensive or derogatory terms, made fun of because of age or disability, or threatened with racial violence generally doesn't welcome the conduct. However, the question of welcomeness sometimes comes up in sexual harassment cases, because some sexual advances, comments, or jokes might not offend their target. Welcomeness may be an issue in other types of harassment cases, too. For example, if an older worker frequently refers to himself as "gramps" or "the old-timer" and makes jokes about his "senior moments," other employees may feel that he doesn't mind being teased about his age.

Severe or pervasive conduct. A single act can constitute harassment if it is extreme, such as a sexual assault or racially motivated attack. Typically, however, there must be a pattern of harassment or a series of incidents over time. One teasing comment, request for a date, or even use of a bigoted epithet probably does not constitute harassment by itself. There's no clear line or magic number of incidents when name-calling, teasing, and such cross the line to become harassment. The court will consider all of the incidents in context. Generally, the more egregious each incident is, the fewer will be necessary for a harassment claim.

Terms and conditions of employment. For a court to decide that harassment occurred, the conduct must affect the terms and conditions of the victim's employment. If the harasser is a supervisor, for example, harassment might take the form of a negative job action, such as firing, failure to promote, demotion, discipline, a pay cut, an undesirable transfer, a reassignment, or a change in job duties or title. Even if there is no negative job action, a victim can prove harassment if he or she reasonably finds the workplace to be hostile or abusive. The key word here is "reasonable." It isn't enough that the victim finds the workplace to be hostile; the circumstances must be such that a reasonable worker in the victim's position would also find the workplace hostile.

Related terms: *Faragher-Ellerth* defense; protected characteristic; sexual harassment; tangible employment action.

health care reform

Health care reform is the popular term for the Patient Protection and Affordable Care Act of 2010. The law makes substantial changes to the health insurance system in this country. Because many people currently receive their health insurance through their jobs, the law will have a significant impact on employers and employees alike. However, most changes don't take effect for several years after passage of the law.

Tax credit for small businesses that offer health insurance. Beginning in tax year 2010, small businesses—defined as those with fewer than 25 full-time employees (or the equivalent) and an average annual salary of less than $50,000 per employee—are eligible for a tax credit if they provide health insurance to their employees. To qualify, the business must pay at least half of the premium for covering a single person (not a family). Businesses can get a credit of up to 35% of the premiums they paid; nonprofit employers can get a credit of up to 25% of the premiums they paid (these percentages are set to increase in 2014). The maximum credit is available to the smallest employers (those with ten or fewer employees and annual wages of less than $25,000).

Temporary reimbursement to employers that provide retiree health coverage. A provision of the law called the Early Retiree Reinsurance

Program gives a subsidy to employers that provide health care coverage to retirees who do not yet qualify for Medicare (those between the ages of 55 and 64). Coverage for spouses, surviving spouses, and dependents of the retiree is also covered. The subsidy will cover up to 80% of claims incurred after June 1, 2010, but only after the retiree has made at least $15,000 in annual claims. (And the subsidy cuts off once the retiree has made $90,000 in annual claims.)

Plan sponsors must apply for this subsidy. This is a temporary program, scheduled to end on January 1, 2014, when retirees will be able to get insurance through state insurance exchanges. However, the program has a limited budget, to be paid out on a first-come, first-served basis.

H

New Moms Get Lactation Breaks

In keeping with the health care reform law's emphasis on preventive health care and promoting healthy habits, the health care reform law requires employers to allow new mothers to express breast milk. For up to one year after birth, employers must provide reasonable break time for nursing mothers to pump. The employer need not pay for this time unless state law requires it; many states already require employers to offer lactation breaks. The employer must provide private space (other than a bathroom) for this purpose.

Employers with fewer than 50 employees don't have to provide lactation breaks if doing so would impose an "undue hardship"—meaning it would take significant expense or difficulty, considering the employer's size, structure, and resources. Because the law didn't set a future date when the lactation break requirement will take effect, most experts agree that it became effective immediately upon the President's signature.

Requirements and restrictions on health care plans. For plan years that begin on October 1, 2010 or later, new restrictions and requirements apply to health care plans. There are more requirements for new plans; existing (grandfathered) plans won't have to comply with all of these requirements right away.

Here are some of the requirements that will apply to **existing plans:**

- There can be no lifetime dollar limits on the care provided for essential health benefits. Which benefits go on this list will be decided by the Department of Health and Human Services (HHS), but the list must include certain items, such as emergency care, hospitalization, maternity and newborn care, prescription drugs, laboratory services, mental health, and preventive care.
- Insurers can apply annual benefit limits, subject to certain restrictions in order to ensure access to necessary services.
- Children up to the age of 26 who are not covered at their own jobs must be allowed to enroll in a parent's plan. (The IRS recently issued guidance explaining that this additional benefit is tax-free to the parent/employee.)
- Children up to the age of 18 may not be denied coverage for preexisting conditions.
- Plans may rescind (cancel) coverage only if the insured commits fraud or intentionally misrepresents a material fact.

Additional requirements for grandfathered plans will start in 2014.

New plans will have to comply with the rules for existing plans, along with some additional requirements, including:

- Plans must fully cover preventive care, with no deductible or co-pay.
- Employers that choose to offer wellness programs must pay the full cost, with no deductible or co-pay.
- Employees must be able to go to the emergency room and ob-gyn visits without prior authorization; participation in clinical trials must be covered.
- Group health plans may not discriminate in favor of highly compensated employees.

Again, additional requirements will apply in 2014.

Long-term care. The health care reform law includes the Community Living Assistance Service and Supports Act (the CLASS Act), a new program that provides limited payments for long-term care. The CLASS Act is a federal insurance program, like Social Security or Medicare. Unlike those programs, however, participation is voluntary for both employers and employees.

Beginning in January 2011, employers who choose to participate in the program may allow employees to opt in or may automatically enroll employees and allow them to opt out of the program. Employees pay the full price of the premiums, which are withheld as a regular payroll deduction. Once employees have paid into the program for at least five years, they are eligible for cash benefits (estimated at about $50 per day) if they are limited in at least two daily living activities, such as bathing, dressing, or caring for themselves.

Changes to HSAs and FSAs. Beginning in 2011, over-the-counter drugs are no longer reimbursable through flexible savings accounts (FSAs) or health savings accounts (HSAs) unless the drugs are prescribed by a doctor. The health care reform law also caps annual contributions to an FSA to $2,500 beginning in 2013. And employees under the age of 65 who make nonqualified withdrawals from their HSA (in other words, they don't use the money for health care purposes) will have to pay a 20% penalty.

Reporting and notice requirements. The health care reform law imposes several new informational requirements on employers. They include:

- Employers must report the value of the health benefits they provide to employees on each employee's W-2 Form. This requirement kicks in at the beginning of 2012 for benefits provided in 2011.
- Employers must give employees information about the state insurance exchange program, including how to get premium assistance if necessary. This requirement starts in 2013.

- Beginning in 2014, larger employers must report certain information about the health coverage they provide to employees.

Play or pay: The employer mandate. Beginning in 2014, the individual mandate will kick in. Everyone will have to be covered by health insurance or pay a fine; those who can't afford insurance will be eligible for assistance.

The employer mandate kicks in at the same time. Employers with at least 50 employees must provide health care benefits or pay a penalty. Employers who provide benefits may still have to pay a penalty, depending on the cost of benefits to employees and employee ability to pay. Here are the basics:

- Employers that have more than 50 employees and don't offer coverage must pay an annual fine of $2,000 per full-time employee (those working at least 30 hours a week). The first 30 employees are "free"; the fine begins with employee number 31.

- Even employers that offer coverage may face a penalty if the employer doesn't pay for at least 60% of the actuarial value of the benefits the plan provides or the employee's cost for coverage is more than 9.5% of the employee's household income. In this situation, a full-time employee would be eligible to receive government-subsidized coverage—and, if this happens, the employer would have to pay a penalty of $3,000 per full-time employee who receives the subsidy, up to a limit.

- Employers must offer a voucher to employees who (1) have an income that is less than four times the federal poverty level, (2) would have to pay more than 8% of their income for employer-provided coverage, and (3) choose to enroll in a plan from a state insurance exchange. The voucher requires the employer to pay what it would have paid to enroll the employee in its own plan.

Larger employers will also have to automatically enroll employees in their health insurance plan.

Related terms: benefits; COBRA; lactation break.

holiday

A holiday is a day off work in observance of a patriotic, religious, or other event. The federal government, state governments, and even local governments declare certain days "legal" holidays, which means that government offices and other public institutions (such as schools) are generally closed on that day.

Private employers are not required to give employees any days off, even legal holidays. According to the 2010 Employee Benefits Survey conducted by the federal Bureau of Labor Statistics, however, more than ¾ of private industry employers give employees paid holidays, an average of eight days off per year.

honesty test

An honesty test (sometimes called an "integrity" test) is a pencil-and-paper (or keyboard-and-screen) test intended to reveal the test taker's truthfulness. The Employee Polygraph Protection Act (EPPA), passed by Congress in 1988, essentially banned polygraph testing in the hiring process for the vast majority of private employers. Following this ban, employers that still wanted to assess the truthfulness of applicants for hire or promotion had to turn to psychological and personality tests, such as honesty tests.

> **EXAMPLE:** Here's an example of a question that might be asked on an honesty test (try to guess which answer prospective employers want to see!):
>
> If I were ever to receive payment in excess of the work I had done, I would immediately tell my boss about the excess payment.
> - a. This statement about me is completely true
> - b. This statement about me is mostly true
> - c. This statement about me may be true or false
> - d. This statement about me is mostly false
> - e. This statement about me is completely false

Related term: Employee Polygraph Protection Act.

hostile work environment

See harassment.

hot cargo agreement

A hot cargo agreement is an agreement between an employer and a union in which the employer promises to stop doing business with another employer, with whom the union has a dispute. Under the National Labor Relations Act (NLRA), it is an unfair labor practice for an employer or a union to enter into a hot cargo agreement. It is also an unfair labor practice for a union to strike for the purpose of forcing an employer to enter into a hot cargo agreement.

Related terms: National Labor Relations Act; strike; unfair labor practice.

hour worked

Under the Fair Labor Standards Act and state laws that govern wages and hours, an "hour worked" is an hour for which an employee is entitled to be paid. For most of the time an employee works, there's no dispute over whether the employee should be paid: If the worker is doing his or her job, the employer must pay for that time. The question of whether time counts as hours worked or not comes up when the employee isn't doing his or her regular work but isn't exactly off-duty, either, such as time spent in training programs, traveling, on call, or eating lunch.

Under federal law, employees are entitled to earn pay for the time they spend under their employer's control or for their employer's benefit, even if they are not performing their jobs. Generally, this does not include time employees spend commuting to and from work each day. It does, however, include other time that employees cannot spend as they wish, even if they do not spend that time actually performing their regular job duties. Here, we explain some of the rules under federal law; many states have their own rules, and employers must follow whichever rule is most protective to the employee.

Training and education programs. Time spent attending lectures, meetings, training programs, or classes must be paid if attendance is mandatory. An employee need not be paid only if all of the following are true:

- The program is outside of normal work hours.
- Attendance is voluntary.
- The program is not job related.
- The employee doesn't perform any other work at the same time.

EXAMPLE 1: Bob works for a software company. Every month, the company invites a speaker to give an evening seminar on practical issues that might be of interest to employees. Attendance is voluntary, no work is done during the lectures, and the topics include things like cleaning up your credit report, household budgeting, planning a home remodeling project, and estate planning. The company doesn't have to pay employees who choose to attend these seminars.

EXAMPLE 2: Bob's company wants everyone to learn how to use every feature of its various software packages. It creates a training program for employees. Employees who are already familiar with a particular program must pass an online test demonstrating their knowledge. Those who pass the test are excused from attendance; everyone else must attend. Because attendance is mandatory and the program is job related, the company must pay employees for the time they spend in training.

Travel time. Although employees are not entitled to be paid for time spent commuting, they must be paid for travel time that is part of the job. For example, if an employee is required to go out on service calls, the time spent traveling to and from the customers must be paid. Also, if employees have to take employer-provided transportation from a central location to the worksite, they may be entitled to pay for this time. Even if an employee's job does not ordinarily involve travel, the employer may have to pay for travel time if the employee is required to come to the workplace at odd hours to deal with emergency situations.

What about business trips? Special rules apply to employees who occasionally travel to another location for business. The rules depend on whether the trip includes an overnight stay.

- **One-day trips.** If an employee goes on a one-day business trip, the employee must be paid for all time spent traveling. However, the employer can subtract the time it takes the employee to get to the airport or public transportation hub as commuting time, even if it takes the employee longer than his or her ordinary commute to work.

  EXAMPLE: Tom lives in Greenbrae, California, and regularly commutes to his job in San Francisco. His commute takes about ½ hour each way by bus. His employer sends him to Los Angeles for a business trip. Tom leaves home at 6 a.m. to catch an 8 a.m. flight. He spends all day with a customer in Los Angeles, then dashes off to the airport to catch his 6:30 p.m. flight, which lands at 8 p.m. Tom arrives home by 9 p.m. He is entitled to be paid for 12 hours of work; the time he spends commuting between his home and the airport is considered noncompensable commuting time, even though it's quite a bit longer than his usual commute.

- **Overnight trips.** When an employee spends more than a day out of town, the rules are different. The employee must be paid for all time spent actually working. However, whether the employee is entitled to pay for time spent in transit depends on when the travel takes place. Employees are entitled to pay for time spent traveling during the hours when they regularly work (the period of the day they regularly work), even if they ordinarily work Monday through Friday but travel on the weekend.

EXAMPLE: If Tom usually works 9 to 5, and leaves the office at 3 p.m. to catch a flight for an overnight business trip, he should be paid for the two remaining hours in his day, but not for the rest of the time he spends traveling that evening. But if Tom returns home on a 10 a.m. Saturday flight that takes four hours, he is entitled to be paid for all of that time. Even though he traveled on the weekend, the flight took place during his ordinary hours of weekday work.

On-call time. If an employee is required to stay on the employer's premises while waiting for a work assignment, the employer must pay for that time, even if the employee isn't actually performing job tasks. If an employee must be on call elsewhere, the employer must pay for hours over which the employee has little or no control and which the employee cannot use for personal enjoyment or benefit. In other words, if an employer places significant restrictions on employees who are on call, then they may be entitled to pay, especially if they get called into work fairly often. For example, an employee who must remain close to the workplace, cannot drink alcohol, and is called into work several times during each on-call shift is probably entitled to compensation for all of those on-call hours.

Meal and rest breaks. Many states have laws that require employers to provide meal and/or rest breaks. These laws specify the minimum time that must be allowed and whether that time must be paid. In the states that do not require paid breaks, employees must be free of all job responsibilities during breaks. If an employee must perform any job duties during a regularly scheduled break (such as covering phones or staffing a reception area), that time must be paid.

Related terms: meal break; on-call time; rest break.

Immigration Reform and Control Act

The Immigration Reform and Control Act of 1986 (IRCA) is a sweeping immigration law. IRCA addresses a number of issues that are unrelated to the employment relationship, which aren't covered here. Among the employment-related issues it covers are rules for hiring agricultural workers and securing temporary employment visas for foreign workers (such as H-1B visas).

Form I-9. IRCA requires employers to verify that all employees are legally authorized to work in the United States by requiring new employees to complete part of the I-9 Form and provide documentation proving their identity and work authorization. The employer must sign the form verifying that the employee has presented the proper documents. Once the I-9 Form is complete, the employer must update it if necessary (for example, if the employee's work authorization document expires), retain it for three years after the employee is hired or one year after the employee is terminated, whichever is later, and make it available for inspection by federal government officials.

Discrimination is prohibited. IRCA also prohibits employers from discriminating against employees on the basis of citizenship status or national origin unless a federal law explicitly declares that U.S. citizenship is an essential requirement of the job. If two applicants are equally qualified for a position, IRCA allows an employer to give preference to a citizen or national of the United States. However, an employer may not institute a blanket policy of preferring U.S. citizens for all job openings.

Related terms: *Employment Eligibility Verification Form* (I-9); national origin discrimination.

impairment

Under the Americans with Disabilities Act (ADA), a disability is defined as an impairment that substantially limits a major life activity. An impairment may be physical or mental. A physical impairment means a disorder, condition, cosmetic disfigurement, or anatomical loss that affects the functioning of the body's systems, such as the lymphatic, reproductive, neurological, or respiratory system. A mental impairment is any mental or psychological disorder, such as organic brain syndrome, emotional or mental illness, learning disability, or intellectual disability.

An impairment is different from a condition or trait. Only impairments can be disabilities; conditions and traits cannot. For example, height and weight, when they are within the normal range, are traits, not impairments. Personality traits such as poor judgment or a quick temper are also not impairments, unless they are a symptom of a mental or psychological disorder. Social conditions, such as poverty or lack of education are also not impairments.

Related terms: Americans with Disabilities Act; disability; major life activity.

implied contract

An implied contract is an agreement that is neither written down nor explicitly spoken aloud, but is implied from all of the facts and circumstances. In the employment law field, the existence of an implied contract is a question that typically comes up after an employee has been fired. The employer argues that the employee worked at will, and so can't sue for breach of an employment contract; the employee counters that the employer's actions and statements led the employee to believe that the employee would be fired only for good cause, and were sufficient to create a contract to that effect. Here are some of the factors courts consider in deciding whether an implied employment contract was created (different states apply different standards when considering implied contract claims):

- Whether the employer told the employee that he or she had job security, would be fired only for good cause, would have a job as long as he or she performed well, and so on.
- Whether the employer's policies limit its right to fire at will. For example, a mandatory progressive discipline policy that doesn't give the employer leeway to depart from the stated procedures, policies providing that new employees become "permanent" after completing a probationary period, policies promising regular promotions and raises if performance meets a certain standard, and policies requiring good cause to fire might be used as evidence that the employer had given up the right to fire at will.
- The employee's tenure. A long-term employee who has received regular promotions, raises, and positive performance evaluations has a better shot at making an implied contract claim than a short-term employee.

Related terms: employment contract; good cause.

In re Oakwood Healthcare

See manager.

incapacity

Incapacity refers to someone's inability to work or perform other regular daily activities. Incapacity may determine an employee's eligibility for certain benefits. For example, in many states, an employee is entitled to workers' compensation wage replacement during the period of incapacity—inability to work—caused by a workplace injury or illness. Under the Family and Medical Leave Act (FMLA), several of the definitions of a serious health condition (for which an employee may take leave) involve incapacity. For instance, if an employee or employee's family member has an illness, injury, impairment, or condition that involves more than three full days of incapacity and continuing treatment by a health care provider, that employee may be entitled to FMLA leave.

Related terms: Family and Medical Leave Act; workers' compensation.

independent contractor

An independent contractor is a self-employed business person who performs services for other people or businesses. The federal Bureau of Labor Statistics estimates that more than ten million people work as independent contractors in occupations ranging from the trades (such as plumbers, electricians, and carpenters) to computer technology, from farming to freelance writing. Contractors go by a number of names—entrepreneurs, consultants, freelancers, the self-employed, and business owners—but regardless of the title or field, they all have two things in common: They are in business for themselves, and they don't rely on a single employer for their livelihood.

From an employment law perspective, the important thing about independent contractors is that they are not employees. This means, among other things, that those who hire independent contractors don't have to withhold or pay payroll taxes, provide benefits, get workers' compensation coverage, pay unemployment claims, or abide by a number of laws intended to protect employees. To make sure employers aren't taking advantage of workers (and skipping out on their tax obligations) by calling them contractors when they should really be classified as employees, state and federal government agencies closely scrutinize the relationship between employers and the independent contractors they hire.

Different government agencies have different tests to determine whether a worker is an independent contractor or an employee. What these tests have in common is that they seek to determine how much control the hiring firm has over the worker. The more control the firm has over how the worker does the job, the more likely that worker is to be classified as an employee.

The IRS test. The IRS looks at a number of factors to determine how much control a hiring firm has over a worker. There are three main areas the IRS reviews in making this decision: the worker's behavior on the job, finances, and relationship with the hiring firm.

- **Behavior on the job.** A worker is more likely to be considered an employee if the hiring firm has the right to control how the worker does specific tasks. For example, a worker who receives training from the hiring firm or is given instructions that must be followed about how to do the job is more likely to be classified as an employee.

- **Financial situation.** A worker who controls his or her own work-related expenses is more likely to be considered an independent contractor. For example, a worker who has a significant investment in equipment and facilities, pays his or her own travel and business expenses, is paid by the job (rather than by the hour or week), and has the opportunity to earn a profit or to lose money on a job is more likely to be classified as a contractor.

- **Relationship between the worker and the hiring firm.** The more a worker is treated like an employee, the more likely he or she is to be classified as such. For example, a worker who receives benefits, can quit or be fired at any time, and is hired to perform services that are part of the firm's core business is more likely to be classified as an employee.

intermittent leave

Under the Family and Medical Leave Act (FMLA), intermittent leave is FMLA leave that is taken in separate blocks of time for the same qualifying reason. For example, an employee who is receiving chemotherapy spread over several months may need one day off every few weeks for treatment, or an employee may need time off when a chronic illness flares up.

Employees are allowed to take intermittent leave if it's medically necessary for the employee's own serious health condition, a family member's serious health condition, or a family service member's injury or illness suffered while on active military duty. Employees may also take intermittent leave to handle qualifying exigencies relating to a family member's call to active duty in the military. Employees are entitled to take intermittent leave to care for a new child only if the employer agrees.

Related terms: Family and Medical Leave Act; military caregiver leave; military family leave; qualifying exigency; serious health condition.

intern

An intern is a type of temporary worker, generally a student or person who is new to the field, who takes the position to learn what the job is like and get some hands-on experience. Interns may be paid or unpaid, depending on the employer and practice in the industry. If an internship is unpaid or paid less than the minimum wage (and any overtime due), however, it must meet certain requirements intended to make sure that the internship really is a valuable learning opportunity rather than a form of exploitation.

The Department of Labor's six-part test. The federal Department of Labor looks at six factors to determine whether a true internship exists (meaning the intern is not legally considered an employee entitled to minimum wage and overtime). Generally, these factors are intended to uncover whether the internship is a benefit to the intern or to the employer:

- **The internship must be similar to training that would be provided in an educational environment.** An internship that centers on an academic experience is more likely to meet this test, as is one that trains the intern for multiple employment settings rather than just to do the work of the employer.
- **The internship must be for the benefit of the intern.** The more the business depends on the work of the intern, and the more time the intern spends on routine, regular work of the business, the more likely the intern will be considered an employee who is entitled to minimum wage and overtime.
- **The intern must not displace regular employees, and must work under close supervision of existing staff.** A company that is using

interns instead of regular employees (either because it has let employees go or put off hiring) is likely to be seen as an employer that owes wage and hour obligations. Similarly, if an intern receives the same supervision as regular employees, that argues against a true internship experience.

- **The employer gets no immediate advantage from the intern's work—and may, on occasion, find its operations impeded by the internship.** Having to provide an intern with extra training, special learning opportunities, and additional supervision and guidance, for example, will entail time and expense taken away from other activities, and is less likely to indicate an employment relationship.

- **The intern is not necessarily entitled to a job once the internship ends.** An internship that is actually a trial period, the successful completion of which will lead to a job, will be considered regular employment.

- **Both employer and intern understand that the intern is not entitled to wages for time spent in the internship.**

Where the Rich and Famous Interned

In addition to those who became famous while they were interns (like Lauren Conrad, of MTV's *The Hills*, or Monica Lewinsky of the famous blue dress), plenty of people who were destined for fame started out as interns. According to Inc.com, the list includes:

- Oprah Winfrey: While in college, this media mogul interned at a Nashville television station.
- Brooke Shields: She was already famous as a young actress, but Ms. Shields scored a high school internship at the San Diego Zoo.
- Patrick Ewing: While already a star on Georgetown's basketball team (but before he became the starting center for the New York Knicks), Ewing was a summer intern for the Senate Finance Committee.

International Union, UAW v. Johnson Controls

See bona fide occupational qualification.

investigation

An investigation is the process by which an employer determines whether misconduct took place, who was responsible, and what should be done about it. (Sometimes, an employer's own investigation is referred to as an "internal" investigation, to distinguish it from outside investigations that might be conducted by a government agency, such as the Equal Employment Opportunity Commission or the Department of Labor.)

For example, if an employee complains that she was sexually harassed, the employer might ask the HR director to investigate by interviewing the employee, interviewing the alleged wrongdoer and any witnesses to the harassment, reviewing documents associated with the harassment (such as email messages or handwritten notes), and reaching a conclusion about what actually happened. Or, a company that is experiencing a high rate of "shrinkage" (products disappearing that have not been paid for) might ask an investigator to figure out who had an opportunity to take the items, interview those employees, review documents associated with the property (such as shipping invoices, purchase orders, and so on), and determine who is responsible for the loss.

Related term: retaliation.

Retaliation Against Investigation Witnesses: The *Crawford* Case

Title VII prohibits employers from retaliating against—taking a negative employment action, such as firing, demoting, or transferring to a less desirable position—an employee for opposing illegal practices under the law, such as discrimination and harassment. Clearly, this protects employees who make a complaint, whether to the employer or to an outside agency, such as the Equal Employment Opportunity Commission. The U.S. Supreme Court recently held that witnesses and others who speak out against illegal practices during a workplace investigation are also protected.

In 2001, Vicky Crawford, an employee of the Metro School District, was interviewed during an investigation into allegations of sexual harassment against Gene Hughes, the District's employee relations director. In response to questions from a District human resources officer, Crawford described several incidents in which Hughes had acted inappropriately. She said that Hughes pulled her head into his crotch, asked to see her breasts, and grabbed his own crotch, saying "You know what's up." Two other witnesses also described inappropriate behavior by Hughes. When the investigation was complete, the District took no action against Hughes, but fired Crawford (a 30-year employee) and the other two witnesses.

When Crawford sued for illegal retaliation, both the federal district court and the federal Court of Appeals found that she had no case. Because she wasn't the person who originally complained about Hughes, she couldn't bring a retaliation claim. The Supreme Court disagreed, finding that these holdings would create a "freakish rule" that would protect someone who reports harassment on her own initiative, but not someone who reports harassment in response to a question from her boss. The Court found that Crawford's statements to the investigator were sufficient to show that she was opposed to Hughes's behavior, and that she was therefore protected from retaliation. Once Crawford's case was allowed to go to a jury, she was awarded $1.5 million in damages.

Crawford v. Metropolitan Government of Nashville and Davidson County, Tennessee, 129 S.Ct. 846 (2009).

investigative consumer report

An investigative consumer report is a consumer report (as defined under the Fair Credit Reporting Act or FCRA) that is based at least in part on personal interviews that go beyond simply verifying facts that the employee or applicant has provided to the employer. Employers that request and use investigative consumer reports on employees or applicants must follow special rules set out in the FCRA. Like a regular consumer report, an investigative consumer report must come from a consumer reporting agency, such as a private investigator or background checking firm, to fall within the coverage of the FCRA.

Related terms: background check; consumer report; consumer reporting agency; Fair Credit Reporting Act.

Jespersen v. Harrah's Operating Co.

See dress codes.

job description

A job description is a document that sets forth the duties, requirements, and prerequisites of a position. Typically, a manager prepares a job description when hiring for a new position or replacing a departing employee. The description helps applicants understand what the position entails and helps hiring companies make sure that applicants have the necessary skills, degrees, and experience for the job.

joint employer

A joint employer is an employer that shares control over an employee with another employer. In a joint employment situation, both companies are considered "employers," both are responsible for complying with applicable employment laws, and both can be sued for violating the employee's legal rights. Typically, joint employment comes up when one company is undisputedly the employer of a group of employees, and a second company is alleged to also be their employer (by an employee who wants to sue the second company for violating his or her rights). For example, a company that contracts with a temporary agency to supply employees or shares employees with a contractor or subcontractor might be a joint employer to those employees.

Who's a joint employer? In determining whether a company is a joint employer, courts look at all of the circumstances, particularly the relationship between the two companies, to determine whether the company is acting as an employer or not. The rules depend in part on which laws are involved. For example, some state statutes explicitly spell out what courts should consider in determining joint employer status. Generally speaking, the main factors courts look at include whether the alleged joint employer:

- has the right to hire and fire some employees of the other company
- has the power to set pay rates and pay methods for employees of the other company
- has the right to supervise the work and schedules of employees of the other company, and
- is responsible for maintaining employment records for employees of the other company.

J

jury duty (time off for)

Almost every state prohibits employers from firing or disciplining employees for taking time off work to serve on a jury. A few states go further and make it illegal for employees to discourage or intimidate an employee from serving on a jury.

Just because employees are entitled to time off doesn't mean they have a right to be paid for that time, however: In most states, unless an employer has promised otherwise in its policies or handbook, it does not have to pay employees for leave taken to serve on a jury. A few states require employers to pay for at least some of this time (for example, to pay the employee's regular salary for at least a few days).

key employee

Under the Family and Medical Leave Act (FMLA), a key employee is a salaried employee who is among the highest paid 10% of the company's employees within 75 miles of that employee's worksite. Although employees who take FMLA leave are ordinarily entitled to be reinstated to their jobs upon returning from leave, key employees may be denied reinstatement if their return to work would cause an employer substantial and grievous injury.

Employers must provide notice to key employees, shortly after they request leave, that they may be denied reinstatement. Another notice is required if the employer intends to deny reinstatement, and yet another notice must be provided if a key employee requests reinstatement at the end of his or her leave. Although key employees may be denied reinstatement, they are still entitled to the other rights provided by the FMLA. For example, the employer must continue the key employee's health benefits while that employee is on leave, even if the employer doesn't plan to reinstate the employee.

Related terms: Family and Medical Leave Act; reinstatement.

Kolstad v. American Dental Association

In *Kolstad v. American Dental Association*, 527 U.S. 526 (1999), the Supreme Court decided what facts an employee has to prove to get punitive damages for discrimination under Title VII.

The Civil Rights Act of 1991 amended Title VII to allow punitive damages awards against employers who violate Title VII, up to an amount ranging from $50,000 to $300,000, depending on the size of the employer. Under the Act, punitive damages may be awarded against an employer who engages in intentional discrimination, "with malice or with reckless indifference" to the rights of the victim. The Supreme Court interpreted this language to mean:

- **The employer must know that its actions might violate federal law.** If the employer believes that its actions are legal, or doesn't realize that they are illegal (because it is unaware of Title VII's prohibitions, for example), no punitive damages may be awarded. The employer need not know for certain that it is acting illegally, but it must have some idea that it could be violating the law.
- **An employer that makes good faith efforts to comply with Title VII won't be liable for punitive damages based on discrimination by managers and supervisors.** The Court didn't specify exactly what constitutes good faith efforts, but suggested that having a policy prohibiting discrimination and responding appropriately to complaints of discrimination—by performing an investigation and taking effective disciplinary action against wrongdoers—could protect an employer from punitive damages.

Related terms: Civil Rights Act of 1991; damages; discrimination; manager; Title VII.

Labor Management Relations Act

See Taft-Hartley Act.

Labor Management Reporting and Disclosure Act

The Labor Management Reporting and Disclosure Act (LMRDA), also known as the Landrum-Griffin Act, was passed by Congress in 1959 to regulate internal union affairs and the relationship between union officials and union members. It covers how union officers are elected, what information the union must provide to its members and the government, and the rights of union members vis-à-vis the union. The law also imposes restrictions on certain types of strikes and picketing.

The LMRDA passed as a result of Senate hearings to investigate criminal activities (particularly the influence of organized crime) and corruption in unions, especially the International Brotherhood of Teamsters. The hearings led not only to the passage of the LMRDA, but also to a number of convictions of union officials and the expulsion of the Teamsters from the American Federation of Labor and Congress of Industrial Organizations (AFL-CIO).

Related terms: National Labor Relations Act; Taft-Hartley Act.

lactation break

A lactation break is time off provided during the workday to allow new mothers to breastfeed or pump breast milk. Some states require employers to give new mothers a reasonable amount of time off for lactation; generally, this time is unpaid unless the employee uses her paid lunch or rest breaks for this purpose.

Starting in 2010, the federal Patient Protection and Affordable Care Act (the health care reform law) also requires larger employers to provide lactation breaks. In keeping with the health care reform law's emphasis on preventive health care and promoting healthy habits, it includes a provision requiring employers to allow new mothers to express breast milk. For up to one year after an employee gives birth, employers must provide reasonable break time for nursing mothers to pump. The employer need not pay for this time unless state law requires it. The employer must provide private space (other than a bathroom) for this purpose.

Employers with fewer than 50 employees don't have to provide lactation breaks if doing so would impose an "undue hardship." In other words, if providing breaks would entail significant expense or difficulty, considering the employer's size, structure, and resources, the employer doesn't have to allow them.

Related terms: health care reform; meal break; rest break.

Landrum-Griffin Act

See Labor Management Reporting and Disclosure Act.

layoff

A layoff occurs when an employer discharges an employee for reasons relating to the needs of the business rather than the employee's performance or conduct. Typically, layoffs take place because of declining business, a plant closing, cost cutting, restructuring that makes some employees unnecessary or duplicative, or other changes in a company's direction and goals (for example, getting rid of one product line to focus on another or consolidating business operations).

The term "layoff" was once used more typically to refer to a temporary situation. For example, in seasonal jobs or industries that experience wide fluctuations in work loads, employees might be laid off when work is scarce, only to return to the payroll when business picks up again. Particularly in a union setting, employees who are laid off temporarily might retain contract rights, including their seniority and the right to be recalled to work according to set rules. These days, however, layoffs refer more commonly to a permanent job loss.

Related terms: mass layoff; plant closing; Worker Adjustment and Retraining Notification Act (WARN).

leave year

Under the Family and Medical Leave Act, an employee may take up to 12 weeks of leave (or up to 26 weeks of military caregiver leave) in a 12-month period called the "leave year." Although military caregiver leave does not automatically renew, the 12-week leave provisions of the FMLA do: In other words, employees are entitled to 12 weeks of leave every 12 months, as long as they meet the other eligibility requirements.

The leave year need not be a calendar year. The FMLA includes four different ways of measuring the leave year, and allows employers to choose among them. However, once an employer chooses a method, it must use it for all employees consistently. Otherwise, employees will be free to choose whichever method works best for them. These methods are:

- **The calendar year.** Employers can choose to measure the leave year by the calendar. Most don't, however, because this could allow employees to take 24 weeks of continuous leave in a row if the leave spans the last 12 weeks of one year and the first 12 weeks of the next.
- **Any fixed 12-month period.** For example, a company could use its fiscal year or a year starting on the anniversary of an employee's hire. This method presents the same lengthy leave possibility as the calendar-year method, and so is also rarely used.
- **A 12-month period counting forward from the employee's first day of leave.** This method may also allow employees to take more

than 12 weeks of leave at a time, if some leave is saved for the end of the leave year. This method must be used for military caregiver leave.

- **A "rolling" leave year.** Using this method, an employee's leave entitlement is measured backward from the first day that FMLA leave is taken. Each time the employee takes leave, any part of the 12-week entitlement that was not used in the immediately preceding 12 months is available. This is the only method that doesn't allow employees to take more than 12 weeks of leave at a time.

> **EXAMPLE:** Mario takes one week of FMLA leave beginning February 12, 2011; four more weeks beginning March 2, 2011; three more weeks beginning May 7, 2011; and four more weeks beginning July 10, 2011. Under the rolling leave year method, Mario's next leave year will begin February 12, 2012. At that time, Mario will be entitled to one week of leave; four more weeks beginning March 2, 2012; three more weeks beginning May 7, 2012; and four more weeks beginning July 10, 2012.

Related terms: Family and Medical Leave Act; military caregiver leave; military family leave; rolling leave year.

light duty

In employment law, light duty refers to a temporary job that is less physically demanding than an employee's usual job, offered when the employee is unable to perform his or her regular work due to an injury, illness, disability, or pregnancy. For example, an employee who usually drives a route but is temporarily unable to do so because of a back injury might be offered a light-duty position doing paperwork until he is cleared to drive again. Whether an employee is entitled to light duty—and whether the employee has to accept a light-duty position—depends on the situation and the applicable law.

Pregnant employees. Under the federal Pregnancy Discrimination Act (PDA), pregnant employees who are temporarily unable to do their jobs because of pregnancy have the right to be treated like employees who are temporarily disabled for any other reason. If an employer provides light-duty assignments to all temporarily disabled employees, it must give light-duty work to employees whose temporary disability stems from pregnancy. If, however, an employer limits light-duty work to those who are injured on the job or who would otherwise be out on workers' compensation leave, some courts have held that the employer may deny light-duty work to pregnant employees, along with all other employees whose temporary disabilities are not work-related.

> EXAMPLE: Amanda worked as a truck driver. When she applied for the job, she was told that she had to be able to push or pull items weighing up to 200 pounds using a dolly. She also stated on her application that she could lift 75 pounds and carry it 56 feet, and that she could lift 60 pounds over her head. After a few months of work, Amanda discovered that she was pregnant. Her doctor restricted her to lifting no more than 20 pounds. Amanda told her employer of the restriction, and her employer sent her home, stating it had no light-duty work for her to do. After a couple of weeks, during which Amanda called in every day to request light duty and her employer told her there was none, she was fired.
>
> Amanda sued for pregnancy discrimination. She claimed that her employer offered light-duty assignments to employees who were on workers' compensation leave, and should have done the same for her. However, the federal Court of Appeals disagreed. Because the company denied light duty to all employees whose inability to work was not job-related (in other words, it did not single out only pregnant employees), its policy was not discriminatory. To require the company to provide light duty to pregnant employees, the court said, would force it to treat pregnant women better than other employees who were injured

off the job. The PDA requires employers only to "ignore" an employee's pregnancy, not to accommodate it in ways that are not available to other employees who are similarly situated. *Reeves v. Swift Transportation Co. Inc.*, 446 F.3d 637 (6th Cir. 2006).

State laws also prohibit pregnancy discrimination, and some states require employers to accommodate an employee's pregnancy. In these states, light-duty work may be required as a reasonable accommodation.

Workers' compensation. State laws require most employers to carry workers' compensation insurance, which pays medical bills and provides some replacement income for employees who suffer work-related injuries or illnesses. To keep costs down and return employees work as soon as possible, many employers offer light duty to employees who are out on workers' comp leave. Although state laws differ, an employee who unjustifiably refuses a light-duty position may lose the right to receive workers' comp benefits.

Disabilities. An employee who has a disability as defined by the Americans with Disabilities Act (ADA) may be entitled to a light-duty position, depending on the circumstances. Generally, an employee is protected from disability discrimination only if he or she can perform the job's essential functions, with or without a reasonable accommodation. If the job's essential functions are physically demanding and an employee cannot perform them because of a disability, that employee doesn't have a right to require the employer to fundamentally restructure the job or create a different light-duty position.

However, an employee with a disability may be entitled to a light-duty position if:

- the employee suffers a job-related injury and the employer makes light-duty positions available to other employees in the same situation, or
- the employer has light-duty positions available and providing such a position to an employee with a disability would not

create an undue hardship for the employer. Although the ADA does not require employers to create positions for employees with disabilities, it may require an employer to reassign them to vacant positions as a reasonable accommodation.

Related terms: Americans with Disabilities Act; Pregnancy Discrimination Act; workers' compensation.

Lilly Ledbetter Fair Pay Act

In *Ledbetter v. Goodyear Tire & Rubber Co.,* 550 U.S. 618 (2007), the U.S. Supreme Court found that Lilly Ledbetter's claims of sex discrimination in pay under Title VII were barred. The Court found that Ledbetter's claims weren't timely because she didn't file charges of discrimination with the Equal Employment Opportunity Commission (a prerequisite to bringing a discrimination lawsuit) within 180 days after the performance evaluations and related compensation decisions that she felt were discriminatory. Congress later overturned the Court's decision when it passed the Lilly Ledbetter Fair Pay Act.

Ledbetter was a supervisor at a Goodyear plant in Alabama from 1979 until she retired, in 1998. By the time she retired, she was the only woman in her position, and she earned $3,727 per month. The lowest paid man in her position earned $4,286, and the highest paid earned $5,236. After her retirement, she filed charges with the EEOC alleging that she was paid lower wages because of her sex. She won at trial, but the federal Court of Appeals overturned that decision, finding that her charges were filed too late. Because Goodyear's annual pay raises were based on annual performance evaluations, the Court found that Ledbetter should have filed charges when each of those decisions were made. The Court disregarded any allegedly discriminatory acts that occurred more than 180 days before Ledbetter filed her EEOC charges, and found that no discrimination had taken place within the relevant time period.

The U.S. Supreme Court agreed, finding that Ledbetter was entitled to bring claims based only on incidents that took place within the 180-day time limit, and that no discrimination occurred during that time. Ledbetter argued—and the dissent agreed—that each paycheck she received was a separate act of discrimination, carrying forward the effects of the earlier discriminatory decisions. The dissent also pointed out that evidence of pay discrimination tends to accrue over time, beginning in small increments and only later growing to a disparity large enough to suggest discrimination. This argument didn't carry the day in court, but it was persuasive to members of Congress, who overturned the *Ledbetter* case.

The Lilly Ledbetter Fair Pay Act was the first bill signed into law by President Obama in 2009. The Act amends Title VII to state that a separate violation of the law occurs each time an employee receives wages, benefits, or other compensation resulting from a discriminatory pay practice. The Act also states that an employee who is subject to discrimination in pay may recover back pay for up to two years before filing an EEOC charge, as long as the discriminatory acts that occurred during the 180-day charging period are similar or related to the acts that occurred before the charging period.

Related terms: charge; exhaustion (of remedies); sex discrimination; Title VII.

living wage laws

Living wage laws require employers to pay employees who work within the city or county covered by the law more than the federal or state minimum wage. The living wage rate is typically based on how much a full-time worker would have to earn to support a family of four at or above the poverty line in the geographical area covered by the law. Some living wage laws also require employers to provide certain job benefits or allow employers to pay less than the living wage if they already provide benefits.

City and county governments often pass living wage ordinances in areas where the cost of living has skyrocketed beyond that of the rest of the country (such as New York City or San Francisco). Many living wage laws cover only companies that have contracts with, or receive subsidies from, the local government, but some apply more broadly to all private employers in the area.

Related terms: minimum wage.

LMRDA

See Labor Management Reporting and Disclosure Act.

major life activity

To have a disability under the Americans with Disabilities Act, a person must have a physical or mental impairment that substantially limits at least one major life activity. Major life activities include (but are not limited to) caring for oneself, performing manual tasks, seeing, hearing, eating, sleeping, walking, standing, lifting, bending, speaking, breathing, learning, reading, concentrating, thinking, communicating, and working. They also include major bodily functions, such as the proper functioning of the immune system, normal cell growth, and digestive, bowel, bladder, neurological, brain, respiratory, circulatory, endocrine, and reproductive functions.

Related terms: Americans with Disabilities Act; disability; impairment.

manager

A manager (sometimes referred to as a "supervisor") is an employee who has the authority to make certain decisions regarding other employees on behalf of the employer. Generally speaking, the actions of managers are considered to be the actions of the employer, and the employer can be sued based on those actions. A company can really only act through its managers, so their decisions (for example, to fire, demote, or transfer someone) are imputed to the employer.

Whether an employee qualifies as a manager is an important distinction for several employment and labor laws. Managers not only have the legal authority to act for the employer, but they are also subject to certain legal restrictions. For example, managers may not be in the same bargaining unit with rank and file employees, and they are not entitled to overtime if they work more than 40 hours in a week. Although each law defines the role of manager a bit differently, all of them focus on the manager's authority to make employment decisions regarding other employees.

M

The Rights to Assign and Responsibly Direct: *In re Oakwood Healthcare*

In *In re Oakwood Healthcare Inc.*, 348 N.L.R.B. 37 (2006), the National Labor Relations Board (NLRB) found that employees who have the authority to make work assignments or direct the work of other employees may be supervisors if those tasks require some independent judgment and discretion, even if they spend only 10% to 15% of their time on these supervisory duties and the rest of their time performing the same job duties as other employees. This decision represents a change from previous NLRB decisions, which interpreted the term "supervisor" more narrowly.

Previously, the NLRB found that employees who used ordinary professional or technical judgment in directing less-skilled employees to provide services were not exercising independent judgment, and therefore did not qualify as supervisors. But the U.S. Supreme Court rejected this interpretation as too limited (in *NLRB v. Kentucky River Community Care, Inc.*, 532 U.S. 706 (2001)). In response to the Supreme Court's ruling, the NLRB decided, in the *Oakwood* case, to adopt a less restrictive standard.

In *Oakwood*, the NLRB focused on two supervisory responsibilities: assigning work and directing the work of other employees. The NLRB found that an employee who assigns others to particular departments, shifts, or significant tasks is a supervisor, as long as making those assignments requires some independent judgment and discretion and is not simply clerical or routine in nature. An employee who responsibly directs others—that is, who oversees the work of other employees and is held accountable for their performance—also qualifies as a supervisor.

Title VII and other antidiscrimination laws. The U.S. Supreme Court and the Equal Employment Opportunity Commission have found that employers are always liable for harassment committed by managers (called "supervisors" in this context) if the harassment results in a tangible employment action, such as job termination; demotion; denial of a raise, bonus, or promotion; and so on. For purposes of these laws, a supervisor is someone who has the authority to recommend or carry out tangible employment actions affecting the employee or the authority to direct the employee's daily work activities, such as supervising the employee, making work assignments and schedules, and so on.

Fair Labor Standards Act (FLSA). Under the FLSA, managerial employees are exempt from the minimum wage and overtime requirements. Even if they work more than 40 hours a week, managerial employees aren't entitled to get overtime. Two requirements must be met for an employee to be an exempt managerial employee: a salary test and a job duties test. Under the salary test, the employee must earn at least $455 per week and be paid on a salary basis. Workers are paid on a salary basis if they receive their full salary for any week in which they perform any work, regardless of how many hours they work or the quality or amount of work they do. (There are a handful of exceptions to this rule; see "pay docking.")

An employee must also perform certain job duties to qualify. Managerial employees (also called "executive" employees) must meet all of the following requirements:

- The employee's primary duty must be managing the company or a recognized department or subdivision of the company.
- The employee must customarily and regularly supervise at least two full-time employees (or their equivalent).
- The employee must have the authority to hire and fire, or the employee's recommendations as to hiring, firing, promotions, or any other change in employee status must be given particular weight.

National Labor Relations Act (NLRA). Under the NLRA, "supervisors" are not considered employees under the law, which means they are not protected by the NLRA and may not join a union. The NLRA defines supervisors as those who have the authority, in the interest of the employer, to perform or effectively recommend at least one of the 12 actions listed below regarding other employees, if their exercise of that authority requires independent judgment and is not merely routine or clerical in nature:

- hire
- transfer
- suspend
- lay off
- recall
- promote
- discharge
- assign
- reward
- discipline
- responsibly direct, or
- adjust grievances.

Related terms: bargaining unit; exempt employee; National Labor Relations Act; National Labor Relations Board; pay docking; salary basis; tangible employment action.

mandatory subjects of bargaining

Mandatory subjects of bargaining are topics that are central to the employment relationship and must be negotiated between the union and the employer, rather than adopted unilaterally by the employer. Such subjects include wages, hours, production quotas, grievance procedures, and selection methods for layoff.

Related terms: collective bargaining.

Manuel v. Westlake Polymers

See absenteeism.

marital status discrimination

Marital status discrimination occurs when an employer makes job decisions based on whether someone is married, single, divorced, or widowed. Federal laws don't prohibit discrimination based on marital status, but many state laws do. In these states, employers may not make employment decisions, including decisions about benefits or pay, based on an employee's marital status or position as head of the household.

Nepotism rules. Some employers have policies against nepotism, which prohibit (among other things) one spouse from supervising or working closely with another. In states that prohibit marital status discrimination, the legality of these policies depends on the reasons behind them. A flat ban on spouses working at the same company— for example, a policy stating that no spouses of current employees will be hired—would most likely be found illegal in a state that prohibits discrimination based on marital status. However, a policy that prohibits one spouse from reporting to the other, in order to maintain employee morale and department productivity, would likely be upheld.

Related terms: discrimination; nepotism; protected characteristic.

mass layoff

Under the Worker Adjustment and Retraining Notification Act (WARN), a mass layoff is a reduction in force that results in an employment loss (termination or an hours cut of more than 50%) at a single employment site during any 30-day period for:
- 500 or more employees, or
- 50 to 499 employees if the laid-off employees make up at least one-third of the employer's active workforce.

Mass layoffs are covered by WARN, which means the employer must give written notice of the layoff, 60 days in advance, to the affected employees, the bargaining representative of all union members who are affected, and state and local government officials.

There are some exceptions to the WARN requirements, which allow employers to give shorter notice or even no notice in certain situations. If no exception applies, however, an employer that doesn't give the required notice may be ordered to pay employees for up to 60 days.

Layoffs in the Recession

The Bureau of Labor Statistics collects data on mass layoffs, defined for these purposes as when at least 50 initial claims for unemployment are filed against the same establishment in a five-week period. During the current recession, the numbers of workers who have lost their jobs in such a mass layoff event climbed to more than 1.5 million in 2008 and more than 2 million in 2009. This compares to less than 1 million in 2006 and 2007. To learn more, go to www.bls.gov/mls.

M

Related terms: plant closing; Worker Adjustment and Retraining Notification Act (WARN).

McKennon v. Nashville Banner Publishing Co.

See after-acquired evidence.

meal break

A meal break is time off work to eat lunch or another meal during a shift. Federal law doesn't require employers to provide meal breaks. However, if an employer doesn't pay an employee for a meal break and the employee ends up having to work during the break, that time must be paid. For example, a receptionist who has to answer phones during her lunch must be paid for that time, even if her employer doesn't otherwise pay employees for meal creaks.

Fewer than half the states require employers to provide a meal break. In those states that require meal breaks, employees who work more than five or six hours at a time typically must be allowed to take a half hour to eat. Some states prohibit employers from giving this time off near the beginning or end of the work shift.

Related terms: hour worked; rest break.

mediation

Mediation is a form of alternative dispute resolution in which two (or more) parties involved in a dispute come together to try to work out a solution to their problem with the help of a neutral third person, called the mediator. Unlike a judge or an arbitrator, the mediator doesn't have the authority to decide who "wins" or "loses," or to make any other decisions about the dispute. The mediator's job is to help the participants evaluate their own goals and options in order to find their own solution.

When does mediation take place? In employment disputes, mediation may occur at any point after a problem first arises. Some companies have in-house mediation programs, which can help employees work out issues with coworkers or supervisors before they become too serious. The Equal Employment Opportunity Commission (EEOC), the federal agency that enforces the laws prohibiting discrimination, has its own mediation program for discrimination charges, and many courts require the parties to a lawsuit to try mediation before taking their claims to court.

When does mediation make sense? Because of its informality, speed, and low-cost, mediation is often a good option if:

- **Time is of the essence.** To resolve a dispute quickly, mediation can be the best way to go. For example, if a company is planning an initial public offering and an employee is threatening to sue, the company probably wants a speedy, private resolution. Similarly, an employee who is facing workplace mistreatment, such as harassment or bullying, often needs a quick solution to the problem.
- **The dispute is between coworkers.** The law doesn't offer much help to those who are fighting with coworkers. These disputes

M

can be mightily unpleasant, but they often don't constitute legal violations (unless sexual harassment or an assault is involved). And, unless the coworker causing the problem is independently wealthy, there isn't likely to be much money in bringing the case to court.

- **There is an ongoing employment relationship between the parties.** Because mediation has the potential to help build and repair relationships, it can be especially helpful in disputes involving current employees. Unlike litigation, which encourages the parties to take extreme positions and go all out to win, mediation encourages collaboration and emphasizes how the parties will get along in the future. This makes it a good process for resolving disputes among people who will continue working together.

- **Mediation is available free or at low cost.** Many larger private employers, government agencies, and courts offer mediation free or at very low cost. If a program like this is available, it makes sense to give it a try. Because mediation isn't binding, the parties are always free to continue their dispute if the mediation isn't successful.

- **Confidentiality is important.** Confidentiality is often a significant concern in employment disputes. The employer may have trade secrets, business practices, or plain old dirty laundry that it doesn't want to air in public. Employees may not want their every workplace lapse discussed and debated in open court. Mediation offers everyone a way to keep these issues confidential.

Mediation may not be right in some situations. For example, if violence has occurred or been threatened, the victim may not feel comfortable sitting down at a negotiating table with the perpetrator. Or, if either party wants to break new legal ground by setting a precedent, mediation won't further that goal.

Related terms: alternative dispute resolution; arbitration; Equal Employment Opportunity Commission.

medical certification

Under the Family and Medical Leave Act, an employer may ask an employee who needs leave to provide a medical certification: a document completed by the employee and a health care provider that gives some basic information about the employee's need for leave. There are three types of medical certifications: certification of the employee's own serious health condition, certification of a family member's serious health condition, and certification of a family member's serious illness or injury suffered in the line of active military duty, entitling the employee to take military caregiver leave. (An employer can also request nonmedical certifications, such as proof of a family relationship or proof of the need for qualifying exigency need.) The federal Department of Labor has certification forms for each of these types of leave.

Related terms: Department of Labor; Family and Medical Leave Act; military caregiver leave; qualifying exigency; serious health condition.

M

medical marijuana

More than a dozen states allow residents to use marijuana for medical purposes. Called "medical marijuana" or "compassionate use" laws, these measures typically require the user to have a doctor's written authorization to use marijuana, often for particular diseases or disabilities. If a patient meets the criteria, he or she cannot be prosecuted under state law for crimes relating go the use, possession, or cultivation of a certain amount of marijuana. Federal drug laws still apply, however.

But I have a prescription. These laws raise questions for employees with marijuana prescriptions and their employers: If an employee uses marijuana at work, arrives at work obviously under the influence, or tests positive for marijuana use on a drug test, what are the rules? Is the employer legally required to accommodate the employee's drug use? What if marijuana was prescribed for a disability? Can an employee be fired for using marijuana as legally prescribed by a doctor?

Pot country rules against the employee. So far, only a couple of states have weighed in on these questions, and both have found that employees who test positive for marijuana may be fired, even if they have a valid prescription under the state's law. The Oregon Supreme Court found that, even though an employee had a valid registry card allowing him to use marijuana for a medical condition, he could be fired for doing so. Because marijuana use is still illegal under federal law, the Court found that the employee was fired for the current use of illegal drugs, which both the federal ADA and Oregon law allow. (*Emerald Steel Fabricators v. Bureau of Labor and Industries*, 230 P.3d 518 (2010).)

The California Supreme Court found that the state's medical marijuana law protected legal users only from criminal prosecution, not from an employer's enforcement of its own rules on drug use. In that case, Gary Ross used marijuana, with a prescription, to relieve pain and spasms caused by a back injury he suffered while serving in the Air Force. He was fired when he failed a drug test shortly after he began work at Ragingwire. He sued, claiming that Ragingwire was legally required to accommodate his off-duty use of marijuana because it was prescribed for his disability. The Court disagreed, holding that employers have no duty to accommodate an employee's use of marijuana, a drug that is still illegal under federal law. Although the state's law protected Ross from criminal charges, it didn't protect his job. (*Ross v. Ragingwire Telecommunications*, 42 Cal.4th 920 (2008).)

Related terms: Americans with Disabilities Act; disability; drug testing; reasonable accommodation.

medical records

Medical records are written information regarding the medical history or condition of an employee. Under the Americans with Disabilities Act (ADA), medical records must be kept confidential.

This means they must be kept separate from regular personnel files and security measures must be taken to restrict access (such as using a locked file cabinet or a password-protected database).

Under the ADA, information in employee medical records may be revealed only to

- safety and first aid workers, if necessary to treat the employee or provide for evacuation procedures
- the employee's supervisor, if the employee's disability requires restricted duties or a reasonable accommodation
- government officials as required by law, and
- insurance companies that require a medical exam.

Related terms: Americans with Disabilities Act; disability; reasonable accommodation.

military caregiver leave

Under 2008 amendments to the Family and Medical Leave Act (FMLA), an employee may take military caregiver leave to care for a family member who suffers or aggravates a serious injury or illness while on active military duty. Another amendment in 2009 expanded this entitlement to cover leave to care for a family member who is a veteran, was a member of the Armed Forces within the past five years, and suffers from a service-related injury or illness.

Although this provision is part of the FMLA, it differs from the other types of leave available under the law because it covers more family members, lasts for a longer period of time, and is a one-time-only entitlement, rather than renewing each year like regular FMLA leave.

Who is covered. The same general coverage and eligibility requirements that apply to the FMLA apply to the military caregiver provisions. However, employees may take leave only to care for:

- a covered servicemember (one who is an active member of the regular Armed Forces, National Guard, and Reserves, or is on the temporary disability retired list) or a veteran (one who was a member of the Armed Forces within the past five years)

M

- with a serious illness or injury (one that may render the servicemember unfit to perform the duties of his or her office, grade, rank, or rating)
- incurred or aggravated in the line of duty on active duty (while serving full-time duty in the active military)
- for which the servicemember or veteran is undergoing medical treatment, recuperation, or therapy. Active servicemembers also qualify if they are not currently undergoing treatment, recuperation, or therapy, but are otherwise in outpatient status or on the temporary disability retired list.

More family members are covered. Caregiver leave is available only if the servicemember who needs care is the employee's family member. As is true for the other provisions of the FMLA, a family member includes the employee's spouse, parent, or child. However, the caregiver entitlement also includes adult children and "next of kin." If a servicemember has designated a blood relative as his or her next of kin for purposes of this leave, that person qualifies for leave. If not, the servicemember's next of kin is his or her nearest blood relative (other than a parent, child, or spouse) in this following order of priority:

- blood relatives who have legal custody of the servicemember
- siblings
- grandparents
- aunts and uncles, and
- first cousins.

All blood relatives within the same level of the highest priority relationship are considered the servicemember's next of kin. For example, if no one has legal custody of a servicemember with three siblings, all three siblings are considered next of kin. All three, along with the servicemember's spouse, parent, and child, may take leave to care for the same servicemember, if necessary. The purpose of this rule is simply to make sure that someone, or more than one person, will be available to provide care.

More leave is available. For this provision only, an employee is entitled to 26 weeks of leave, rather than the 12 weeks allowed for other types of FMLA leave. Unlike other types of FMLA leave, however, military caregiver leave isn't an annually renewed entitlement. Instead, it's a per-servicemember, per-injury requirement. An employee may take up to 26 weeks of leave in a single 12-month period. The employee may be entitled to an additional 26 weeks of leave only if:

- the servicemember suffers a different serious injury or illness in the line of duty, or
- a different family member suffers a serious injury or illness in the line of active duty.

Even if the servicemember's injury is such that he or she will need ongoing care, an employee is entitled to only one 26-week period of leave.

If the employee takes FMLA leave for other reasons during the same 12-month period, those types of leave count toward the employee's 26-week entitlement. For example, if an employee already used six weeks of leave for the adoption of a child, the employee has only 20 weeks of military caregiver leave available in the same 12-month period.

Related terms: Family and Medical Leave; leave year; military family leave; qualifying exigency.

military family leave

Military family leave is time taken off work because of a family member's military service. Amendments to the federal Family and Medical Leave Act (FMLA) in 2008 give employees the right to two types of military family leave:

- qualifying exigency leave, which is available when an employee needs to handle particular issues relating to a family member's active duty or call to active duty in the military, and
- military caregiver leave, which is available to care for a family member who suffers a serious injury or illness while on active military duty.

Related terms: Family and Medical Leave Act; military caregiver leave; qualifying exigency leave.

military leave

Military leave is time taken off work to serve in the Armed Forces. The right to military leave is protected by federal law and the laws of many states, in recognition of the fact that about half of our country's total military power comes from the National Guard and Reserves—employees who serve in the military while holding nonmilitary jobs in the private or public sector—rather than career military personnel.

The federal Uniformed Services Employment and Reemployment Rights Act (USERRA) gives employees the right to reinstatement after taking up to five years of leave to serve in the military, including active service, inactive service, and training. Most states also give employees the right to take time off to serve in the state's militia or guard.

Related term: Uniformed Services Employment and Reemployment Rights Act.

minimum wage

The minimum wage is the lowest amount an employer may legally pay most employees per hour. Employers may pay more than the applicable minimum wage where they do business, but they may not pay less: It's the legal floor below which wages may not fall.

Federal, state, or local? The federal minimum wage, set by Congress, is currently $7.25 an hour. This limit applies to virtually all employers. Many states have their own minimum wages, and some local governments have minimum wages as well. Whenever there are multiple employment laws covering the same issue, employers must follow the one that provides the most protections to workers. In this case, that means employers must pay the highest applicable minimum wage.

EXAMPLE: An employer that does business in San Francisco, California, is subject to the $7.25 federal minimum wage, California's minimum wage of $8, and San Francisco's minimum wage of $9.92. This means the company must pay its San Francisco-based employees the highest amount, $9.92.

Some employees can be paid less than the minimum. The minimum wage laws do not protect some workers. For example, the federal minimum wage law doesn't cover outside salespeople, independent contractors, employees of seasonal amusement businesses, or newspaper deliverers, among others. State and local laws may also exclude certain employees.

Kids are cheaper. Even if an employee is otherwise covered, employers may sometimes pay employees less than the minimum wage, at least for a certain period of time. For example, federal law allows employers to pay a "youth minimum wage" of $4.25 an hour to employees under the age of 20 for their first 90 calendar days of employment. Once the worker turns 20 or the 90-day limit has passed (whichever comes first), the employee is entitled to the full regular minimum wage. Some states require employers to pay all employees the minimum wage, regardless of their age.

Subminimum wage certificates. Employers may apply to the federal Department of Labor for a certificate allowing them to pay certain employees less than the minimum wage. Such a certificate is available only if necessary to prevent the curtailment of employment opportunities for these workers, who include:

- messengers: those employed primarily in delivering letters and messages for a company whose principal business is providing these services
- apprentices: employees who are at least 16 years old and are employed to learn a skilled trade
- full-time students: students who are employed in retail, a service industry, or agriculture, or who work for the institution in which they are enrolled

M

- student learners: students who are receiving instruction in an accredited school and working part time in a vocational training program
- learners: employees being trained for certain occupations for which skill, dexterity, and judgment must be learned, and who produce little or nothing of value when initially employed, and
- employees with disabilities: workers whose earnings or productive capacity is impaired by a physical or mental disability.

Here's a tip: Under federal law and the laws of some states, employees who earn tips may be paid less than the minimum wage, as long as the wage they are paid plus the tips they actually receive add up to at least the minimum wage. (For more information, see "tips.")

Room and board. Under federal law, employers may withhold money from an employee's paycheck to satisfy a debt the employee owes the employer or to cover the cost of certain employment expenses (such as uniforms or tools), but only if the amount the employee receives after these deductions is at least equal to the minimum wage. (Some states don't allow these types of deductions, even if the employee earns more than the minimum wage.) However, an employer may deduct the reasonable cost of meals and housing provided to the employee, even if these deductions cause the employee's pay to fall below the minimum wage. These deductions are allowed only if all of the following requirements are met:

- The employer customarily pays the expenses.
- The items are provided for the benefit of the employee.
- The employee is told in advance about the deductions.
- The employee voluntarily agrees to accept less than the minimum wage in exchange for the food and lodging provided.

Related terms: exempt employee; Fair Labor Standards Act; independent contractor; living wage; outside salesperson; tips; uniforms.

moonlighting

Moonlighting refers to working a second job (sometimes secretly, to avoid displeasing a primary employer or avoid reporting the income). Usually, moonlighting takes place at different times of day (for example, working one job during the day and another at night or by the light of the moon, which is where the term comes from). If someone works one job while on leave from another, it may also be referred to as moonlighting.

Some employers prohibit employees from moonlighting for a competitor or at a job that interferes with their work for the employer. Restrictions like these are likely legal. However, more restrictive policies—such as one that prohibits all moonlighting or allows moonlighting only with approval—might not be legal in states that have passed off-duty conduct laws protecting employees from discrimination based on what they do on their own time, as long as those activities are not illegal. In these states, an employer that imposes restrictions beyond what's necessary to protect its own interests might run afoul of the law.

M

Who Moonlights?

Recent data from the Bureau of Labor Statistics show that 5.2% of employees held more than one job in 2009. Since the start of the recession in December 2007, these numbers have stayed fairly steady. Moonlighting was more common in the mid-1990s, when the percentage of employees with multiple jobs peaked at 6.2%. Women are more likely to moonlight than men, and whites are more likely to moonlight than those of other races.

Related term: off-duty conduct laws.

National Labor Relations Act

The National Labor Relations Act of 1935 (NLRA), also known as the Wagner Act, established workers' right to organize and bargain collectively with employers. It also outlawed certain employer efforts to prevent union organizing and bust up existing unions (called "unfair labor practices"), and it established the National Labor Relations Board.

The NLRA was amended in 1947 by the Taft-Hartley Act, which imposed a number of restrictions and requirements on unions, and again in 1959 by the Labor Management Reporting and Disclosure Act, which regulated internal union affairs and the relationship between union officials and union members. As originally passed, however, the NLRA voiced strong support for the rights of employees to join a union and to collectively bargain with their employer to improve their working conditions.

Which employers are subject to the NLRA. The NLRA applies to all private employers whose operations affect commerce between the states—that is, whose employees handle, sell, produce, or otherwise work on goods or materials that have come from or will go to another state, or whose employees use the mail, telephone, Internet, or other equipment to communicate across state lines. This means all but the smallest and most local employers are covered. It doesn't apply to governments, religious schools, or employers subject to the Railway Labor Act (railroad and airline industries).

Jurisdictional standards. Although the National Labor Relations Board (NLRB) has the right to take action to enforce the NLRA against virtually all employers, it intervenes only in larger disputes. In its discretion, the NLRB has set minimum business volume thresholds, which it calls "jurisdictional" requirements, that an employer's business must meet before the NLRB will step in. Here are some of the jurisdictional limits that apply to some common industries (it's by no means a complete list):

- Nonretail businesses: at least $50,000 in direct sales of goods or services to consumers in other states, indirect sales (through other sellers), direct purchases of goods or services from suppliers in other states, or indirect purchases (through other purchasers)
- Retail enterprises: at least $500,000 in total gross annual business volume
- Management and operation of office buildings and shopping centers: at least $100,000 in total annual revenue, of which $25,000 or more must come from organizations that meet any of the other jurisdictional standards (not including the indirect sale or purchase of goods for nonretail businesses)
- Newspapers: at least $200,000 in total annual business volume
- Hotels, motels, and residential apartment buildings: at least $500,000 in total annual business volume
- Law firms and legal assistance programs: at least $250,000 in gross annual revenue
- Employers that provide social services (such as groups that solicit and distribute charitable contributions): at least $250,000 in gross annual revenue
- Private universities and colleges: at least $1,000,000 in gross annual revenue from all sources (except contributions not available for operating expenses at the grantor's request), and
- National defense: any enterprise affecting commerce whose operations have a substantial impact on nation defense.

Which employees does the NLRA protect? The NLRA generally protects all employees of a covered employer. However, certain workers are not protected by the NLRA, including agricultural workers, domestic servants, anyone employed by a spouse or parent, independent contractors, and managers and supervisors.

Unfair labor practices. The NLRA prohibits employers from engaging in certain activities, including:

- interfering with an employee's right to organize, join, or assist a union; engage in collective bargaining; or engage in protected concerted activities (actions or communications by two or more employees to improve, protest, or otherwise change the terms and conditions of their employment, such as wages, benefits, workplace rules, supervision, working conditions, and so on)
- dominating or providing illegal assistance or support to a labor union, including creating a company or sham union
- discriminating against employees to encourage or discourage membership in a labor organization
- retaliating against an employee for filing a charge with or giving testimony to the NLRB, and
- refusing to engage in good faith, collective bargaining with a duly elected union.

Organizing and representation elections. The NLRA establishes workers' basic right to organize: to form, join, or assist a union; to choose their own representatives to negotiate with their employer about terms and conditions of employment; and to engage in other collective efforts to improve their work situations. To this end, the law establishes procedures for determining whether a particular union should have the right to represent a group of workers.

To represent workers in negotiations with an employer, a union must have the support of a majority of workers in an appropriate bargaining unit. Unions generally demonstrate this support by asking workers to sign authorization cards: forms indicating a desire to be represented by the union in dealings with the employer. If the union gets the support of a majority of bargaining unit workers, it will often ask the employer to recognize the union voluntarily.

If the employer refuses to recognize the union, the workers or the union may petition the NLRB and ask it to hold an election. The petition must be accompanied by signed statements of union support from at least 30% of the workers in the proposed bargaining

N

unit. The NLRB will hold a secret election (one in which workers cast their ballots privately). If the union receives a majority of the votes cast, it will be certified as the bargaining representative of the unit.

The NLRA prohibits employers from unfairly influencing their workers' decision to join or form a union and from using threats or coercive tactics to influence the outcome of an election. Such tactics might include punishing or threatening union supporters, promising or giving benefits to workers who oppose the union, infiltrating or spying on union meetings, or questioning workers about their support for the union.

Related terms: bargaining unit; collective bargaining; company union; decertification; Labor Management Reporting and Disclosure Act; National Labor Relations Board; strike; Taft-Hartley Act; unfair labor practice.

National Labor Relations Board

N

The National Labor Relations Board (NLRB) is the federal agency that administers and enforces the National Labor Relations Act (NLRA). The NLRB has two missions: to resolve representation disputes (disagreements over whether a group of employees has chosen a union to represent it—and, if so, which union) and to prevent and remedy unfair labor practices.

Structure of the NLRB. The NLRB has a number of regional offices throughout the country, which process and investigate unfair labor practice charges and election petitions. The actual Board is a five-member panel (appointed by the President of the United States) that issues decisions in labor disputes, like a court. If either side is unhappy with the Board's decision, it can appeal to the federal court system. The NLRB also has an Office of General Counsel, which is independent from the Board and is responsible for investigating and prosecuting labor cases. This Office also oversees the work of the regional offices.

A Funny Thing Happened on the Way to a Quorum: Supreme Court Invalidates 600 NLRB Decisions

Because the NLRB handles issues that are often fiercely contested, and because its members are appointed for five-year terms by the President and then must be confirmed by the Senate, politics has a way of holding up appointments to the Board. It often happens that the Board is operating at less than full strength while the President, Senate, or both decide whether to support a particular candidate. In the meantime, however, labor disputes keep happening, and cases keep coming before the Board. So how many sitting members must the Board have to decide a case?

At least three, the Supreme Court decided in *New Process Steel v. NLRB*, 130 S.Ct. 1117 (2010). For more than two years, starting at the end of 2007, the NLRB was down to only two members. These two, one appointed by a Republican and the other by a Democrat, issued about 600 cases on which they could agree on the outcome. If the two split, no decision was issued. A few parties who weren't pleased with the Board's decision filed appeals to federal court, challenging the Board's authority to issue decisions with only two members. One appeals court said the Board had this authority; another said it did not. The Supreme Court agreed to decide the matter.

The case turned on the NLRB's authority to delegate its powers to a smaller group, and how large that smaller group must be. The NLRA allows the full Board to delegate any of its powers to a group of at least three members (a quorum). The Act also says that two members may constitute a quorum on issues that the full Board delegates to a three-member group. For those of us who skipped the student council and model U.N. meetings, all this talk of delegations and quorums can numb the brain. But the issue boiled down to this: Can the NLRB act with only two members or does it need at least three? Or, as the petition for certiorari put it more dramatically, "Does the NLRB exist?"

The Supreme Court decided that the provision about two members acting was effective only if everyone in the three-member quorum was still on the Board. So, for example, if a three-member quorum had properly been delegated the right to hear cases, and one of the members withdrew from hearing a particular case (say, because of a conflict of interest), the

---

A Funny Thing Happened on the Way to a Quorum: Supreme Court Invalidates 600 NLRB Decisions (continued)

remaining two members could issue a decision—but only if the third member was still on the Board. Once the Board had only two members, they were no longer authorized to issue decisions.

It's not yet clear what will happen to the 600 decisions the two-member Board nonetheless issued. The cases that were appealed to federal court were returned to the NLRB for reconsideration once it got a third member. But in cases that weren't appealed, the parties have presumably already altered their behavior to conform to the decision, which may no longer be valid.

---

national origin discrimination

An employer discriminates based on national origin when it treats an employee differently because of ethnicity or country of ancestry, or because of traits closely linked to ethnicity (such as surname, accent, cultural identity, and so on). National origin discrimination is prohibited by Title VII and the laws of many states. Here are some examples of national origin discrimination:

- An airline doesn't allow anyone who appears to be from the Middle East to work in any position that involves dealing with passengers.
- A hardware store that serves a predominantly white neighborhood refuses to promote an employee who has adopted a traditional African style of dress.
- A Chinese restaurant hires only people with Asian features and surnames to wait on customers.
- An automotive supply store disciplines Latino employees more severely than white employees for unexcused absences and tardiness.

Accent rules. Because accent is closely associated with national origin, employers can legitimately make job decisions based on an employee's accent only if the accent significantly interferes with the employee's ability to do the job. For example, a business might transfer an employee with a heavy accent from a software help desk position to a job that doesn't require customer contact. Such a transfer would be legitimate if customers had complained that they could not understand his instructions; the same transfer would be illegal if the employee was transferred simply because he had an accent or a particular type of accent, not because the accent impaired his ability to do the job.

Fluency and language requirements. An employer may be able to prohibit on-duty employees from speaking any language other than English if it can show that the rule is necessary for business reasons. Similarly, an employer may require fluency in a language (such as the ability to speak Cantonese or Spanish) if necessary for business reasons.

Related terms: discrimination; English-only rules, Title VII.

negligent hiring

If a third party is injured (or worse) by an employee, and the employer knew or should have known that the employee posed a danger to others or was otherwise unfit for the job, the third party may be able to sue the employer for negligent hiring. This legal theory applies even to actions that are well beyond the scope of the employee's job. In fact, it is often used to hold an employer responsible for an employee's violent criminal acts on the job, such as robbery, rape, or even murder. Here are some examples:

- A pizza company hired a delivery driver without looking into his criminal past, which included a sexual assault conviction and an arrest for stalking a women he met while delivering pizza for another company. After he raped a customer, he was sent to jail for 25 years—and the pizza franchise was liable to the victim for negligent hiring.
- A car rental company hired a man who later raped a coworker. Had the company verified his résumé claims, it would have

discovered that he was in prison for robbery during the years he claimed to be in high school and college. The company was liable to the coworker.

- A furniture company hired a deliveryman without requiring him to fill out an application or performing a background check. The employee assaulted a female customer in her home with a knife. The company was liable to the customer for negligent hiring.

The employer must be careless. To win a negligent hiring claim, the injured person must show that the employer didn't take reasonable care in hiring employees. If there was no reasonable way the employer could have known that an employee was dangerous, then the employer wasn't careless—and won't be liable for negligent hiring. In contrast, an injured third party can sue an employer under a legal theory called "respondeat superior" (let the superior answer) even if the employer exercised proper care in hiring, but only if the employee caused the injury while acting in the course and scope of employment. The difference is based on the underlying purpose of each claim: Respondeat superior holds the employer responsible for the costs of doing business, including damages caused by the employees while on the job; negligent hiring holds the employer responsible for its own careless actions in placing a dangerous person in a position to harm others.

Coming to a courtroom near you? Although not all states have allowed these types of claims, the clear legal trend is to allow injured third parties to sue for negligent hiring.

Related terms: background check; course and scope of employment; negligent retention; respondeat superior.

negligent retention

Negligent retention is a legal claim similar to negligent hiring, except the injured third party claims that the employer was careless in keeping an employee on the payroll after the employer knew, or should have known, that the employee posed a danger. This type of claim might be brought when the employer had no way of knowing that the employee was dangerous when hiring, but should have known later, through the employee's actions or newly discovered information about the employee's past acts, that the employee posed a risk. For example, a company that retains a delivery employee who is convicted of driving while intoxicated and fails a random workplace drug test could well be liable to a pedestrian the employee hits while driving under the influence.

Related term: negligent hiring.

nepotism

Nepotism occurs when an employer favors relatives or friends when making job decisions. Usually nepotism is familial, as when the CEO hires his sister-in-law or his son over more qualified candidates. The term, which comes from the Latin word for nephew or grandchild, is said to derive from the Catholic Church practice during the Middle Ages of popes and bishops giving their nephews positions of preference (often, as Cardinals) that would ordinarily be given from father to son.

Sometimes, nepotism is used as a synonym for "cronyism," to refer to any process of favoring those with whom one is connected (for example, an employer who hires his buddies from the Elks Club, Alcoholics Anonymous, the local gym, or a college fraternity).

new hire reporting

Whenever any employer in the United States hires a new employee, the employer must report basic identifying and contact information for the employee to a state agency called the State Directory of New Hires. The information is then used within the state and nationwide to try to track down parents who aren't meeting their child support obligations. This requirement was part of the Personal Responsibility and Work Opportunity Reconciliation Act of 1996, President Clinton's sweeping welfare reform law.

What information is required. The employer must provide the employee's name, address, and Social Security number, along with the employer's name, address, and federal employer identification number. State agencies may require employers to submit additional information on new hires, such as the date of hire and the employee's birth date. Some states require employers to report on independent contractors, too.

New Process Steel v. NLRB

See National Labor Relations Board.

NLRA

See National Labor Relations Act.

NLRB

See National Labor Relations Board.

no-fault attendance policies

See absenteeism.

noncompete agreement

See covenant not to compete.

nondisclosure agreement

A nondisclosure agreement (also called an NDA or confidentiality agreement) is a contract in which the parties promise to protect the confidentiality of secret information that they learn during employment or another type of business transaction. An employer can ask an employee or independent contractor to enter into an NDA to protect any type of trade secret or other confidential information. For example, an NDA can prohibit someone from disclosing a secret invention design, an idea for a new website, or confidential financial information. If either side reveals the information in violation of the NDA, the other side can ask a court to immediately stop the violator from making any further disclosures and sue for damages.

An NDA will not protect information that the employer does not treat as confidential. For example, if an employer leaves "secret" information in plain view of the cleaning staff or available on publicly accessible websites, an NDA won't protect that information.

What's in an NDA? There are five important elements in an NDA:

- **Definition of confidential information.** Every NDA provides a general description of the types or categories of confidential information or trade secrets that the agreement covers. The purpose is to establish the boundaries or subject matter of the information, without actually disclosing the secrets.
- **Exclusions from confidential information.** An NDA typically excludes certain information from protection. The party that learns the trade secret has no obligation to protect this excluded information. Typical types of excluded information include:
  - information that is already generally known outside of the business at the time the NDA is signed
  - information that becomes known outside of the business through no fault of the employee or independent contractor
  - information the employee or contractor already knew, and
  - information the employee or contractor learns independently.
- **Obligations of the receiving party.** The employee or contractor generally must keep the information in confidence and limit its use. Under most state laws, the receiving party can neither reveal the information nor assist others in acquiring it improperly or revealing it.
- **Time period.** Most NDAs provide that the employee or contractor cannot disclose confidential information during

N

employment or for a period after the employment or contractual relationship ends.

- **Miscellaneous provisions.** Miscellaneous standard terms are usually included at the end of the agreement. They include things like which state's law will apply if the agreement is breached, whether the parties will use arbitration to settle disagreements about the contract, and whether attorney fees will be awarded to the party who wins.

Who needs an NDA? Under state trade secret law, current and former employees have a duty not to disclose a company's trade secrets whether or not they sign an NDA. Nonetheless, many employers require employees to sign an NDA, to make sure employees are aware of this obligation, show a court (if necessary) that the company makes every effort to protect its trade secrets, clearly specify which information must be kept secret, and set out the rules and procedures for resolving disputes, including whether alternative dispute resolution methods (such as arbitration or mediation) will be used, which state's law will apply, and where lawsuits to enforce the agreement must be brought.

Independent contractors are under no obligation to maintain a hiring company's trade secrets, nor are customers, vendors, prospective business partners, or other outside parties. Therefore, any employer that will disclose confidential business information to someone other than an employee should insist on an NDA.

Related terms: covenant not to compete; employment contract; nonsolicitation agreement; trade secret.

nonexempt employee

A nonexempt employee is one who is entitled to earn overtime under the Fair Labor Standards Act (FLSA). All employees are nonexempt, unless they fall within one of the law's exemptions. You can find a list of exemptions in the entry for exempt employees.

Related terms: exempt employees; Fair Labor Standards Act; minimum wage; overtime.

nonsolicitation agreement

A nonsolicitation agreement is a contract in which an employee agrees not to solicit a company's clients or customers, for his or her own benefit or the benefit of a competitor, after leaving the company. A nonsolicitation agreement can also include an agreement by the employee not to solicit other employees to leave when he or she quits or otherwise moves on.

Often, a nonsolicitation agreement is part of a larger document, such as an employment contract, a noncompete agreement, or a nondisclosure agreement. But it doesn't have to be. For example, if an employer isn't concerned about a former employee opening a competing business or working for a competitor but just wants to make sure the employee doesn't take any of its customers or employees, a nonsolicitation agreement alone will serve its purpose.

When a nonsolicitation agreement is used. Nonsolicitation agreements are especially common in service or sales businesses, particularly when the customer pool is limited. For example, a company that specializes in providing parts and service for an expensive model of hybrid SUV can't just go out and drum up more business: Unless people own that vehicle, they have no need for the company's services. Even if there are many customers for a company's products, it might want a nonsolicitation agreement if it sells something that isn't unique and competes primarily on price. In this situation, an employee who knows the company's pricing schedule has a unique advantage in soliciting customers, because he or she knows exactly how sweet the offer has to be to woo customers away.

What makes a nonsolicitation agreement enforceable. Courts sometimes won't enforce a nonsolicitation agreement that makes it too difficult for an employee to earn a living or unfairly limits a competitor's ability to hire workers or attract customers through legitimate means. To be enforceable, an agreement must meet these requirements:

- **The employer must have a valid business reason.** Such a reason might include protecting a valuable customer list, protecting

N

trade secrets or other valuable information, or protecting the company from the mass departure of valuable employees with specialized skills, knowledge, and access to trade secrets.

- **The customer list must be worth protecting.** If the purpose of a nonsolicitation is to protect the company's customer list, the company must have spent time, energy, and money establishing its client database—and it must contain information that isn't readily available to the general public. If anyone could figure out who a company's customers or clients are just by looking in the phone book, a court probably won't protect the customer list.

- **Employees and customers can leave voluntarily.** Nonsolicitation agreements can't prevent a client, customer, or employee from moving to a competitor voluntarily. There isn't much a company can do to stop its other employees from leaving to join a former employee at a new company, as long as the departing employee hasn't improperly solicited them (and the other employees aren't subject to noncompete agreements). Similarly, if customers want to take their business to a competitor, a nonsolicitation agreement isn't going to be much help, unless the departing employee has improperly pressured them or used the former employer's information (such as a price list) to get their business.

Related terms: covenant not to compete; employment contract; nondisclosure agreement; trade secret.

Occupational Safety and Health Act

The Occupational Safety and Health Act (OSH Act) of 1970 is a federal law that requires employers to provide safe working conditions for employees. The OSH Act covers virtually all private employers, regardless of size, and all of their employees. The law is enforced by the Occupational Safety and Health Administration (OSHA).

What the OSH Act requires. The law imposes these requirements:

- **Compliance with industry standards.** All employers must comply with the standards for their industry issued by OSHA or their state agency. OSHA has issued a number of standards for construction, maritime and longshoring, agricultural work, and general industry. Within these broad categories, the standards may govern certain types of business (such as sawmills, bakeries, or telecommunications companies); use of particular tools and equipment; handling certain potentially hazardous materials; safety gear; safety requirements for walking surfaces, exits, and platforms; and much, much more.

- **Safety.** Employers must provide a workplace that is free of "recognized hazards" that are likely to cause serious harm or death to employees. Employers must also conduct safety training sessions to educate employees about the materials and equipment they will be using, any workplace hazards they face (especially toxic chemicals), and steps the company is taking to control those hazards.

- **Inspection.** OSHA enforces the OSH Act through inspections, conducted at random or in response to complaints of unsafe conditions. Employers must submit to these inspections if the inspector has a warrant; if not, the employer may consent to the inspection or demand that a warrant be obtained.

- **Employee rights.** The OSH Act gives employees the right to receive certain information about their workplace, such as the presence or use of toxic substances. It also gives employees the right to file a complaint with OSHA about unsafe working conditions, and prohibits employers from retaliating against employees who exercise this right. And, the OSH Act gives employees the right to refuse to work if they are faced with imminent danger, the employer will not correct the situation, and there is no time to eliminate the danger through other channels, such as requesting an OSHA inspection.

- **Record keeping.** The OSH Act requires employers to post notices about the law, current citations that OSHA inspectors have issued to the employer, and a log and summary of occupational illnesses and injuries. In addition, employers must keep records of their efforts to comply with the law and prevent injuries and illness; records of work-related deaths, injuries, and illnesses; and records of employee exposure to potentially toxic substances or harmful physical agents. Certain employers don't have to keep all of these records, including those with ten or fewer employees and those that have low-hazard retail and service industries, such as banks, art galleries, and restaurants.

State laws on workplace safety and health. When the OSH Act was passed it preempted all then-existing state job safety and health laws. Each state then had the option of submitting its own plan to the Secretary of Labor for approval. If the secretary found the plan acceptable, then the state's law could stand and that state retains the right to govern workplace health and safety within its borders with its own laws, regulations, and standards. (These states are called "state plan states.") In states without an approved plan, the OSH Act preempts all state laws, regulations, and standards that relate to job health and safety, unless the OSH Act doesn't cover a particular issue. For example, if the federal laws don't cover elevators, states may regulate on that topic, even if they didn't submit a state plan.

All states—even those that aren't state plan states—may enforce laws that protect a wider class of people than just employees. These laws include fire codes, occupancy standards, building codes, and so on. All states can also have laws that protect its state and local government employees, and can train, educate, and consult on job safety and health issues.

Related term: Occupational Safety and Health Administration.

Occupational Safety and Health Administration

The Occupational Safety and Health Administration (OSHA) is the federal agency responsible for implementing and enforcing the Occupational Safety and Health Act (OSH Act). OSHA issues workplace safety regulations and standards, conducts inspections, investigates complaints of violations, and issues citations and proposed penalties against employers who violate the OSH Act.

OSHA is also responsible for enforcing various laws that protect those who complain of wrongdoing by their employers, through its Workplace Protection Program. This program covers those who complain of violations of various workplace safety laws, as well as those who complain of internal financial regularities under the Sarbanes-Oxley Act, the health care reform law, and the Dodd-Frank Wall Street Reform and Consumer Protection Act. In this capacity, OSHA takes and investigates complaints and holds hearings before an administrative law judge.

Related terms: Occupational Safety and Health Act; Sarbanes-Oxley Act.

O'Connor v. Consolidated Coin Caterers Corporation

This Supreme Court case holds that the Age Discrimination in Employment Act (ADEA) protects an older employee from

225

discrimination even if the younger employee who replaces him is also over the age of 40—and therefore, also protected by the ADEA.

The ADEA protects only those who are at least 40. The ADEA prohibits employers from making job decisions on the basis of age. However, it protects only employees who are at least 40 years old. The intent of this age limit appears to have been to limit the protections of the act to older workers (regardless of how youthful many of us who are past the threshold may feel), rather than prohibiting any consideration of age. Discrimination against younger workers in favor of older workers isn't illegal, nor is discrimination against those who are not yet 40. For example, a clothing store that wanted to maintain a youthful image might prefer college-age clerks; as long as those who were denied jobs because of their age had not yet reached the big 4-0, they would not have a discrimination claim under the ADEA.

What if the favored employee has also celebrated a 40th birthday? But what of older employees who are discriminated against in favor of younger, but still at least 40-year-old, employees? The U.S. Supreme Court answered that question in the case of *O'Connor v. Consolidated Coin Caterers Corp.*, 517 U.S. 308 (1996). James O'Connor worked for Consolidated Coin for 18 years before he was fired, at the age of 56. He brought an age discrimination claim, alleging that the company fired him because of his age and replaced him with a younger worker. Because that younger worker was 40 years old and therefore also protected by the ADEA, the lower court threw out his case.

In a unanimous decision, the Supreme Court overturned that decision and allowed O'Connor to proceed with his lawsuit. The Court found that an employee who is in the protected class—those who are at least 40—can bring an age discrimination claim if the employer's decision was based on age, whether or not that employee's replacement is also at least 40: "Or to put the point more concretely, there can be no greater inference of age discrimination ... when a 40-year-old is replaced by a 39-year-old than when a 56-year-old is replaced by a 40-year-old."

Related terms: age discrimination; Age Discrimination in Employment Act; reverse discrimination.

off-duty conduct laws

Off-duty conduct laws prohibit employers from taking action against employees based on what they choose to do on their own time, as long as those activities are not illegal. Not every state has an off-duty conduct law, and the form these protections take vary. Some states protect an employee's right to engage in any lawful activity, some protect an employee's right to use lawful products off the job, and some explicitly protect only an employee's right to smoke or use other tobacco products off the job.

Although these laws are often invoked to prohibit employers from firing or refusing to hire those who smoke, the broader version—the laws that protect employees who engage in lawful activities—applies to a wide range of conduct. For example, such a law would protect an employee who works for a particular political candidate, collects signatures for a controversial ballot measure, or maintains a blog with unpopular views.

Older Workers Benefit Protection Act

Passed in 1990, the Older Workers Benefit Protection Act (OWBPA) amended the Age Discrimination in Employment Act (ADEA) to address two issues:

- **Benefits.** The OWBPA provides guidance on the ADEA requirement that the benefits employers offer to older workers must be "equal" to the benefits offered to younger workers.
- **Waivers.** The OWBPA also provides standards that an employee's waiver of the right to sue for age discrimination must meet in order to be upheld by a court.

Equal benefits must be provided ... mostly. The OWBPA prohibits age discrimination in the provision of fringe benefits, such as life insurance, health insurance, disability benefits, pensions, and retirement benefits. In most situations, this means that employers must provide equal benefits to older and younger workers. For benefits that cost more to provide as workers age, however, employers can sometimes meet the nondiscrimination requirement by spending the same amount on the benefit provided to older and younger employees, even if this means older workers receive lesser benefits. Employers are also allowed, in some circumstances, to provide lesser benefits to older workers if they receive additional benefits from the employer or the government (called "offsets") to make up the difference.

The equal cost defense. An employer may offer a lesser benefit to older workers if it costs the same as the benefit offered to younger workers. However, this defense applies only to certain benefits and only if a number of conditions are met. An employer may use the equal cost defense only if all of the following are true:

- **The benefit becomes more costly to provide as workers age.** This is often true of life insurance, health insurance, and disability insurance, for example. As workers age, it becomes more likely that they will use these benefits, and insurers often charge more for coverage to guard against this possibility. Because benefits such as severance pay or paid vacations do not cost more to provide to older workers, however, the defense does not apply to these benefits.

- **The benefit is not a retirement benefit.** The equal cost defense doesn't apply to retirement benefits.

- **The benefit is part of a bona fide employee benefit plan.** A bona fide employee benefit plan is one that has been accurately described, in writing, to all employees and that actually provides the benefits promised.

- **The benefit plan explicitly requires lower benefits for older workers.** An employer may use the equal cost defense only if the benefit plan requires benefits to diminish for older workers. If the plan gives the employer discretion to provide lower benefits to older workers if it chooses, the employer may not rely on the equal cost defense.

- **The employer pays the same amount for coverage for older and younger workers.** This is where the "equal cost" part comes in.
- **Benefit levels for older workers have not been reduced more than necessary to achieve the goal of equal cost for coverage of older and younger workers.** In other words, the employer may not rely on the equal cost defense to cut older workers' benefits beyond what's required to achieve cost parity.
- **When comparing coverage costs, the employer has not used age brackets of more than five years.** In other words, an employer that plans to reduce a benefit for workers ages 61 through 65 must compare the cost of covering those workers to the cost of covering workers ages 56 through 60, not the cost of covering workers in their 20s or 30s.

The offset defense. In some cases, employers may offer older employees lesser benefits if those employees receive additional benefits from the employer or the government that make up the difference. The employer may use these additional benefits to offset the shortfall and bring the older workers' benefits up to the same level offered to younger employees. The rules for using offsets are quite detailed, and they don't apply to all types of benefits. You can find out more at the EEOC's website, www.eeoc.gov, or in *The Essential Guide to Federal Employment Laws*, by Lisa Guerin and Amy DelPo (Nolo).

Special requirements for certain benefits. The OWBPA includes detailed rules for particular types of benefits, including employee contribution plans, long-term disability benefits, retiree health benefits, pensions, and early retirement incentive plans. These rules attempt to accommodate employers' benefit programs (and to avoid creating disincentives to employers who provide these benefits) while ensuring that older workers are not discriminated against. (You can find all of the details in the portion of the Equal Employment Opportunity Commission's Compliance Manual that addresses non-discrimination in benefits, www.eeoc.gov/policy/docs/benefits.html.)

Rules for waivers. The OWBPA also spells out requirements for employee waivers of the right to sue for age discrimination. Employers often ask employees to sign such waivers as a condition of receiving severance on termination of employment. Employee waivers of the right to sue for age discrimination must meet all of the following requirements to be knowing and voluntary (and, therefore, valid):

- The waiver must be part of a written agreement between the employer and the employee.
- It must be written in language understandable to the employee (or in the case of an offer made to a group, understandable to the average employee eligible to participate).
- The waiver must specifically refer to the worker's rights or claims under the ADEA.
- The employee may not be required to waive any rights or claims that may arise after the agreement is signed.
- The employee must receive something of value (such as cash or continued benefits) in exchange for the waiver, over and above anything to which the employee is already entitled. For example, if all employees receive a set amount of severance pay, the employer must give an employee who signs an ADEA waiver additional compensation or benefits.
- The employer must advise the employee, in writing, to consult with an attorney before signing the agreement.
- The employer must give the employee at least 21 days to consider the agreement, or 45 days if the waiver is requested in connection with an exit incentive program or other employment termination program offered to a group of employees. (The employee can accept the agreement after a shorter period of deliberation, as long as the waiver agreement gave the employee the opportunity to take as long as the law allows.)
- The employee must have at least seven days to revoke the agreement after signing it.

More information must be provided for group layoffs. If a waiver is requested in connection with an exit incentive program or other employment termination program offered to a group of employees, the employer must provide additional information, intended to reveal the age demographics of the group. The employer must inform the employee, in writing, of:

- any class, unit, or group covered by the program, any eligibility rules for the program, and any time limits applicable to the program, and
- the job titles and ages of all employees eligible or selected for the program, and the ages of all employees in the same job classification or organizational unit who are not eligible or selected for the program.

Related terms: Age Discrimination in Employment Act; benefits; release; severance agreement.

ombudsperson

See alternative dispute resolution.

Oncale v. Sundowner Offshore Service, Inc.

In the short and unanimous opinion of *Oncale v. Sundowner Offshore Service, Inc.,* 523 U.S. 75 (1998), the U.S. Supreme Court decided for the first time that same-sex harassment is illegal under Title VII.

Background. Title VII, the main federal law that prohibits employment discrimination, protects employees from discrimination and harassment based on gender, among other things. Courts have held that this prohibition applies whether a man or a woman is the harasser. Although men are more likely to be the perpetrators of sexual harassment and women the victims, harassment is an equal opportunity offense, as a legal matter. However, as courts have held repeatedly, Title VII does not prohibit harassment based on sexual orientation. This raises the question of whether harassment of a man by a man, or of a woman by a woman, is prohibited by Title VII as sexual harassment.

The facts. The Supreme Court's opinion states that "the precise details (of the alleged harassment) are irrelevant … in the interest of both brevity and dignity we shall describe them only generally." Those facts are truly shocking. In his three-month stint working as a roustabout on an oil rig in the Gulf of Louisiana, married father of two Joseph Oncale was repeatedly threatened with rape by his male coworkers, was restrained on at least two occasions while a coworker touched him with his penis, and was forcibly sodomized with a bar of soap, all in full view of other employees. He quit his job, telling the company that it was because of sexual harassment and verbal abuse, because he feared that he would be forcibly raped otherwise.

The Court's decision. The Court found that any harassment that takes place "because of sex" is actionable, whether the perpetrator and victim are of the same or the opposite sex. The critical issue, to the Court, is whether employees of one sex are exposed to disadvantageous working conditions while employees of the opposite sex are not. In the case of explicitly sexual overtures, it's easy to infer that the harasser would not have so treated someone of the opposite sex. In a same-sex harassment case that appears to be motivated by enmity rather than attraction, the court stated that the harassment might take such a sex-specific and derogatory form as to make clear that the harasser was motivated by general hostility to others of his or her gender in the workplace. Regardless of what form the evidence takes, however, the court established once and for all that same-sex harassment is actionable, as long as it is based on sex.

The court remanded the case back to the lower courts, to reconsider the facts in light of its legal ruling that the case should not be thrown out simply because the harassers and the victim were all men. About six months later, the case settled for an undisclosed amount.

Related terms: harassment; sexual harassment; Title VII.

on-call time

On-call time is time when an employee is not actually performing job duties, but must be available to work if called upon. For example, a trauma nurse who must carry a pager and return to the hospital immediately if paged is on call, as is a computer technician who must respond to help calls over the weekend.

Paid to wait or waiting to be paid? Are employees entitled to be paid for time spent on call? The answer depends on where the employee has to be and any other restrictions placed on the employee. An employee who must stay at the workplace waiting for work is entitled to be paid for that time. For example, an employee who repairs appliances and waits in the office to be called out on a job is entitled to be paid for that time, as is a secretary who does a crossword in the office while waiting for an assignment.

Employees who don't have to stay at work are entitled to pay for hours over which the employees have little or no control and which they cannot spend as they wish. If an employee is actually called and has to work, the employee is always entitled to pay for that actual work time. As for the hours that are spent on call and not actually working, the more restrictions an employer places on an employee who is on call, the more likely that employee is entitled to be paid. Here are some of the factors courts consider:

- **How many calls an employee gets while on call.** The more calls an employee has to respond to, the more likely he or she is entitled to pay, particularly if any of the calls require the employee to report to work or give advice or guidance over the phone. An employee who is frequently interrupted like this would have difficulty planning and using his or her time as desired.

- **How long an employee has to respond after a call.** If an employer requires employees to report in immediately after being paged, for example, such employees have a better argument that they should be paid for their time.

- **Where the employee can go while on call.** Employees who must stay within a limited distance from work are more likely to be entitled to compensation.

- **What the employee may do while on call.** If an employer sets a lot of rules for on-call workers, such as a ban on alcohol or a requirement that they respond quickly and in person to calls (which can be difficult if the employee is at the gym or taking the kids to school), the employer may have to pay for this time.

Related term: hour worked.

open shop

An open shop is a company at which employees are free to decide whether or not to join or support the union. Employees who decide not to join the union cannot be required to pay any union-related fees, and cannot be fired or otherwise penalized for failing to do so.

"Closed shops," in which all employees must join the union and remain a member as a condition of employment, are no longer legal. However, "agency shops," in which all employees must either join the union or pay fees to it, are legal except in states that prohibit them. In these states, called "right to work" states, every unionized workplace must be an open shop.

Related terms: agency shop; closed shop; right to work; union security agreement.

OSHA

See Occupational Safety and Health Act; Occupational Safety and Health Administration.

OSH Act

See Occupational Safety and Health Act.

outside salesperson

An outside salesperson is an employee who customarily and regularly works away from the employer's place(s) of business, and whose primary duty is making sales or taking orders to sell goods, services, or the use of facilities. Outside salespeople are exempt from the minimum wage and overtime requirements of the Fair Labor

Standards Act (that is, they are not entitled to the minimum wage or overtime).

Related terms: exempt employee; Fair Labor Standards Act; minimum wage; overtime.

overtime

Overtime refers both to the hours an employee works beyond a limit set by law and to the pay an employee is entitled to receive for those hours. Employers that want employees to work extra hours must pay for the privilege: Under the federal Fair Labor Standards Act (FLSA), employees who work more than 40 hours in a week are entitled to their usual hourly wage for those extra hours and a 50% overtime premium, which means they must be paid 150% of their usual wages—typically referred to as "time and a half"—for their overtime hours.

Not all employees are entitled to earn overtime, however. And, many states have their own overtime laws that differ from the FLSA. As is always true in wage and hour matters, the employer must follow the law that offers the most protections to employees.

Who is entitled to earn overtime pay. All nonexempt employees covered by the FLSA are entitled to overtime, with the following exceptions:

- rail, air, and motor carrier employees
- employees who buy poultry, eggs, cream, or milk in their unprocessed state
- those who sell cars, trucks, farm implements, trailers, boats, or aircraft
- mechanics or parts persons who service cars, trucks, or farm implements
- announcers, news editors, and chief engineers of certain broadcasting stations
- local delivery drivers or drivers' helpers who are compensated on a trip rate plan
- agricultural workers

- taxi drivers
- domestic service workers who live in the employer's home, and
- movie theater employees.

Exempt employees, including outside salespeople; salaried executive, administrative, and professional employees; and certain computer specialists are not entitled to earn overtime pay. (See "exempt employees" for more information.)

When overtime is due. Under the FLSA, employees who work more than 40 hours in a week are entitled to overtime pay. Some states have different ways of calculating overtime, however. For example, some states use a daily overtime standard, which entitles eligible employees to earn overtime after they've worked eight hours in one day, even if their total hours in the week are less than 40. Some states also require employers to pay a premium if the employee has to work a seventh or even a sixth day during the same week, even if the employee's total hours are less than 40.

How overtime pay is calculated. As noted above, employees are entitled to an overtime premium of an additional 50% of their regular hourly rate for overtime hours worked. An employee's regular rate of pay includes all compensation for work, such as wages, commissions, performance-based bonuses and prizes, and shift differentials. It doesn't include money or items that aren't intended as part of an employee's compensation, such as expense reimbursements, discretionary bonuses, or gifts from an employer (such as a holiday bonuses). It also doesn't include overtime pay. The employee's hourly rate is calculated by adding up the employee's entire compensation for the week and dividing by the total number of hours worked.

> **EXAMPLE:** Rick works at a call center for a software company. In one week, he works 45 hours, for which he is paid ten dollars an hour, or $450. His employer pays a $50 bonus each week to the employee who earns the highest customer satisfaction ratings in the week; customers are asked for their feedback at the end of each call. Rick earned the bonus for this week, so his total

compensation is $500. His hourly rate for the week is $500 divided by 45 hours, or $11.11 an hour, so he is entitled to an additional $27.78 in overtime pay: half of his $11.11 hourly rate (the overtime premium) times five hours. If Rick hadn't received the bonus, he would be entitled to $25: half of his regular $10 hourly rate times five hours.

What about comp time? Compensatory time, usually shortened to "comp" time, refers to the common practice of giving employees time off at some later date rather than paying overtime. Common doesn't mean legal, however: Private employers may not give employees straight compensatory time—an hour off for every extra hour worked—instead of overtime because this deprives employees of the 50% overtime premium. Employers that want to offer time off rather than pay overtime have two options:

- Adjust an employee's hours within a week so the employee doesn't work overtime. For example, an employee who has worked four ten-hour days could be allowed to take the rest of the week off, resulting in a 40-hour workweek for which no overtime is due. In states that have a daily overtime standard, however, this won't work.

- Give an employee an hour and a half off for every extra hour worked in the pay period. This preserves the overtime premium. For example, if an employee who usually earns $1,600 every two weeks (or $20 an hour) works an extra ten hours during the first week of the pay period, the employee is entitled to $300 in overtime pay—ten hours multiplied by one-and-a-half times the employee's hourly rate, or $30. If the employee took 15 hours off in the second week of the pay period, however, his or her paycheck would remain the same. The employee would receive $300 in overtime pay, but would be docked $300 (15 hours multiplied by $20 an hour) for the time not worked.

Related terms: exempt employees; hour worked.

OWBPA

See Older Workers Benefit Protection Act.

O

paid time off (PTO)

Paid time off (PTO) refers to a leave entitlement that is all-inclusive. Rather than offering separate sick leave, vacation days, personal days, and so on, an employer grants employees a certain amount of PTO each year, to be used for any reason.

Benefits of PTO. For many employers, adopting a PTO policy reduces paperwork and record-keeping hassles. It also reduces the need for management oversight of how employees actually use their leave, particular sick days. Because employees are entitled to take PTO for any reason, no one will have to make sure that they are really sick—and they won't feel compelled to prove it ("(cough), I have a really bad cold (sniffle)"). Depending on how they use their leave, employees may also benefit by having more control over their time. And, because many employees don't use their full allotment of sick days, employees may have more total usable days off under a PTO system.

PTO and vacation cash-outs. Some states require employers to pay out an employee's accrued unused vacation time (but not sick time) when the employee quits or is fired. In these states, an employer that has a PTO policy will likely have to pay out the employee's entire allotment of PTO, even though some of it was intended to cover sick time and other absences.

Related terms: sick leave; vacation.

Patient Protection and Affordable Care Act of 2010

See health care reform.

Patterson v. McLean Credit Union

See Civil Rights Act of 1991.

pay docking

Pay docking is the practice of cutting an employee's pay for absences or workplace infractions, such as tardiness or misconduct. Used as a disciplinary measure, pay docking is subject to strict legal limits when employers impose it on exempt employees (those who are not entitled to earn overtime). Pay docking can have the effect of transforming exempt employees to nonexempt employees, entitling them to earn overtime for working more than 40 hours in a week.

How does pay docking cause a problem? To qualify as exempt, employees have to be paid a set amount each pay period, without any reductions based on the quantity or quality of work they do. An employer who docks their pay is treating these employees like nonexempt employees. Depending on the reasons for the employer's actions, the law might require the employer to treat these employees as if they were nonexempt for all purposes, which means the employees are entitled to earn overtime.

Who qualifies as a salaried employee? Under federal law, exempt employees—those who are not entitled to overtime—must earn at least $455 per week (or $23,660 per year). These employees must also be paid on a salary basis. This means that the employee's salary is a fixed amount that doesn't depend on how many hours the employee works, how much work the employee accomplishes, or the quality of that work. As long as employees do some work during the week, they are entitled to their full weekly pay, unless the time they take off falls into one of the exceptions described below.

Permissible salary deductions. Employers may make salary deductions (without jeopardizing the employee's exempt status) for one or more full days an employee takes off for the following reasons:
- to handle personal affairs
- to go on unpaid family or medical leave under the Family and Medical Leave Act (FMLA)

- for disability or illness, if the employer has a plan (such as disability insurance or sick leave) that compensates employees for this time off
- to serve on a jury, as a witness, or on temporary military leave, but the employer may deduct only any amount that the employee receives as jury or witness fees or as military pay
- during the employee's first or last week of work, if the employee does not work a full week
- as a penalty imposed in good faith for infractions of safety rules of major significance (rules that prevent serious danger in the workplace or to other employees)
- to serve an unpaid disciplinary suspension imposed in good faith for infractions of workplace conduct rules, but only if the employer has a written policy regarding such suspensions that applies to all employees.

Penalties for improper deductions. An employer that makes improper deductions from a salaried employee's pay can get into big trouble. However, the law contains a "safe harbor" provision, which offers employers some protection if they make improper deductions inadvertently.

An employer will be penalized if it has an "actual practice" of making improper deductions—actions that show the employer didn't intend to pay employees on a salary basis. Among the factors a court or government agency will consider when making this determination are:

- the number of improper deductions
- the time period during which the employer made improper deductions
- how many employees were subjected to improper salary deductions and where those employees worked
- how many managers were responsible for taking improper deductions and where those managers worked, and
- whether the employer has a clearly communicated policy that either permits or prohibits improper deductions.

P

An employer with an actual practice of making improper deductions will lose the overtime exemption for all employees who work in the job classification(s) for which the deductions were made and work for the managers responsible for making the deductions. In other words, the employer will have to pay overtime (if earned by the employees) to everyone who holds the position from which improper deductions were taken.

Safe harbor protections. An employer will not be subject to the penalties noted above if either of the following is true:

- Any improper deductions were either isolated or inadvertent, and the employer reimburses the employees for the money improperly withheld.
- The employer has a clearly communicated policy prohibiting improper deductions (including a complaint procedure), reimburses employees for the money improperly withheld, and makes a good faith effort to comply with the law in the future.

Related terms: exempt employee; Family and Medical Leave Act; overtime; sick leave; vacation.

PDA

See Pregnancy Discrimination Act.

peer review program

See alternative dispute resolution.

per diem

Per diem means "per day," and it refers to the maximum amount an employer will reimburse an employee for expenses incurred while away from home. An employer might pay the per diem amount without question, or might reimburse the employee only for expenses actually incurred. Most often, employees will have a per diem for business trips; employees who are temporarily posted away from home (for example, who are sent out of state for a couple of months to oversee a building project) might also receive a per diem.

The federal General Services Administration establishes the per diem rates for federal employees, and many private employers also use these rates. The rates differ by city, depending on the cost of living. The per diem is expected to cover lodging, meals, and incidental expenses, which include tips. For 2011, the per diem rate for most counties is a total of $123: $77 for lodging, $41 for meals, and $5 for incidentals (which doesn't leave room for any big tippers).

Related term: hour worked.

performance evaluation

A performance evaluation is a review of an employee's work. The term is used to refer to a document in which the employee's performance is evaluated as well as the meeting in which the employee and manager meet to discuss performance.

permanent employee

Permanent employee is a designation sometimes used to distinguish an employer's regular staff from its contingent workers, such as temps, leased employees, or independent contractors. Some employers have also used this term to create a distinction between new employees and employees who have successfully completed an initial orientation or probationary period.

The term has fallen into disuse in private industry in recent years, and with good reason: It strongly suggests that the employee has job security, and most private employers want to maintain their right to fire employees at will, at any time and for any reason that is not illegal. Some employees have pointed to their title of "permanent," or to their transition from a "probationary" employee (who can be fired at any time) to a "permanent" employee as evidence of an implied contract that they would be fired only for good cause. The designation of "permanent employee" may still be used in

P

workplaces that do offer some form of job security, or at least the right to be fired only for good cause, such as government employers, university settings, or unionized workplaces.

Related terms: at-will employment; employment contract; implied contract.

Personal Responsibility and Work Opportunity Reconciliation Act

Passed in 1996 as part of former President Clinton's welfare reform effort, the Personal Responsibility and Work Opportunity Reconciliation Act (PRWORA) changed many aspects of the welfare system, most notably by imposing "welfare-to-work" requirements. The law also includes provisions on nutrition programs, teen pregnancy prevention, child care, foster care, food stamps, and more. In addition, PROWRA requires employers to report all new hires to a state registry, which uses it to try to track down parents who aren't paying their child support.

Related term: new hire reporting.

personnel file

An employee's personnel file is a collection of the company's paperwork regarding that employee. It typically includes:

- hiring documents, such as the job application, résumé, and offer letter
- benefits documents, including enrollment forms, next of kin designations, and so on
- tax records, such as the employee's IRS Form W-4 and similar state withholding form
- performance documents, including evaluations, commendations, written warnings, and other disciplinary paperwork
- records of promotions, pay raises, transfers, and other job changes

- any acknowledgments or contracts the employee has signed, such as an employee handbook acknowledgment, noncompete agreement, employment contract, or nondisclosure agreement, and
- documents relating to the employee's departure from the company (if applicable), such as unemployment documents, COBRA forms, any written reasons for the employee's departure, notes from an exit interview, and so on.

What's usually not in a personnel file. There are a few types of documents that should not go in the regular personnel file, primarily because employers are required or advised to keep them confidential. These include:

- **Medical records and records of genetic information.** These must be kept confidential, in a separate file. Access to these records must be strictly limited according to the dictates of the Americans with Disabilities Act (ADA) and the Genetic Information Nondiscrimination Act (GINA).
- **I-9 forms.** These must be completed for each employee, verifying that they are eligible to work in the United States. I-9 forms are often also kept in a separate file, so they are easily accessed (without compromising employee privacy) in case of an audit. Also, because I-9 forms reveal an employee's citizenship status and perhaps national origin, keeping them out of the employee's personnel file limits the number of people in the company with access to this information.
- **Confidential statements about others.** Many employers also segregate records that include confidential statements about the employee by others, such as an investigation report that includes witness statements or notes from conversations with an employee's references.

Employee access to personnel files. Most states give employees some right to view the contents of their own personnel files. This right may be limited, however. In some states, employers have to provide employees with copies of certain documents in their files. In others, the employee may only review the file in person, sometimes in the presence of a company representative. And in some states, the company can withhold certain documents that might compromise another person's privacy.

Related terms: Americans with Disabilities Act; COBRA; Employee Eligibility Verification Form; Genetic Information Nondiscrimination Act; investigation; reference.

picket

A picket occurs when people (sometimes also called "pickets") congregate outside of a place of business to publicize their dispute with that business. Often, a picket is carried on by striking workers, to protest the company's actions and discourage temporary workers and customers from patronizing the business ("crossing the picket line"). A picket may also precede a strike, as a way to publicize a dispute and pressure the employer to make concessions.

A picket need not be part of a work action, however. For example, a group that disagrees with a company's animal testing practices might picket the company's factory and stores to publicize the issue and encourage customers to boycott the company's products.

Related terms: boycott; strike.

pink slip

When a boss starts handing out pink slips, look out: The people who receive them are getting fired. This colloquial term has been used to refer to firing or being fired for a long time, but its derivation isn't clear. According to Jesse Sheidlower, editor at large of the *Oxford English Dictionary*, the term was used in the early 1900s to refer to rejection of various kinds, although there's no evidence that workers were actually handed pink pieces of paper when they were fired. For example, a pink slip was a note sent to a typographer, indicating that he's made a mistake. It also referred to a rejection letter from a magazine to an author.

plant closing

A plant closing takes place when an employer shuts down an entire facility or work site. Sometimes, the employer closes a plant without relocating the business done there (for example, if the employer decides to stop manufacturing a particular product line). Sometimes, the employer closes a plant in one location and outsources the work to another location.

Under the Worker Adjustment and Retraining Notification Act (WARN), employers are required to give employees advance notice of a plant closing. For the purposes of this law, a plant closing is defined more specifically as the permanent or temporary shutdown of a single site of employment, or one or more facilities or operating units within such a site, which results in at least 50 full-time employees losing their job in a 30-day period.

Related terms: mass layoff; Worker Adjustment and Retraining Notification Act.

Pollard v. E.I. duPont de Nemours & Co.

See front pay.

Portal to Portal Act

The federal Portal to Portal Act, passed in 1947, defined the circumstances in which employees can be paid for activities immediately preceding and following the actual work they were hired to do (for example, putting on a uniform, donning or doffing protective gear, or traveling to a job site). The law expressed Congress's concern that courts (including the Supreme Court) were interpreting the Fair Labor Standards Act (FLSA) to require pay for all time an employee had to spend on the employer's premises, regardless of what the employee was doing. Congress found that this contravened long-standing customs and collective bargaining agreements, "thereby creating wholly unexpected liabilities, immense in amount and retroactive in operation, upon employers." Congress further opined that this employer liability could result in financial ruin, impaired credit, industrial uncertainty, interference with collective bargaining, and even the "derangement" of public finance.

Which activities must be paid? The Portal to Portal Act states that, absent a contract or existing custom or practice, employees are not entitled to be paid for:

- walking, riding, or otherwise traveling to and from the place where the employee's principal activities are performed, or
- activities that are "preliminary or postliminary" to the employee's principal activities, if they occur before the employee starts or after the employee finishes those principal activities for the day.

These rules apply only to time before the employee's workday begins and after it ends, however. If the employee must travel from one worksite to another during the workday, for example, that time doesn't fall under the Portal to Portal Act and still must be compensated.

Integral and indispensable activities. Disputes over the Portal to Portal Act often come down to whether a particular activity is preliminary or postliminary, or instead is part and parcel of the employee's principal activities. The Supreme Court has said that activities that are integral and indispensable to the employee's principal activities must be paid. For example, the Court has held that donning and doffing specialized protective gear and company-required bathing to remove the toxic lead associated with producing batteries were compensable as part of the employee's principal activities. (*Steiner v. Mitchell*, 350 U.S. 247 (1956).) The Court has also held that the time slaughterhouse employees spend walking from the locker room—where they change into specialized protective gear—to the production area, and time they spend walking back again at the end of the day, is compensable. The donning and doffing time, which must be paid, marks the start and finish of the workday, so walking time within those limits must also be paid. (*IBP, Inc. v. Alvarez*, 546 U.S. 21 (2005).)

Related terms: Fair Labor Standards Act; hour worked.

Pregnancy Discrimination Act

Congress passed the Pregnancy Discrimination Act (or PDA, not to be confused with "public displays of affection") in 1978 as an amendment to Title VII. The PDA was a direct response to the case of *General Electric Co. v. Gilbert*, 429 U.S. 125 (1976), in which the Supreme Court decided that pregnancy discrimination was not necessarily sex discrimination—and, therefore, was not necessarily illegal under Title VII.

Pregnant women and nonpregnant persons. In the *Gilbert* case, the Supreme Court found that GE's disability program, which paid some wage replacement while employees were unable to work, did not discriminate against women, even though it didn't pay benefits for disability due to pregnancy or childbirth. The Court found that the plan did not discriminate because it offered the same benefits package to men and women: If a man and a woman both suffered the same disability, both would be covered by the plan. That only women can become pregnant didn't constitute sex discrimination because not all women do. Quoting an earlier decision on a similar issue (although decided based on the Constitution, not Title VII), the Court stated that the pregnancy exclusion and the protected class (women) were not the same in that the plan didn't differentiate between men and women, but between pregnant women and non-pregnant persons, who might be male or female.

Congress to Supreme Court: Nice try. The PDA takes on *Gilbert* directly. After stating that discrimination based on sex includes discrimination based on pregnancy, childbirth, and related conditions in any aspect of employment, the law gets more specific to state that this includes "receipt of benefits under fringe benefit programs, as other persons not so affected but similar in their ability or inability to work." Under the PDA, employers must treat employees who are temporarily unable to work due to pregnancy just as they treat employees who are temporarily disabled for other reasons, no worse and no better. In addition, employers may not engage in the many types of discrimination that used to occur regularly, such as firing

P

women or requiring them to stop working when they were "showing," refusing to hire pregnant women on the assumption that they would stop working once they had a child, and so on.

Women are also protected from discrimination based on their potential to become pregnant. For example, an employer cannot exclude all women of childbearing years from jobs that require contact with toxic chemicals or other substances that could lead to birth defects.

Related terms: bona fide occupational qualification; sex discrimination; Title VII.

pregnancy leave

Pregnancy leave is time off for a female employee who is temporarily unable to work due to pregnancy, childbirth, and related conditions. Many employers have policies that allow employees to take pregnancy leave; in this situation, the employer must follow its own policy. Even if an employer doesn't have a pregnancy leave policy, however, pregnancy leave might be required by several different laws:

- **The Pregnancy Discrimination Act (PDA).** The PDA doesn't require pregnancy leave per se, but it does require employers to give employees who are temporarily unable to work due to pregnancy the same leave it offers to other temporarily disabled employees.
- **The Family and Medical Leave Act (FMLA).** Pregnancy and disability associated with childbirth are considered serious health conditions under the FMLA, for which employees may take FMLA leave.
- **State leave laws.** Some states require employers to allow time off for pregnancy and childbirth. Some are similar to the FMLA, in that they include pregnancy along with other reasons for leave. Some explicitly require pregnancy disability leave, either up to a limit (California allows employees to take up to four months off, for example) or for a "reasonable" time.

- **State temporary disability provisions.** A handful of states offer temporary disability insurance, which provides some wage replacement, from a state fund, to employees who are temporarily unable to work for any reason, including pregnancy.

Related terms: Family and Medical Leave; Pregnancy Discrimination Act; temporary disability insurance.

presenteeism

Presenteeism happens when employees who should be at home sick come to work (as distinguished from absenteeism, which happens when employees who should be at work stay home). Although it's usually nice to have employees at work, presenteeism can be a big problem because the sick employee doesn't get much done—except to infect coworkers. One employee who shows up with the flu can soon lead to half the department out for the same reason. To discourage presenteeism, some employers state in their attendance policies that they expect employees to stay home when they are ill; some even back up this requirement by sending employees home who show up to work obviously sick.

Thanks for Sharing ... Your Virus

According to a briefing paper prepared by the Institute for Women's Policy Research, almost 26 million employees were infected with the H1N1 virus during the peak months of the pandemic, September 2009 through November 2009. Almost 18 million of them took at least some time off work. Memo to the remaining eight million from their colleagues: It's called "contagious" for a reason. Employees who came in to work with the virus infected an estimated seven million of their coworkers.

Sick at Work: Infected Employees in the Workplace During the H1N1 Epidemic, by Robert Drago and Kevin Miller, Institute for Women's Policy Research Briefing Paper No. B264 (February 2010).

P

pretext

A pretext is an explanation or a justification that is put forward to conceal an underlying motive. In employment law, pretext comes up in disparate treatment discrimination cases. If the employer produces evidence of a legitimate, nondiscriminatory reason for a challenged employment decision, the employee must prove that the employer's reason is only a pretext: a subterfuge to hide the employer's discrimination.

> **EXAMPLE:** Jose is fired from his position as a teller at a bank. Ron, his manager, tell Jose that he is being fired because he was late twice in a month. At trial, Jose's lawyer presents evidence that four other employees were late at least twice in the same month, and only one was fired. The other employee fired is also Latino, and the other three are white. Jose's lawyer also presents two witnesses who overheard Ron talking to his district manager on the phone, saying "The customers in this neighborhood want Mexicans to mow their lawns, not to manage their money." This is probably enough evidence to show that Ron's explanation that he fired Jose for tardiness is a pretext for discrimination.

Related terms: discrimination; disparate treatment.

privacy

Privacy refers to the age-old right to be left alone. In a workplace context, privacy refers to employees' right to be free from overly intrusive actions by employers that delve into their activities, beliefs, communications, and personal lives.

Privacy is one of the more complex areas of workplace law, largely because the rights associated with it come from different sources. There is no one federal statute that lays out the content and limits of the right to privacy. Instead, privacy principles derive mainly from the U.S. Constitution, some state constitutions, various state and federal statutes, and court decisions by state and federal judges.

The common law balancing test. Generally speaking, courts recognize that employees have a right to be free from unjustified intrusions by their employers. If an employee claims that his or her right to privacy has been violated, courts generally sort it out by weighing two competing concerns. On the one hand, the court will consider the employee's legitimate expectations of privacy: whether the employee reasonably believed that the area searched or monitored (such as a locker, desk drawer, email messages, or off-duty conduct) was private, and on what basis. On the other hand, the court will look at the reason for the intrusion: whether the employer had a legitimate, job-related reason for searching or monitoring, and whether the employer could have gathered the same information in a less intrusive way.

Constitutional protections. The U.S. Constitution does not explicitly grant a right to privacy. Nonetheless, the U.S. Supreme Court has decided, in a series of decisions dealing primarily with sex and reproductive choice, that the Bill of Rights implies a right to privacy. However, private employers and employees don't have to worry too much about exactly what this evolving right entails: It applies mostly to the government. Private employers generally cannot be sued for violating the federal constitution.

However, some state constitutions contain an explicit right to privacy—and some apply this right to private employers as well as state governments. Provisions like these can put more weight on the employee's side of the scale when a court balances the employee's right to privacy against the employer's reasons for intruding.

Federal protections. No single federal law lays out comprehensive rules on privacy. However, some federal laws set down specific privacy guidelines for employers. For example, the Americans with Disabilities Act and the Genetic Information Nondiscrimination Act require employers to keep employee medical information confidential. The Fair Credit Reporting Act requires employers to get written consent from an employee or applicant before checking that person's credit report. The Employee Polygraph Protection Act prohibits employers from requiring employees to take lie detector

P

tests. And, the National Labor Relations Act prohibits employers from monitoring a worker's union activity, including off-the-job meetings.

State protections. Many states have laws outlawing particular privacy violations. For example, some states prohibit employers from considering an applicant's arrest records, require employers to notify workers when they listen in to a worker's telephone conversations, prevent employers from making job decisions based on what employees do with their own time, or prohibit employers from using particular surveillance techniques (such as one-way mirrors or video cameras) in areas like restrooms and locker rooms.

Sexting on the SWAT Team

In 2010, the U.S. Supreme Court decided its first case on workplace electronic monitoring. The case involved Jeff Quon, a member of a city SWAT team, who—along with the rest of the team—was issued a pager with texting capabilities. The city had a written policy informing employees that their email and Internet use was not private, and told employees that same policy applied to the pagers. However, employees were also told that their usage wouldn't be monitored as long as they paid any fees imposed for going over the character limit each month.

After Quon exceeded the limit several times, the city decided to audit his messages for the past two months to determine whether the city should raise its character limit. The audit revealed that Quon had used his pager extensively for personal messages, including sexually explicit messages. Quon and several people with whom he had texted sued, alleging invasion of privacy.

The U.S. Court of Appeal for the Ninth Circuit found in Quon's favor. It found that Quon had a reasonable expectation of privacy in his text messages, based on his supervisor's statements that those messages would not be read. It also found that the city had a reasonable justification for searching. In the end, the Court found that the city should have used less intrusive means of determining whether

Sexting on the SWAT Team (continued)

to raise its character limit, such as asking Quon to perform the audit himself or warning Quon that his messages would be audited going forward, rather than reading messages that had already been sent.

The U.S. Supreme Court disagreed, finding that the city's monitoring was justified and that Quon had no legal claim that he had been subjected to an unreasonable "search" under the Fourth Amendment of the Constitution. The outcome doesn't mark a change from prior cases: Courts have largely upheld the rights of employers to monitor employee communications, in the public and private sector. The Ninth Circuit's decision was the outlier in this regard.

What was more interesting, however, was the Court's discussion of how the law should treat technology. Justice Kennedy's opinion for the majority says:

"The Court must proceed with care when considering the whole concept of privacy expectations on communications made on electronic equipment owned by a government employer. The judiciary risks error by elaborating too fully on the Fourth Amendment implications of emerging technology before its role in society has become clear … . Cell phone and text communications are so pervasive that some persons may consider them to be essential means or necessary instruments for self-expression, even self-identification. That may strengthen the case for an expectation of privacy."

Because *Quon* involved a public employer, it doesn't apply directly to the private sector, which is not bound by the Fourth Amendment. However, courts have generally followed similar principles in analyzing these cases against private employers.

City of Ontario, California v. Quon, 130 S.Ct. 2619 (2010).

Related terms: Americans with Disabilities Act; email monitoring; Employee Polygraph Protection Act; Fair Credit Reporting Act; Genetic Information Nondiscrimination Act; National Labor Relations Act; off-duty conduct laws; surveillance.

professional employee

Under the Fair Labor Standards Act (FLSA), a professional employee is exempt from the minimum wage and overtime requirements of the federal Fair Labor Standards Act (FLSA). Even if professional employees work more than 40 hours a week, they aren't entitled to overtime pay. Two requirements must be met for an employee to be an exempt professional employee: a salary test and a job duties test.

Salary test. Under the salary test, the employee must earn at least $455 per week and be paid on a salary basis. Workers are paid on a salary basis if they receive their full salary for any week in which they perform any work, regardless of how many hours they work or the quality or amount of work they do. (There are a handful of exceptions to this rule, covered in "pay docking.")

Duties test. An employee must also perform certain job duties to qualify. There are two types of professional employees: creative professionals and learned professionals. Creative professionals must have the primary duty of performing work that requires invention, imagination, originality, or talent in a recognized artistic or creative field. Learned professionals must meet all of these requirements:

- The employee's primary duty is performing work that requires advanced knowledge, is predominantly intellectual in nature, and requires the consistent exercise of discretion and judgment.
- The advanced knowledge is in a field of science or learning.
- The advanced knowledge is customarily acquired through a prolonged course of instruction.

Related terms: exempt employee; Fair Labor Standards Act; minimum wage; pay docking; salary basis.

progressive discipline

Progressive discipline is any employee discipline system that provides a graduated range of responses to employee performance or conduct problems. These disciplinary measures range from mild to severe, depending on the nature and frequency of the problem. For example, an informal coaching session or verbal warning might be appropriate for an employee who violates a minor work rule, while a more serious intervention—even termination—might be called for if an employee commits serious misconduct (such as sexual harassment) or does not improve a performance or conduct problem after receiving several opportunities to do so.

Most large companies use some form of progressive discipline, although they don't necessarily call it by that name. Whether they are called positive discipline programs, performance improvement plans, corrective action procedures, or something else, these systems are all similar at their core, although they may vary in the details. For example, companies might adopt different types of disciplinary measures (or different names for these measures), might require managers to give employees a certain number of opportunities to improve before termination becomes an option, or might require particular forms of documentation. However, all progressive discipline systems are based on the principle that the company's disciplinary response should be appropriate and proportionate to the employee's conduct.

protected activity

Protected activity refers to actions for which an employee may not be disciplined or retaliated against by an employer. Generally, if a law gives employees the right to do something, such as complain about working conditions or take time off, then an employer may not discipline or fire employees for exercising that right. Here are some examples of protected activities:

- Joining with another employee to talk about, improve, protest, or otherwise change the terms and conditions of employment is a protected activity under the National Labor Relations Act. (These are often referred to as protected concerted activities, because employees engage in them together.)

P

- Under Title VII and other antidiscrimination laws, employees who file a complaint (in court, with an administrative agency, or internally with their employer) of discrimination are protected from retaliation, as are employees who participate in an investigation of discrimination.
- Under the Occupational Safety and Health Act and other federal and state laws regulating employee safety, complaining of unsafe working conditions is a protected activity for which employees may not be disciplined.
- Exercising the right to vote and serving on a jury are protected activities.
- Exercising the right to take time off under the Family and Medical Leave Act and similar state laws is a protected activity, as is taking military leave for which reinstatement is guaranteed by the Uniformed Services Employment and Reemployment Rights Act and similar state laws.

Related terms: discrimination; Family and Medical Leave Act; National Labor Relations Act; Occupational Safety and Health Act; retaliation; Title VII; Uniformed Services Employment and Reemployment Rights Act.

protected characteristic

A protected characteristic is a trait or attribute that a legislative body has put off limits as a basis for making decisions. In other words, it is discriminatory to make a decision based on someone's protected characteristic, such as race, national origin, or color.

Related term: discrimination.

protected class

A protected class is a group of people that are legally protected from discrimination based on their shared characteristic, such as race, sex, religion, disability, or age.

Related terms: discrimination; protected characteristic.

qualified individual with a disability

The Americans with Disabilities Act (ADA) protects only qualified individuals with disabilities. A qualified individual with a disability must meet these requirements:

- The person must have a disability as defined by the ADA.
- The person must satisfy the prerequisites for the position, such as educational degrees, employment experience, skills, licenses, and other job-related requirements.
- The person must be able to perform the essential functions of the position, with or without a reasonable accommodation.

The ADA doesn't require employers to hire anyone who isn't qualified or can't do the job. Someone who doesn't satisfy the job requirements for the position or can't perform its essential functions, even with a reasonable accommodation, cannot bring a disability discrimination claim against the employer.

Related terms: Americans with Disabilities Act; disability; essential functions; reasonable accommodation.

qualifying exigency

The Family and Medical Leave Act (FMLA) gives covered employees the right to take time off to handle qualifying exigencies: specified matters relating to a family member's deployment to a foreign country on active duty in the military. Leave for a qualifying exigency is a type of FMLA leave for which an employee may take a total of 12 weeks off per year, along with leave for the employee's own serious health condition, for a family member's serious health condition, or to bond with a new child. The employee is entitled to a combined total of 12 weeks off for any or all of these reasons.

Qualifying exigency leave was added to the FMLA in 2008, along with a provision that allows employees to take up to 26 weeks of leave in a single one-year period to care for a family member who suffers a serious injury in the line of duty. These provisions were further expanded in 2009.

What counts as a qualifying exigency? The FMLA identifies seven categories of qualifying exigencies. For some of these exigencies, the amount of leave available is limited or restrictions apply to when the employee may take leave. There is also an eighth category for additional activities, which applies to any situation that the employer and employee agree should count as a qualifying exigency. The qualifying exigency categories are:

- **Short-notice deployment.** An employee may take leave to address any issue arising from a family's member's notification of an impending call or order to active duty within seven or fewer calendar days before the date of deployment. This type of leave may be taken for only seven calendar days, beginning on the day when the family member is notified of his or her deployment.

- **Military events and related activities.** An employee may take leave to attend an official ceremony, program, or event sponsored by the military and relating to the family member's active duty service. An employee may also take leave to attend family support or assistance programs and informational briefings sponsored or promoted by the military, military service organizations, or the American Red Cross.

- **Child care and school activities.** When required by a family member's active duty, an employee may take time to arrange alternative child care for the family member's child; to provide child care for the family member's child on an urgent, immediate-need basis (not regularly or every day); to enroll the family member's child in, or transfer the child to, a new school or day care facility; or to attend meetings with school or day care staff (such as disciplinary meetings, parent-teacher conferences, or meetings with a school counselor).

- **Financial and legal arrangements.** An employee may take time off to handle financial or legal issues that might need attention when a family member is called to active duty, such as preparing or updating a will or living trust, preparing or executing financial and health care powers of attorney, transferring bank account signature authority, obtaining military identification cards, or enrolling in the Defense Enrollment Eligibility Reporting System.
- **Counseling.** An employee may take leave to attend counseling, provided by someone other than a health care provider, for him- or herself, for the family member, or for the family member's child.
- **Rest and recuperation.** An employee may take time off to be with a family member who is on short-term, temporary rest and recuperation leave during deployment. The employee may take a maximum of five days of leave for each rest and recuperation leave.
- **Postdeployment activities.** An employee may take time off to attend ceremonies, reintegration briefings and events, and other official programs or ceremonies sponsored by the military for up to 90 days following the termination of a family member's active duty status. On a sadder note, employees may also take leave to handle issues arising from the death of a family member while on active duty status, such as meeting and recovering the family member's body and making funeral arrangements.
- **Additional activities.** In addition to the categories listed above, an employer and employee may agree to treat other events as qualifying exigencies. For this type of leave, the employer and employee must also agree on the timing and length of the leave.

Q

EXAMPLE: Duquan's father, David, runs a dog board and care service out of his home, taking care of dogs while their owners are out of town. David, a member of the Reserves, is called to report for active duty in ten days. Duquan asks his employer for time off to help his father with the dogs in his care; some owners are not due back until after David deploys. Duquan and his employer agree that Duquan may take one week of qualifying exigency leave to learn the ropes from his father, contact the owners and arrange for them to either pick up their dogs or find other care by the end of the week, and care for the dogs until their owners return.

Related terms: Family and Medical Leave Act; military caregiver leave; military family leave.

quid pro quo harassment

Quid pro quo is Latin for "this for that." In sexual harassment cases, quid pro quo harassment occurs when a supervisor conditions some aspect of an employee's work—such as getting hired or promoted, getting chosen for plum assignments or opportunities, or just keeping a job—on submitting to the supervisor's sexual advances.

Related terms: harassment; sexual harassment.

Q

race discrimination

Race discrimination occurs when an employer makes a job decision based on an employee's race or adopts a policy that appears neutral but disproportionately affects members of a certain race. Race discrimination in employment is prohibited by Title VII and similar state laws. It's also prohibited by Section 1981, a post-Civil War era statute that prohibits race discrimination in contracts, including the employment relationship.

Related terms: Civil Rights Act of 1991; discrimination; disparate treatment; disparate impact; harassment; Section 1981; Title VII.

Randi W. v. Muroc Joint Unified School District

See defamation.

reasonable accommodation

A reasonable accommodation is assistance or changes to a position or workplace that will enable an employee to do his or her job despite having a disability. Under the Americans with Disabilities Act (ADA), employers are legally required to provide reasonable accommodations to employees with disabilities, unless doing so would pose an undue hardship.

Types of accommodations. Reasonable accommodations fall into three broad categories:

- **Application process:** changes to the job application process that enable a qualified individual with a disability to apply and be considered for the position. For example, if an employer requires all applicants for jobs in its call center to take a written test demonstrating their understanding of the company's products, it should offer to administer the test orally to an employee with impaired vision.

- **Work environment:** changes to the work environment, the circumstances in which the work is performed (for example, work hours or working conditions), or the manner in which the job is performed that allow a qualified individual with a disability to perform the job's essential functions. Examples include providing a hearing-impaired employee with TDD telephone equipment, lowering worktops for an employee in a wheelchair, or allowing an employee who is taking antidepressants to work a later shift.

- **Benefits and privileges:** changes that allow an employee with a disability to enjoy the same benefits and privileges that other employees enjoy. For example, if the company provides a lunchroom for employees, it should make sure that the room is accessible to employees who use wheelchairs.

What's an Accommodation Cost?

When the EEOC drafted its proposed regulations for the Americans with Disabilities Act Amendments Act in 2009, it pulled together various statistics and studies on the cost of reasonable accommodations. Those studies show significant variations in the reported mean cost of an accommodation, ranging from $462 up to more than $1,400. Where the studies agree, however, is that many (the majority, in some studies) reasonable accommodations are free.

Employees must request an accommodation. It is the applicant's or employee's responsibility to request the accommodation initially. The employer doesn't have to anticipate this need. The request need not be made in writing, nor does it have to include particular words. For example, an employee need not mention the ADA or use the words "reasonable accommodation." As long as an employee requests a change due to a medical condition or impairment, that's enough to start the process in motion.

Flexible interactive process. Once an employee or applicant requests an accommodation, the employer and employee must talk and work together to see if a reasonable accommodation is possible. The employer does not have to grant the specific accommodation the employee requests, as long as the employer works with the employee to find an effective solution. If the disability or need for accommodation isn't obvious, the employer may ask the employee to submit medical verification of the disability and limitations.

What isn't required. The following accommodations are considered unreasonable, and an employer is not required to make these changes:

- eliminating an essential function of the job
- lowering production or performance standards, or
- providing personal use items, such as a wheelchair, eyeglasses, hearing aid, or prosthetic limb.

Related terms: Americans with Disabilities Act; Americans with Disabilities Act Amendments Act; disability; essential job functions; qualified individual with a disability; undue hardship.

reasonable factor other than age

A reasonable factor other than age (RFOA) is an employer's defense to a claim of age discrimination based on disparate impact. If the employer can prove that its policy or practice was based on an RFOA, even one that often correlates with age (such as seniority), then the employer can escape liability for age discrimination. An RFOA is an affirmative defense, which means the employer bears the burden of proving it at trial; the employee doesn't have to show that the employer's practice was unreasonable.

Related terms: age discrimination; Age Discrimination in Employment Act; disparate impact.

R

reference

In the employment context, a reference is a statement made to a prospective employer about an applicant's skills, abilities, or past employment, usually by a former employer, teacher, or other person who is familiar with the applicant. (Often, the person who gives the reference is also called a reference.)

Some employers do not provide detailed references for former employees, instead giving prospective employers only bare-bones data, such as the dates the employee worked for the company, the positions the employee held, and the employee's salary. The purpose of a policy like this is to avoid allegations by the former employee that the company spoke falsely and damaged the employee's reputation (leading to a claim of defamation). To encourage full disclosure, a number of states have passed laws that protect reference providers with a qualified privilege: As long as the speaker is not acting maliciously, a former employer may not be sued for defamation based on information it provided in response to a reference request from a prospective employer.

Related term: defamation.

Reid v. Google

See age discrimination.

reinstatement

Reinstatement is returning an employee to the position the employee held prior to going out on leave or being fired. Under the Family and Medical Leave Act (FMLA) and the Uniformed Services Employment and Reemployment Rights Act (USERRA), an employee who takes protected leave is entitled to reinstatement when that leave is over. USERRA requires the employer to return the employee to the "escalator" position: the position the employee would have held had he or she been continuously employed rather than taking leave, including any raises or promotions that would have happened during that time. The FMLA requires only that the employee be reinstated to the formerly held position.

Reinstatement as a remedy. Sometimes, a court orders reinstatement as a remedy for wrongful termination. If the court finds that the employee was fired illegally (for example, for discriminatory reasons or in retaliation for complaining of unsafe working conditions), the court can order the employer to reinstate the employee, pay the employee all of the compensation that should have been paid while the employee was not working (back pay), and perhaps pay other damages, such as for emotional distress.

When reinstatement isn't appropriate. Even if a court finds that an employee was illegally fired, it won't order reinstatement if the employment relationship is so irreparably damaged that reinstatement isn't possible. In this situation, a court might award front pay: damages intended to compensate the employee for lost wages going forward from the date of trial. Front pay may also be awarded if reinstatement will be delayed. For example, if the employer has replaced the fired employee and no comparable position is immediately available, the court might award front pay for the period of time between the trial and the date when the employee can be reinstated.

Related terms: damages; escalator position; Family and Medical Leave Act; front pay; Uniformed Services Employment and Reemployment Rights Act; wrongful discharge.

R

release

A release is a contract that excuses one party from liability for particular actions. It's sometimes called a waiver, because the party who releases the other from liability is waiving (giving up) the right to sue. In the employment law context, a release typically enters the picture at one of two times: when an employment relationship is terminated or when a dispute between an employee and employer is settled.

Termination of employment. Many employers ask employees to sign a release when they are fired or laid off, to avoid any possibility of future lawsuits. Because a release is a contract, the parties have to exchange something of value in order for it to be binding. One party's promise to do something, absent any promise, payment, or other consideration from the other party, doesn't create a legally binding contract. In exchange for the employee's promise not to sue, the employer must provide something the employee would not have received otherwise. For example, if an employer has a policy of paying one week of severance for every year an employee has been with a company, it must offer something more to an employee who signs a release. It can't simply fork over benefits to which the employee is already entitled.

Settlement agreements. If there's already a dispute between the parties—for example, because a fired employee has threatened to sue, filed an administrative complaint, or brought a lawsuit—any settlement will include a release. After all, the purpose of the settlement is to resolve all of the outstanding issues between the parties, once and for all. A typical settlement requires the employee to give up the right to sue over the settled claims, in exchange for payment (and perhaps other benefits) from the employer.

Requirements for a legally binding release. To be valid, a release must involve an exchange, as explained above; both parties must give something up to create a contract. In addition, a court will enforce a release only if it is knowing and voluntary. In other words, the employee must enter into it freely, knowing that he or she is signing away the right to sue. If the employee is coerced or threatened into signing, or if the agreement is not voluntary for any other reason, it won't be enforced. For example, if the employer withholds benefits to which the employee is entitled with or without the release (such as the employee's final paycheck) until the employee signs, the release is likely to be found invalid.

To make sure both sides understand what the employee is releasing, the release should clearly spell out the claims it covers. Many releases provide an illustrative list of claims, concluding with "and any and all other claims related to his or her employment." There are special rules if the release is to cover unknown claims: issues the employee didn't know about when the release was signed. If an employee signs a release, then learns facts that would support a legal claim—for example, that the employer illegally withheld money from the employee's paycheck or exposed the employee to toxic chemicals—the release may not cover those claims unless it specifically includes unknown claims. State laws dictate the style and substance of a release of unknown claims. A state might require the employer to use particular language, or even particular typeface and font size.

Special Rules for Older Workers

If the employee is at least 40 years old, the federal Older Workers Benefit Protection Act (OWBPA) requires employers to include additional terms in a release. Among other things, the release must:

- specifically refer to the Age Discrimination in Employment Act (ADEA)
- advise the employee to consult with a lawyer before signing the release
- give the employee at least 21 days to consider the release before signing, and
- allow the employee to revoke the agreement (to back out of the deal) for seven days after signing.

What a release may not include. Certain rights may not be waived, which means an employee is legally entitled to claim those rights, whether or not the employee has signed a release. For example, some state laws provide that an employee may not waive the right to collect unemployment benefits. In these states, even if the employee signs a release and receives severance pay from the employer, the employee is still entitled to unemployment.

Related terms: Age Discrimination in Employment Act; Older Workers Benefit Protection Act; severance agreement.

religious discrimination

Religious discrimination occurs when an employer makes decisions based on an employee's religious beliefs (or lack thereof). The laws that prohibit religious discrimination (Title VII and many state laws) also require employers to accommodate an employee's religious practices and beliefs, at least to some extent.

What's different about religion. Religion is unique among the characteristics protected from discrimination because it isn't really a characteristic, like race or gender; it's a belief system. And unlike other protected traits, which are sometimes protected precisely because they are "immutable," religious belief is deeply personal and can change over time. A person might become more religious, convert from one religion to another, or abandon faith entirely. A person might strongly feel like a member of a particular religion, yet not share all of its beliefs or follow all of its teachings. Also, unlike other protected traits, religion sometimes requires particular behavior while adherents are at work, such as prayer; observing certain holidays; wearing specified items, types of clothing, or hair styles; or professing one's faith to others.

The easy part—discrimination is prohibited. Employers may not discriminate based on someone's religion (for example, refuse to hire an employee because he is a Muslim or refuse to promote any Jews to management positions). Reverse religious discrimination is also prohibited. So, an employer may not require employees to hold certain beliefs or be members of a particular church. Atheists may not be discriminated against because they lack religious beliefs entirely, either.

The harder part—accommodations. The requirement that employers accommodate an employee's religious beliefs or practices is easy to state: An employer may not deny a request for reasonable accommodation of an applicant's or employee's sincerely held religious beliefs or practices (or lack thereof) unless the accommodation would result in more than a de minimis cost or burden on business operations.

What makes a religious belief sincere? Once the discussion moves beyond recognized religious affiliations, it can be hard to determine whether a particular employee's belief is actually religious. Vegetarianism, particular styles of dress or hair length, and views on appropriate gender roles, for example, could each be part of a system of religious practices or could simply be a matter of personal opinion or preference. As the Equal Employment Opportunity Commission (EEOC) points out, personal beliefs are not protected by Title VII; that privilege is reserved for religious beliefs, defined as those that are sincere, meaningful, occupy a place for the believer "parallel to that filled by... God," and concern "'ultimate ideas' about 'life, purpose, and death.'"

How much is de minimis? Courts and the EEOC have repeatedly held that employers don't have to pay for anything beyond administrative costs (for example, the payroll processing costs associated with executing a shift transfer or schedule change) to accommodate an employee's religious beliefs. However, in 2008, the EEOC issued guidance stating that an employer could be expected to pay premium wages to accommodate an employee (for example, the cost of overtime pay for another employee to work extra hours to accommodate the employee's need for time off for a religious observance). Employers also don't have to take actions that would substantially harm morale or disrupt workplace routines.

In light of these rules, some accommodations that might be required include:

- scheduling changes to allow an employee to observe a Sabbath or attend a religious ceremony
- changes to usual dress and grooming requirements (for example, allowing an employee to have long hair, a long beard, or particular religious garb), or
- prayer breaks at work.

R

What about proselytizing? Some employees wish to—or believe that their religion requires them to—express their religious beliefs in the workplace by, for example, posting religious messages in their workspace, sharing their antiabortion views, using religious language (such as "Praise the Lord" or "In the name of Jesus of Nazareth") when communicating with coworkers and customers, or even attempting to convert others. According to the EEOC, almost 20% of employees proselytize to coworkers.

Employers may not restrict religious expression more heavily than other forms of expression that have a similar impact on workplace efficiency. Beyond that, however, the legal rules aren't so clear. Statements like these are considered forms of religious expression entitled to accommodation. On the other hand, other employees may find these statements harassing—and the employer itself might legitimately feel that such statements give the public the wrong idea about the company's own values and mission. There are no bright lines: Unlike racist or sexist comments, which an employer can and should stop whether or not they've reached the level of legal harassment, religious comments are not considered legally inappropriate. In fact, they are legally protected to some extent, and an employer who prohibits them absent complaints or other evidence of trouble could face a successful legal challenge.

> **EXAMPLE:** As part of a workplace diversity program, Hewlett-Packard hung posters of employees, including one featuring an employee who was labeled as gay. In response, Richard Peterson posted passages from the Bible condemning homosexuality. Peterson claimed that he had a religious duty to expose evil, and that he intended the messages to be hurtful to his gay and lesbian coworkers, whom he hoped would read the messages, repent, and be saved.
>
> After Peterson was fired for refusing to take down the passages, he sued for discrimination on the basis of religion. A federal Court of Appeals rejected his claim. The Court found that Peterson's desire to express his religious beliefs could not be

accommodated without requiring his employer to allow other employees to be demeaned. *Peterson v. Hewlett-Packard*, 359 F.3d 599 (9th Cir. 2004).

Related terms: discrimination; harassment; reasonable accommodation; Title VII.

Religious Freedom Restoration Act

Congress passed the Religious Freedom Restoration Act (RFRA) in 1993, in direct response to a U.S. Supreme Court case that allowed a state to deny unemployment benefits to employees who were fired for using peyote, without considering the employees' religious justification for using the drug. RFRA states that the government may not substantially burden someone's religious freedom, even through a law of general application (such as a drug criminalization law, which is not specifically aimed at religious practice), unless it has a compelling government interest in doing so and has chosen the least intrusive means of furthering that interest.

Alfred Smith and the sacramental peyote. The Supreme Court case that led to passage of the RFRA, *Employment Division, Dept. of Human Resources of Oregon v. Smith*, 494 U.S. 872 (1990), involved two men, Alfred Smith and Galen Black, who were fired from their jobs with a private drug rehabilitation organization because they took peyote for sacramental purposes during a ceremony of the Native American Church, of which both men were members. They were then denied unemployment benefits, because the state unemployment department found that they were fired for work-related misconduct. They appealed the decision, arguing that the state's decision to deny benefits interfered with their First Amendment right to freely exercise their religion.

The Supreme Court found against the two men. The Court found that Oregon's criminal law prohibiting the use of peyote was a valid, neutral law of general application. In other words, it was not aimed at deterring the practice of a particular religion. In the Court's words, "if prohibiting the exercise of religion ... is not the

R

object of the [statute] but merely the incidental effect of a generally applicable and otherwise valid provision, the First Amendment has not been offended."

In enacting the RFRA, Congress adopted the views of the dissent in the Smith case (penned by Justice O'Connor). The dissent argued that the effect of the statute on religious exercise should be the focus of the inquiry, not the state's intent in enacting the statute. Whether or not the state intended to target religious practice, its law had the effect of burdening the men's free exercise of their religion, and so had to be justified by a compelling state interest. This is the language Congress adopted in the RFRA: A law, even one of general application, may impose a substantial burden on the free exercise of religion only if it furthers a compelling state interest, and only if it does so by the least restrictive means. (Ironically, Justice O'Connor points out that she would have reached the same result—that the men could be denied unemployment benefits—under this test, based on the state's compelling interest in fair enforcement of its drug laws.)

Related term: religious discrimination.

respondeat superior

Respondeat superior, Latin for "let the superior answer," is a legal theory that holds employers legally liable for the actions its employees take within the course and scope of employment. This is a strict liability rule, which means the employer is responsible whether or not it acted carelessly and whether or not it was aware of the potential for danger. This rule holds employers liable for the costs of doing business, including the expenses associated with their employees injuring people or damaging property while performing their jobs.

Respondeat superior doesn't apply if an employee is acting outside of the course and scope of employment. The employer won't be liable if an employee acts solely for his or her own benefit, particularly if the action is divorced from the employee's job duties.

For example, if an employee hits another car while making a delivery for the employer during work hours, the employer will be liable for the damage. If an employee hits another car while being chased by the cops after robbing a bank, the employer will not be liable.

Related terms: course and scope of employment; frolic and detour; negligent hiring; negligent retention.

rest break

Many employers provide employees with a rest or meal break, whether paid or unpaid. This common practice is not required everywhere, however: The federal wage and hour law, the Fair Labor Standards Act (FLSA), doesn't require employers to provide meal or rest breaks. Some states have stepped into the breach to require such breaks, but others have not.

An employer doesn't have to pay for meal or break time unless:

- state law requires paid rest breaks
- the employee has to to work through the break, or
- the break lasts 20 minutes or less; generally, these shorter breaks are considered part of the employee's workday and must be paid.

Some states require paid breaks. Only a handful of states—California, Colorado, Kentucky, Minnesota, Nevada, Oregon, Vermont, and Washington—currently require employers to allow employees to take rest breaks. With the exception of Minnesota and Vermont, which simply require employers to give employees enough break time to use the restroom, these laws generally provide that employees can take a ten-minute rest break, with pay, for every four hours they work. A few other states allow employers to choose between giving a meal break or rest breaks.

Stricter rules for minors. A number of states require employers to allow younger workers to take meal or rest breaks. In states that already require breaks for adult workers, the rules for minors are sometimes stricter. Some states have special break rules for all

R

minors (employees who are not yet 18 years old); others have special break rules only for minors who are 15 or younger.

Related terms: hour worked; meal break.

restraining order (for employer)

A restraining (often called a "stay away" order) requires a perpetrator of domestic violence to stay a certain distance away from the victim. A restraining order often also requires the batterer to stay away from certain places, such as the victim's home and the school attended by the victim's children, if applicable. The purpose of a restraining order is to allow law enforcement to step in before anyone gets hurt. A batterer who gets too close to the victim has violated the order and can be detained by the police.

Some states allow businesses to get their own restraining orders if they are threatened with violence, and employers can use these laws to get restraining orders against an employee's batterer. Such a restraining order requires the batterer to stay a certain distance away from the employer's property or face arrest. You can find detailed information about workplace restraining orders at the website of Legal Momentum, www.legalmomentum.org.

Related terms: domestic violence leave; workplace violence.

retaliation

Retaliation occurs when an employer punishes an employee for exercising a legal right, such as complaining about harassment, discrimination, unsafe working conditions, or illegal financial dealings. Any negative job action, such as demotion, discipline, firing, salary reduction, negative evaluation, transfer, change in job assignment, or shift change, can constitute retaliation, if the employer did it in response to the employee's actions.

The Supreme Court has said that any materially adverse action against an employee may constitute retaliation under Title VII, if the action might deter a reasonable employee from making a complaint. (*Burlington Northern & Santa Fe Railway v. White*, 548 U.S. 53 (2006).) The Court found that enforcement of Title VII depends on employees' willingness to come forward with complaints, so the statute must be interpreted to provide broad protection from retaliation. Employees are also protected from retaliation for participating in an investigation of discrimination or harassment, even if they weren't the original source of the complaint.

Proving retaliation. To prove retaliation, an employee must show that:

- the employee engaged in a protected activity (such as filing a harassment complaint)
- the employer took action against the employee, and
- there is a causal link between the two events. This element can be demonstrated by timing alone, if the employer disciplined the employee immediately after the employee's legally protected activity. Statements by the employer are often also used to prove causation (for example, if a manager says, "You'll be sorry if you complain about this," and then follows through).

Related terms: discrimination; harassment; investigation; Title VII.

reverse discrimination

Reverse discrimination refers to discrimination against a member of a group that wasn't the intended beneficiary of a discrimination law. For example, Title VII prohibits discrimination on the basis of race, and so protects employees of all races from discrimination based on that characteristic. However, as the Congressional debate and speeches on the Civil Rights Act of 1964 made clear, the racial discrimination provisions in the law were largely intended to remedy ongoing segregation and discrimination against African Americans. Thus, when a white employee claims race discrimination under Title VII, it is sometimes called a reverse discrimination case.

Related terms: affirmative action; discrimination; Title VII.

R

RFRA

See Religious Freedom Restoration Act.

right to sue letter

A right to sue letter is a document issued by the Equal Employment Opportunity Commission or state fair employment practices agency, telling someone who has filed a charge of discrimination that the agency has finished processing the charge and the person is free to file a discrimination lawsuit. The agency may issue a right to sue letter fairly quickly after the employee files a charge; this often happens when the employee intends to sue and has filed the charge as a mere formality. The agency may also issue a right to sue letter following an investigation or effort to settle a claim.

Employees must file a charge with a government agency and receive a right to sue letter before they may file a lawsuit based on the same claims. This requirement is called exhaustion of administrative remedies. Once the agency issues a right to sue letter, the employee has a limited amount of time (90 days, if the EEOC issues the letter) to file a lawsuit.

Related terms: Equal Employment Opportunity Commission; exhaustion (of remedies); FEP laws; Title VII.

right to work laws

The National Labor Relations Act allows states to prohibit union security agreements, which require employees to either join a union or pay fees to it as a condition of getting or keeping a job. States that have passed these laws are called "right to work" states, and the laws are called right to work laws. In these states, workers who decide not to join the union cannot be required to pay any fees to the union and cannot be fired or otherwise penalized for failing to do so.

Related terms: agency shop; closed shop; National Labor Relations Act; open shop; union security agreements.

right to work states

See right to work laws.

rolling leave year

A rolling leave year is one method of determining an employee's entitlement to leave under the Family and Medical Leave Act (FMLA). Under the FMLA, employees are entitled to 12 weeks of leave in a 12-month period for specified reasons (26 weeks of leave are available in a single year if the employee needs to care for a family member who was seriously injured while on active military duty). Employers may choose one of four methods of counting the 12-month period, and one of them is the rolling leave year.

Under the rolling leave year method, an employee's eligibility for leave "rolls out" throughout the year, as leave is taken. When an employee needs leave, the employer looks back over the previous 12 months to see how much leave the employee has taken. Any portion of the employee's 12-week allotment that has not been used in the past 12 months is available to the employee.

> **EXAMPLE:** Juan takes eight weeks of parental leave when he and his wife adopt a child, from January 1 through February 26. The following year, Juan has to have surgery on January 15. Looking back over the 12 previous months, Juan has taken six weeks of leave, from the previous January 15 through February 26. Therefore, he has six weeks of leave remaining.

Related terms: Family and Medical Leave Act; leave year; military caregiver leave.

R

safe harbor

Many statutes contain safe harbors: provisions that reduce or eliminate liability for violating the statute if certain criteria are met. Safe harbors often require the person seeking to avoid liability to have made some good faith attempt to comply with the law, even if that effort failed. For example, copyright law includes a safe harbor that excuses a website provider from liability for infringement claims if the provider made a good faith effort to take down the infringing content.

Here are some important safe harbor provisions in the employment law field:

- **Misclassifying employees as independent contractors.** An employer who misclassifies workers as independent contractors (rather than employees) does not need to fear IRS assessments or penalties if it has a reasonable basis for its classification. A reasonable basis might be founded on longstanding industry practice, reliance on past court decisions or IRS rulings, or advice from an accountant. The employer also must file all necessary 1099 forms for the worker and consistently treat the worker (and all other workers performing substantially similar work) as an independent contractor.

- **Improper pay docking of exempt employees.** A safe harbor exists for an employer that improperly docks the pay of exempt employees (those who are not entitled to earn overtime if they work more than 40 hours per week). Ordinarily, the employer might be found to have converted those employees—and all others in the same job classification who report to the same manager—into nonexempt employees, to whom the employer owes overtime. Under the safe harbor provision, however, an employer won't be liable for any penalties, even if it takes improper deductions, if the employer reimburses the employees for money improperly withheld and either the deductions were isolated or inadvertent, or the employer has a clearly communicated policy that prohibits improper deductions, including a complaint procedure.

- **Acquisition of genetic information.** The Genetic Information Nondiscrimination Act (GINA) prohibits employers from acquiring, requesting, or requiring employees to provide genetic information. However, if an employer receives genetic information in response to a lawful request for medical information, it will be considered inadvertent (and therefore not violate the law) if the employer tells the information provider not to give genetic information. The regulations interpreting GINA provide sample notice language employers can use to make sure they fit into this safe harbor.

Related terms: Genetic Information Nondiscrimination Act; independent contractor; pay docking.

salary basis

A number of categories of employees are exempt from the overtime requirements of the Fair Labor Standards Act, which means they aren't entitled to earn overtime if they work more than 40 hours a week. Some of these employees are exempt simply because of their occupation, regardless of how much they are paid. For certain categories, however, the employee must perform certain job duties and must also meet a salary test in order to be exempt. Under the salary test, the employee must earn at least $455 per week and be paid on a salary basis.

Employees are paid on a salary basis if they receive their full salary for any week in which they perform any work, regardless of how many hours they work or the quality or amount of work they do. There are a handful of exceptions to this rule. For example, an employee who starts or quits a job midweek isn't entitled to be paid for the whole week. Similarly, an employee who takes a few days of unpaid FMLA leave may receive less than his or her full salary for that week. (For more on these exceptions, see "pay docking.")

If the employee is ready, willing, and able to work, an employer may not pay the employee less than a full salary because of the operating needs of the business (for example, because work is slow). During the economic recession that began in 2008, this rule led to questions about whether an employer could legally cut an exempt employee's pay (often along with a cut in hours, as part of a furlough program) without running afoul of the salary basis rule. If an employee is no longer paid on a salary basis, that employee—and possibly, all other employees in the same job category who report to the same supervisor—may no longer be exempt from overtime.

The federal Department of Labor has said that employers may cut the pay of salaried exempt employees without losing the exemption if that cut is prospective and reflects the long-term needs of the business. This means, for example, that an employer may cut an employee's salary from $1,000 to $900 per week, if that cut is intended to continue as long as necessary, in response to the economic downturn. But it may not cut an employee's salary to $900 this week, $800 the next, and bump it back up to $1,000 the following week, based on its day-to-day levels of business. This type of strategy starts to look a lot like simply paying employees for hours worked rather than paying them a salary.

These categories of employees must be paid on a salary basis in order to be exempt from overtime: administrative employees, executive employees, professional employees, outside salespeople, and certain computer employees (who may be paid either at least $455 per week or at least $27.63 an hour).

Related terms: administrative employee; executive employee; Fair Labor Standard Act; outside salesperson; overtime; pay docking; professional employee.

Sarbanes-Oxley Act of 2002

In the wake of corporate scandals involving WorldCom, Enron, and other large companies accused of defrauding shareholders, Congress passed the Sarbanes-Oxley Act of 2002 (SOX). The purpose of the law is to protect investors by improving the accuracy and reliability of corporate disclosures, and the law seeks to further this goal by imposing strict rules for audits and auditors of publicly traded companies, preventing insider trading and deals, requiring companies to adopt strict internal controls, and increasing the penalties for white-collar crimes relating to investor fraud.

Whistleblower protections. Much shareholder fraud is hidden, known only to those inside the company. To encourage reporting of fraud, SOX requires public companies to establish procedures for handling complaints and mechanisms—such as a hotline or Web-based complaint intake system—that allow employees to submit confidential, anonymous complaints and concerns about questionable accounting or auditing matters.

The law also protects employees from retaliation if they come forward with certain types of complaints. To be protected, the employee's complaint must involve conduct that the employee reasonably believes violates SEC rules or regulations, federal law relating to shareholder fraud, or federal law relating to mail fraud, wire fraud, or bank fraud. And, the employee must make the complaint (or provide information) to a federal regulatory or law enforcement agency (such as the SEC), a member of committee of Congress, or someone who has supervisory authority over the employee or has the authority to investigate, discover, or terminate the alleged misconduct. Employees are also protected if they assist, act as a witness, or provide information in an investigation into shareholder fraud by any of the above groups.

Related terms: retaliation; whistleblower.

scab

Scab is a slang term for a worker who is hired to replace an employee who is on strike. It sometimes also refers to employees who refuse to join a strike or who cross a picket line to work during a strike.

Related terms: picket; strike.

second opinion

When an employee takes leave under the Family and Medical Leave Act (FMLA) for a serious health condition (the employee's own or that of a family member), the employer can ask the employee to provide a medical certification from a health care practitioner. A certification provides some basic information about the employee's need for leave, such as some facts about the health condition, when it began, and how long it is expected to last. Once an employee provides a medical certification, the employer can require the employee to get a second opinion: a second certification from a health care provider of the employer's own choosing.

If the original certification supported the employee's request for leave, the employer must provide leave while the second opinion is pending. If the second opinion contradicts the first, the employer has the right to get a third opinion, which will be binding on everyone.

Related terms: Family and Medical Leave Act; medical certification; serious health condition.

secondary boycott

See boycott.

Section 1981

Section 1981 is a federal statute that prohibits racial discrimination in the employment relationship. (The law is known as Section 1981 because of its location in the United States Code.) Section 1981 applies to all private employers and to state and local governments.

A little history. Section 1981 was passed in the Reconstruction era as part of the historic Civil Rights Act of 1866, which declared African Americans to be citizens of the United States, entitled to a series of rights previously reserved for white men. A primary purpose of the law was to undermine the "Black Codes," state laws adopted after the Civil War that restricted the rights of newly freed slaves to own property, make contracts, give evidence in court, or leave a job, among other things.

One of the rights Section 1981 protects is the right to make and enforce contracts, which courts have found prohibits racial discrimination in the employment relationship. (In 1989, the U.S. Supreme Court decided that Section 1981 did not prohibit harassment; however, Congress overturned that decision in the Civil Rights Act of 1991.)

Are at-will employees protected? To sue under Section 1981, an employee must either have an employment contract or have been denied a contract. However, courts disagree as to whether at-will employees—the majority of U.S. workers, who can be fired at any time, for any reason that isn't illegal—have an employment contract for the purposes of Section 1981. Most federal courts to consider the issue have decided that at-will employees do have basic employment contracts (covering, for example, wages and work to be performed), even though those contracts offer no job protection. Therefore, these courts have allowed at-will employees to sue under Section 1981. Other courts have held otherwise, finding that at-will employees don't have contractual rights that they can enforce using Section 1981.

You don't have to be an employee to be protected. Section 1981 protects against discrimination in the making and enforcement of contracts. This covers not only employment contracts, but also partnership contracts and contracts between a business and its independent contractors.

> ### When a Corporation Is Not a Person
>
> A corporation is considered a legal "person," which means it can
> enter into its own contracts, own property, file lawsuits, and be sued,
> separate from its individual owners. One thing it can't do, however, is
> be discriminated against under Section 1981. In 2006, the U.S. Supreme
> Court rejected a black contractor's Section 1981 claim that Domino's
> Pizza had broken several contracts with his corporation because of
> his race. Although the contractor was the sole shareholder of his
> corporation, the Court found that he had no right to sue because
> the contracts were between Domino's and his corporation, not him
> personally.
>
> *Domino's Pizza v. McDonald*, 546 U.S. 470 (2006).

People of all races are protected. Although the law was originally
intended to protect newly freed slaves, courts have consistently
interpreted Section 1981 to protect people of any race (including white
people) from intentional race discrimination. Some courts have also
found that Section 1981 prohibits discrimination based on ethnicity,
but only if that discrimination is racial in character. For example,
courts have held that discrimination against Latin Americans,
Arab Americans, and Asian Americans violates Section 1981, but
discrimination against persons of Slavic or Italian origin does not.

In deciding whether ethnic discrimination constitutes race
discrimination under Section 1981, courts look at a number of
factors, including:

- whether the discriminator perceived or characterized the victim
  as belonging to a separate race because of his or her ethnicity
- whether the victim belongs to an ethnicity that is perceived as
  "nonwhite"
- whether the victim belongs to an ethnicity that has
  traditionally been subject to discrimination, and
- whether the victim is claiming discrimination based on
  characteristics commonly associated with national origin

S

(country of birth, language fluency, or surname, for example), which is not a violation of Section 1981; or on characteristics commonly associated with race (physical characteristics or skin color, for example), which is.

But what about Title VII? Title VII, of the Civil Rights Act of 1964, also prohibits employment discrimination based on race. Although the two statutes overlap, Section 1981 provides some distinct advantages to employees, including:

- **Employees can go straight to court.** To bring a Title VII lawsuit, an employee must first file a discrimination charge with the Equal Employment Opportunity Commission (EEOC). This is called "exhausting" administrative remedies. Employees don't have to do this under Section 1981: They can file a lawsuit right away.

- **Employees have much more time to sue.** Once the EEOC finishes processing an employee's discrimination charge, the employee has only a short period to file a lawsuit: from 90 days to a year, depending on the state. Under Section 1981, an employee has four years to file a lawsuit.

- **Damages are unlimited.** Title VII allows employees to recover all of the money they actually lost (for example, out-of-pocket expenses, back wages, and so on), but caps how much a successful employee can collect for emotional distress and punitive damages. The cap ranges from $50,000 to $300,000, depending on the size of the employer. In contrast, Section 1981 doesn't put any limit on damages.

Related terms: at-will employment; Civil Rights Act of 1991; damages; employment contract; exhaustion (of remedies); independent contractor; Title VII.

serious health condition

Under the Family and Medical Leave Act (FMLA), eligible employees have the right to take leave to care for a family member with a serious health condition or to recuperate from his or her own serious health condition, among other things. Not every illness or injury counts as a serious health condition, however. To be covered by the FMLA, the employee or family member must have an illness, injury, impairment, or physical or mental condition that falls into one of these six categories:

- **Inpatient care (an overnight stay) at a hospital, hospice, or residential medical care facility.** The employee is entitled to leave for the time spent receiving inpatient care and for any period of incapacity or subsequent treatment connected to that care.
- **Incapacity (that is, inability to work or attend to other daily activities) for more than three full calendar days with continuing treatment by a health care provider.** It isn't enough for an employee to be out sick for more than three days: The employees must also receive continuing treatment, defined by the FMLA regulations as either (1) at least two in-person visits to a health care provider within 30 days of the first day of incapacity, or (2) at least one in-person visit that results in a regimen of continuing treatment under the provider's supervision. In either scenario, the first visit must take place within seven days of the first day of incapacity.
- **Incapacity due to pregnancy or prenatal care.** Routine visits to the doctor for prenatal care fall within this category.
- **Incapacity or treatment for a chronic serious health condition.** A chronic condition is one that requires periodic visits (at least twice a year) to a health care provider or nurse, continues over an extended period of time, and may cause episodic, rather than continuous, incapacity. This category is intended to encompass long-lasting conditions that require ongoing management and treatment, such as diabetes, epilepsy, or asthma.
- **Permanent or long-term incapacity.** This category includes conditions for which the person is under the supervision of health care provider, even if the condition isn't amenable to treatment. Examples include Alzheimer's disease, terminal cancer, or advanced amyotrophic lateral sclerosis (also known as ALS or Lou Gehrig's disease).

S

- **Absence for multiple treatments for restorative surgery after an accident or injury, or for a condition that would require an absence of more than three days if not treated.** Examples of conditions in the first category include surgery to reset a broken limb or repair a torn ligament. The second category encompasses treatments for severe arthritis, dialysis for kidney disease, and cancer treatment.

Related terms: Family and Medical Leave Act; medical certification; second opinion.

severance agreement

A severance agreement is an arrangement made between an employer and a departing employee. Typically, the employee receives some compensation and/or benefits, such as cash, continued insurance coverage, the right to keep certain company property (for example, a laptop computer or company car the employee has been using), or outplacement services. In exchange, the employer generally asks the employee to release all legal claims against the company.

Related term: release.

sex discrimination

Sex discrimination occurs when an employer treats employees or applicants differently because of their gender. For example, an employer who promotes only men to managerial positions, pays women less than men for doing the same job, makes decisions based on misconceptions about gender (for example, that men need to be paid more because they are more likely to be supporting families, or that women won't be willing to take overnight business trips because it will mean leaving their children), or adopts neutral policies that disproportionately affect women (such as a lifting requirement) without a legitimate business justification, is engaging in sex discrimination. Pregnancy discrimination is a form of sex discrimination under Title VII, as is sexual harassment.

Sexual stereotyping. Many sex discrimination claims allege that an employer held men and women to different standards based on sexist assumptions about the abilities or desires of the sexes, or based on historic or traditional gender roles. For instance, a manager might fire pregnant employees because he believes that they won't want to return to work after having a baby—or because he believes women should stay home with their children. Women might be relegated to lower paying customer service jobs because their boss believes that women communicate better and are more empathetic than men. Or, a company might refuse to hire a female CEO, believing that customers, competitors, and the public won't take her as seriously as they would a man.

Related terms: pregnancy discrimination; sexual harassment; Title VII.

sexual harassment

Sexual harassment is offensive, unwelcome conduct, based on the victim's sex, which is severe or pervasive enough to affect the terms and conditions of the victim's employment.

Two types of harassment. The U.S. Supreme Court divides harassment into two categories, depending on whether the victim suffers a tangible job action: an action that significantly changes the harassed employee's job status, like getting fired, demoted, or reassigned.

- **If the victim suffers a tangible employment action** at the hands of a supervisor, the company is generally liable for the harm, whether or not the employee complained and whether or not the company knew about the harassment. The logic is that when supervisors make these types of decisions, they are acting for the company. Therefore, if those decisions are influenced by discrimination, the company is responsible. (Harassment that results in a tangible job action is sometimes referred to as "quid pro quo" harassment, Latin for "this for that"; the employee had to put up with the harassment (the "this") in order to get the job benefit (the "that").)

S

- **If the victim doesn't suffer a tangible employment action,** an employer is legally liable for harassment—called "hostile environment" harassment—only in certain circumstances. If the employer exercises reasonable care to prevent and promptly correct any harassment, and the employee unreasonably failed to take advantage of opportunities the employer offered to prevent or correct the harassment (for example, by failing to make a complaint), the company won't be liable for harassment it didn't know about. (For more on these liability issues, see "*Farragher-Ellerth* defense.")

When is harassment unwelcome? Conduct must be unwelcome to the victim to qualify as harassment. This is a requirement in all harassment cases (for example, racial harassment or religious harassment), but it is more often an issue in sexual harassment cases, due to the fact that not all sexual or romantic behavior in the workplace is offensive to the recipient. Some requests for a date are happily accepted, and lead to mutually satisfying relationships. Others—for example, repeated requests after the recipient has clearly indicated a lack of interest or loaded requests by a supervisor with the implication that acceptance is a job requirement—are upsetting, disturbing, or even frightening.

The law defines unwelcome conduct as conduct the victim finds offensive. In other words, unwelcomeness is in the eyes of the beholder. And, two employees in the same circumstances might have different reactions. For example, a group of men enjoy teasing and making sexual jokes with the office receptionist, who finds the jokes amusing and harmless, sometimes even telling one herself. Because the receptionist doesn't find the conduct unwelcome, she isn't being harassed. However, a female secretary who shares space with the receptionist finds these comments offensive and disruptive; she has asked the men to stop, and they have responded that they weren't talking to her, and she should mind her own business. Even though the jokes aren't directed at the secretary, she finds them unwelcome and must put up with them to do her job. She may be a victim of sexual harassment.

Who's Harassing Whom?

The majority of sexual harassment claims involve a male harasser and a female victim. However, courts have recognized harassment claims by male victims of female harassers, male victims of male harassers, and female victims of female harassers. And, the Equal Employment Opportunity Commission (EEOC) reports that harassment claims by men have been steadily increasing: For the last few years, such claims have made up almost 15% of all sexual harassment charges filed under federal law (these statistics don't reveal the gender of the victim).

Severe or pervasive harassment. Harassment is illegal only if it is severe or pervasive. Generally, this means there must be a pattern of harassment or a series of incidents over time. One teasing comment, request for a date, or even use of a bigoted or crude term probably doesn't constitute harassment, by itself. On the other hand, courts have found that a single act can be harassment if the act is truly extreme, such as a sexual assault. There's no "magic number" of incidents when behavior crosses the line to become harassment. Courts look at all of the circumstances in determining whether harassment has occurred. The more egregious each incident is, the fewer will be necessary for a court to decide that they amount to illegal harassment.

Harassment that affects the terms and conditions of employment. Harassment that results in a tangible employment action, as explained above, has affected the terms and conditions of the victim's employment. For hostile environment harassment, however, the lines are less clear. The test is whether the victim reasonably finds the workplace to be abusive or hostile. In other words, it isn't enough that the victim actually believes the workplace is hostile; the circumstances must be such that a reasonable worker in the victim's position would also find the workplace hostile.

S

Sex-Based Harassment

Some courts have recognized claims of sex-based harassment: harassment that is based on sex but is not sexual in nature. In these cases, the harasser is not interested in having a sexual relationship with the victim(s) or otherwise sexualizing the workplace with jokes and stories, but instead wants to create a hostile environment for workers of a particular gender (almost always women). Often, these claims are made by women working in traditionally male professions.

Although women in these cases have clearly been subjected to a hostile work environment because of their sex, there are none of the traditional signs of sexual harassment, like requests for dates, dirty jokes, sexualized comments about women's bodies, and so on. Instead, the harassing conduct in these cases might take the form of sabotaging the tools, vehicles, or work of women employees; soiling or defacing women's workspaces, lockers, or restroom facilities; subjecting women to dangerous working conditions; displaying cartoons or telling jokes that depict violence towards women; and making comments about women's inability to do the job.

Related terms: *Faragher-Ellerth* defense; harassment; tangible employment action; Title VII.

sexual orientation discrimination

Sexual orientation discrimination occurs when an employer makes decisions based on an employee's heterosexuality, homosexuality, or bisexuality. For example, a corporate employer in a conservative area that refuses to hire gay employees is engaging in sexual orientation discrimination, as is an owner of a bar in a gay neighborhood who refuses to allow straight employees to hold positions that involve interaction with customers, such as wait staff or bartending.

It is illegal to discriminate on the basis of sexual orientation in about half the states and the District of Columbia, in both public and private employment. A few states ban sexual orientation discrimination only by public employers. And many cities and counties also ban sexual orientation discrimination in employment.

Never-ending battle over ENDA. Although the federal government may not discriminate against its own employees on the basis of sexual orientation, federal law does not yet prohibit such discrimination in private employment. Congressional efforts to ban such discrimination began in the 1970s and, by 1994, advocates had come up with a catchy title to go along with the legislation: the Employment Non-Discrimination Act, or ENDA. ENDA would amend Title VII to add sexual orientation to the list of protected characteristics that may not form the basis for employment decisions. Some version of the law has been introduced in almost every session of Congress since 1994, but has not yet garnered the votes necessary to pass.

Transgender Rights Added to ENDA

In 2007, a version of ENDA that included protections against discrimination based on gender identity was introduced in the House for the first time. At the same time, a version that did not include gender identity was introduced—and went on to pass in the House, a historic first. The introduction of two bills was a legislative compromise that attempted to recognize that many Democratic supporters of the bill and gay rights organizations wanted it to include gender identity protections, but that such a version of the bill would not pass.

In 2009, only one version of ENDA was introduced, called an "inclusive" version because it includes protection on the basis of gender identity. Prohibiting discrimination based on gender identity, defined as a person's gender-related appearance, mannerisms, characteristics, or identity, with or without regard to the person's designated sex at birth, would protect transgender employees and employees who don't conform to the stereotypes associated with their gender.

Related term: Title VII.

sick leave

Sick leave is time off work for illness or injury. Currently, federal law doesn't require employers to provide paid time off when employees are sick. However, federal law may require employers to offer unpaid time off in some circumstances. In addition, some states and local governments regulate sick leave.

Federal laws on sick leave. Employers that are subject to the Family and Medical Leave Act (FMLA) may have to offer employees FMLA leave, which is unpaid, if they have a serious health condition. The FMLA also allows employees to take leave to care for a family member with a serious health condition. Not every illness or injury qualifies as a serious health condition, however. (For more information, see "serious health condition.") Employees may also be entitled to leave under the Americans with Disabilities Act (ADA), if they have a disability and the leave represents a reasonable accommodation.

State and local laws on sick leave. In a few areas, employers are legally required to provide paid sick leave, at least in some circumstances. In San Francisco and the District of Columbia, for example, employers must provide a certain amount of paid sick leave per year, depending on how many hours the employee works. (The current maximum for the largest employers in D.C. is seven paid days per year; San Francisco employees can accrue a maximum of eight days per year.)

Some states also require employers that make sick leave available to allow employees to use it to care for ill family members. These laws don't require employers to offer paid sick leave in the first place, however.

Even though most employers aren't legally obligated to offer paid sick leave, they do anyway: The most recent numbers from the federal Bureau of Labor Statistics show that more than three-quarters of full-time employees in the private sector receive some paid sick leave, along with more than one-quarter of part-time employees.

Related terms: Americans with Disabilities Act; Family and Medical Leave Act; paid time off (PTO); reasonable accommodation; serious health condition.

similarly situated

Similarly situated means in circumstances that are similar in all legally relevant respects. The term is used in discrimination cases to refer to employees whose situations can be compared to determine whether particular employment decisions were based on discrimination or other factors. If an employee alleging discrimination can point to similarly situated employees who were treated differently, and those employees don't share the employee's protected characteristic (such as race or gender), discrimination might be the cause of the different treatment.

> EXAMPLE: Mihran applied for a promotion to supervisor three times, but each time another employee was selected. Mihran is from Iran, and he believes he has not been promoted because of his ethnicity. If all three of the promoted employees have more experience as supervisors, better performance evaluations, or other characteristics that make them more attractive candidates for promotion, Mihran will have a hard time showing that they were similarly situated. Even if all three are white, their promotions can be explained on the basis of legitimate business criteria; there's no reason to infer that ethnicity played a role. On the other hand, if all three had about the same credentials as Mihran—that is, they were similarly situated—or Mihran was a superior candidate, that more squarely poses the question of whether ethnicity was the reason for the decisions.

Related terms: discrimination; protected characteristic; Title VII.

S

small necessities leave

Small necessities leave is a catchall phrase referring to state laws that require employers to give employees time off for various family needs, such as attending school functions, taking a child to routine dental or medical appointments, or helping with elder care. These laws are intended to recognize and allow employees to handle needs that don't take up much time but play an important role in facilitating work-life balance. Here are a few examples:

- In Illinois, employees can take up to eight hours off in any school year—not to exceed four hours in a single day—to attend a child's school conferences or classroom activities, if those activities can't be scheduled during nonwork hours.
- In Washington, DC, employees can take up to 24 hours off per year to attend a child's school-related events, including parent teacher association (PTA) meetings, student performances, teacher conferences, and sporting events, as long as the parent actually participates and is not just a spectator.
- In Vermont, employees can take a total of 24 hours of leave per year for school activities; to attend or accompany a child, parent, spouse, or parent-in-law to routine medical or dental appointments or other appointments for professional services; or to respond to a medical emergency involving the employee's child, spouse, parent, or parent-in-law.

S

state plan states

See Occupational Safety and Health Act.

statute of limitations

The statute of limitations is the time period during which a lawsuit must be filed. If a lawsuit is filed after the statute of limitations has run out, the case will be dismissed. Statutes of limitations differ depending on the type of legal claim and on state law. For example, many states require that a personal injury lawsuit (such as defamation, wrongful termination, or assault) be filed within one year from the date of injury—or in some instances, from the date when it should reasonably have been discovered—but some states allow two years. Similarly, court claims based on a written contract (including an employment contract) must be filed in court within four or five years from the date the contract was broken, depending on state law.

Related terms: employment contract; exhaustion (of remedies); tort.

step-grievance procedures

See alternative dispute resolution.

strike

A strike is a work stoppage caused by employees' refusal to work, typically to protest an employer decision (to close a plant, freeze wages, cut benefits, impose unpopular work rules, or refuse to improve working conditions, for example). The right to strike is protected by the National Labor Relations Act (NLRA), but not all strikes are legal. Whether a strike is lawful depends on the purpose of the strike, whether the collective bargaining agreement includes a "no-strike" clause, and the conduct of the strikers.

Lawful purposes. A strike is legal—and therefore protected by the NLRA—if the employees are striking for economic reasons or to protest an unfair labor practice by the employer. In the first scenario, strikers are trying to get some economic concession from the employer, like higher wages, increased benefits, or better working conditions. In the second, workers strike because the employer has engaged in some practice that violates the NLRA, like refusing to bargain with the union or discriminating against union members.

No-strike provisions. Even strikes with a legal purpose are not protected by the NLRA If the union's contract with the employer (the collective bargaining agreement) includes a no-strike clause.

S

With a few limited exceptions (for example, if employees are refusing to work because of unusually dangerous working conditions), a strike that violates a no-strike provision is illegal.

Strike misconduct. A strike can also become unlawful if strikers engage in serious misconduct, such as violence or threats, physically preventing others from entering or leaving the workplace, or sit-down strikes, in which employees refuse to leave the workplace and refuse to work. These strikes are not protected by the NLRA.

Employer responses. Although the NLRA protects the right to strike, employers don't have to shut down for the duration of the walkout. Employers are legally allowed to hire replacement workers during the strike. Once the strike ends, the employer's obligation to bring back striking workers depends on the reasons for the strike:

- Employees who strike to protect an unfair labor practice cannot be fired or permanently replaced. When the strike is over, these employees must be reinstated to their jobs, even if means replacement workers have to be let go.

- Employees who strike for economic reasons have lesser reinstatement rights. Although they cannot be fired, they can be replaced. If the employer has hired permanent replacements, economic strikers aren't entitled to immediate reinstatement. Instead, they are entitled to be called back for job openings as they occur.

Related terms: collective bargaining agreement; National Labor Relations Act; scab; unfair labor practice.

S

successor employer

A successor employer (also called a "successor in interest") is a company that buys or merges with another company and assumes the previous employer's obligations and liabilities to its employees. Not every company that takes over or combines with another is a successor employer. There must be a certain amount of continuity and consistency between the two operations, such that it is fair and furthers public policy to hold the new employer legally responsible for the actions or obligations of the previous employer.

The tests for determining whether an employer is a successor employer depend on the law the employee is seeking to enforce. Under the Family and Medical Leave Act, for example, courts are directed to consider these eight factors:

- whether there is substantial continuity of the same business operations
- whether the new employer uses the same plant
- whether there is continuity of the work force
- the similarity of jobs and working conditions under the new and former employer
- the similarity of supervisory personnel
- the similarity in machinery, equipment, and production methods between the two companies
- the similarity in products and services offered by the two companies, and
- the ability of the former employer to provide relief to the employee.

If an employer meets these criteria, the employee's rights are the same as they would have been if the employee had been continuously employed by the same employer. For example, an employee who had worked enough hours for the previous employer to be eligible for FMLA leave would still be eligible once the successor employer took over. Similarly, an employee who went out on leave under the previous employer would be entitled to continued health insurance and reinstatement from the new employer.

Related term: Family and Medical Leave Act.

summary judgment

In a lawsuit, one party may make a motion for summary judgment before trial, asking the judge to rule, based on the undisputed facts, that the moving party must win the case, and therefore, there is no need to have a trial. If a judge grants a motion for summary judgment, the party who made the motion is entitled to have judgment entered in its favor and the case ends there. (A party may also make a motion for summary adjudication, in which it asks the judge to rule in its favor only on certain claims; if the party making the motion wins, it is entitled to judgment in its favor on those claims, and only the remaining claims proceed to trial.)

Judge and jury. In the American justice system, it is not the judge's role to decide the facts of a dispute—who's telling the truth, what really happened, and why, for example—before trial. The judge rules on procedural rules and legal matters, but the facts are decided at trial, usually by a jury. And often, the facts are in controversy. In a "he said, she said" sexual harassment case, for example, the parties tell different versions of the story. In a discrimination case, one person accuses another of discrimination—and the other almost certainly denies it. Whether someone intended to discriminate, acted with malice in giving a false reference, retaliated against someone, or unfairly denied someone a promotion are all factual questions, which typically must be decided at trial.

Summary judgment is appropriate only if there is no possible interpretation of the facts that would allow the other party to win. Employers often file summary judgment motions in employment lawsuits, but they are granted only if there are no facts on which a jury could properly find in the employee's favor. This depends both on the facts both parties rely on and on the law that applies to the case.

> EXAMPLE 1: An employee sues his employer for injuries suffered in a workplace accident. The employer files a summary judgment motion, arguing that the undisputed facts show that the employee was hurt at work, while performing job-related duties, and so must pursue his claims through the workers' compensation system, not through a lawsuit. If the employee can't come up with any facts to the contrary, the employer would be entitled to summary judgment.

EXAMPLE 2: An African American employee sues his employer for racial harassment committed by a manager. The employee claims that the manager repeatedly used racial slurs to refer to him, used "the n-word" frequently in conversation, and told him that he would never be promoted to management because of his race. The manager denies all of these allegations. Some coworkers back the employee's version of events; others support the manager. The employee filed an internal complaint about the manager, but the company never investigated. In this situation, the company's motion for summary judgment should be denied. There are too many disputed facts, and the employee could properly win if a jury decided them in his favor.

supervisor

See manager.

surveillance

Surveillance is the observation or monitoring of a person, group of people, an area, or a communication. Sometimes, surveillance is obvious, as when a video camera is mounted in plain view behind a cash register or a recording informs callers that their conversation may be monitored. Other time, surveillance is secret, as when someone takes photos, video, or recordings without the subjects' knowledge, watches someone through a one-way mirror, or takes on a false identity in order to infiltrate a group, as when a private detective is "hired" to work with—and gather evidence against—a group of employees who are suspected of selling drugs or stealing merchandise.

There ought to be a law. Some types of surveillance are outlawed by statute. For example, some states prohibit employers from using surveillance cameras in rest rooms or areas where employees change clothes. The National Labor Relations Act prohibits employers from sending spies into union meetings. And many states prohibit businesses from recording phone calls unless one or both parties to the call are aware of the monitoring.

For methods of surveillance that aren't specifically prohibited by statute, courts typically assess an employee's claim of invasion of privacy by weighing the employer's reasons for monitoring against the employee's reasonable expectations of privacy, in what's aptly called a "balancing test." The more intrusive the monitoring, the more compelling the employer's reasons for surveillance must be.

Related terms: email monitoring; National Labor Relations Act; privacy.

sweethearting

Sweethearting occurs when a retail employee gives favorite customers (friends or family members, for example) free or heavily discounted merchandise. Sweethearting might be accomplished by under-ringing sales at the register (punching in a lower price) or simply not ringing some items up. These days, when scanners register the price in many stores, it's often accomplished by not scanning every item purchased. A sweethearting scheme is typically given away by increased merchandise shrinkage and shady employee behavior at the register (such as directing the sweetheart customers to wait to have their sales rung up or taking them ahead of other customers, because the employee is waiting for an unsupervised opportunity to do the deal).

S

Taft-Hartley Act

The Taft-Hartley Act (its official title is the Labor Management Relations Act) was passed by Congress in 1947 as an amendment to the National Labor Relations Act (NLRA). This law, widely seen as an effort to rein in the power of unions, covers the following issues:

- **Unfair labor practices by unions.** As originally passed, the NLRA prohibited only unfair labor practices by employers. The Taft-Hartley Act prohibits unions from engaging in certain practices, including certain kinds of strikes (such as secondary boycotts and jurisdictional strikes) and using threats or violence to coerce workers to join the union.
- **Closed shops.** The Taft-Hartley Act outlaws closed shops, in which all employees must join the union to keep their jobs. It also allows states to become "right to work" states, which means that all employers in the state must be open shops. Employees in an open shop are free to choose whether or not to join the union. If they choose not to join, they may not be required to pay any fees to support the union's work.
- **Federal injunctions against strikes.** The law also allows the U.S. Attorney General to seek a federal injunction to suspend a strike that would otherwise imperil national health or safety (in other words, to require employees to go back to work). President Ronald Reagan utilized this provision of the law in 1981, when he got an injunction ordering the Professional Air Traffic Controllers Union to return to work; those who refused to return were fired.

Related terms: agency shop; boycott; closed shop; National Labor Relations Act; open shop; right-to-work states; strike; unfair labor practice; union security agreement.

Tameny v. Atlantic Richfield Company

See wrongful termination in violation of public policy.

tangible employment action

A tangible employment action is an actual adverse job effect that occurs as a result of harassment. Firing, failing to promote, denial of a raise or bonus, or any other decision that causes a significant change in the employee's job status all constitute tangible employment actions, as do less preferable shifts or hours or job or duty changes that result in a perceived demotion. Threats to an employee's continued employment can also be a tangible employment action.

Whether a particular decision constitutes a tangible employment action determines whether or not the employer is strictly liable for the harassment. If a supervisor's harassment results in a tangible employment action, the company is legally responsible for the supervisor's actions, even if it was unaware of the situation or did everything within its power to prevent harassment. On the other hand, if harassment doesn't result in a tangible employment action, an employer might not be liable for harassment it didn't know about, if it took reasonable steps to prevent and correct the harassment and the employee unreasonably failed to take advantage of internal company procedures to deal with the problem (for example, by filing a complaint).

Related terms: *Faragher-Ellerth* defense; harassment; sexual harassment.

telecommuting

Telecommuting (sometimes called "teleworking") is an arrangement in which the employee works offsite for one or more days a week, replacing the physical commute to work with a telecommunications link. It most often refers to working from home, but also covers employees who work from Internet cafes, telework hubs (essentially office space that can be used by the hour or day), and so on. As of 2009, approximately 2% of the U.S. employee workforce (2.8 million people, not including volunteers and the self-employed) considered their home their primary place of work.

Legal issues with telecommuting. Employees who work from home are still employees, entitled to all of the legal protections owed to employees who show up at the office every day. The possibility of legal problems with telecommuting stem from the reality that an employer doesn't control an employee's work-at-home environment or working conditions, but still must meet its legal obligations. Here are some potential trouble spots:

- **Overtime.** If the employee is nonexempt (meaning the employee is entitled to earn overtime for working more than 40 hours in a week, or more than eight hours in a day in some states), the employer must keep careful tabs on the employee's hours. It's easy for employees to put in extra time from home—and even if that time isn't authorized, the employer is legally obligated to pay for it.

- **Workplace safety.** Just because the employee's worksite is a spare bedroom or home office doesn't relieve the employer of liability for dangerous work conditions. And, a telecommuting employee who is injured or falls ill on the job may be entitled to workers' compensation. For example, an employee who suffers chronic neck pain as a result of squinting at a poorly positioned laptop screen while sitting on a folding chair in his dark garage may be eligible for workers' comp.

- **Liability to third parties.** If an employee working at home entertains clients or customers, receives deliveries, or otherwise

T

interacts with outsiders for work, the employer could be legally liable for any injuries those visitors suffer. An overnight delivery service employee who breaks an ankle after tripping on a loose front step may have a cause of action against both the work-at-home employee and the employer.

- **Discrimination.** This issue comes up in the initial decisions about who gets to work from home and how much. Telecommuting is a benefit that must be doled out without regard to race, gender, disability, and so on. A company that allows new mothers to telecommute but doesn't extend the same privilege to new fathers could be acting illegally, for instance. On the other hand, it is not discriminatory for a company to establish company-wide telecommuting policies based on legitimate business decisions—for example, by allowing telecommuting only for employees who have been with the company for at least a year and hold jobs that lend themselves to remote work, or by starting everyone who qualifies to telecommute at one day per week. In addition, the employer may require employees to meet certain performance and accountability standards before they can increase their telecommuting time.

Related terms: discrimination; overtime; workers' compensation.

temporary disability insurance

Temporary disability insurance (TDI) is a state-run benefit program that provides coverage when an employee is temporarily unable to work due to illness or injury. Currently, five states have TDI programs: California, Hawaii, New Jersey, New York, and Rhode Island. Compensation is paid by the state, and coverage is funded by employee contributions (employer contributions are also required in some states). The amounts paid, eligibility rules, and limitations vary by state.

temporary employee

A temporary employee is hired only for a limited period, such as for a company's busy season, to staff a project of limited duration, or to replace an employee who is out on leave. Temporary employees are entitled to all of the protections due employees generally. For example, they are entitled to earn at least the minimum wage, to work free from discrimination and harassment, and to work in conditions that satisfy OSHA standards.

tender-back rule

The tender-back rule is a traditional principle of contract law, which requires someone who wants to challenge the validity of a contract to first return (or tender back) whatever that person received in the deal. The tender-back requirement applies to most releases and waivers signed in connection with a severance agreement. If the employee wants to sue the employer despite the release—in other words, the employee wants to argue that the release is invalid— the employee must first give back whatever he or she received for signing the release. Most courts require the employee to return the consideration (the benefits the employee received for signing the release, typically severance pay) as soon as the employee learns that the release is invalid. Otherwise, the employee has "ratified" (confirmed) the agreement by acting as if it were valid.

Different rules apply to age discrimination cases. However, employees who file lawsuits based on the Age Discrimination in Employment Act (ADEA) are not required to tender back. In *Oubre v. Entergy Operations, Inc.*, 522 U.S. 422 (1998), the U.S. Supreme Court found that requiring age discrimination plaintiffs to tender back before filing a lawsuit would frustrate the purpose of the Older Workers Benefit Protection Act, an amendment to the ADEA that imposes strict requirements on waivers of age discrimination claims. These rules supplant the more lenient tender-back rule that applies to most contracts.

T

As a result of this decision, employees who bring ADEA cases may keep their release money *and* file a lawsuit challenging the release. This doesn't mean the employer is completely out of luck, however. If the employee wins the lawsuit (that is, the employee successfully persuades a jury that the release was invalid), the employer is entitled to reimbursement of the money the employee received for signing the release. The employer can recover either the full amount paid for the release or the full amount awarded to the employee, whichever is less.

Related terms: Age Discrimination in Employment Act; Older Workers Benefit Protection Act; release; severance agreement.

tips (tip credit, tip pooling)

Tips are gratuities: an amount a customer pays for a service, on top of the stated price, to show appreciation to the employees who provide it. Lots of service employees—from waiters, waitresses, and bartenders to gardeners, cleaning staff, movers, doormen, and counter people—receive tips from satisfied customers. In fact, some employees earn more money in tips than in wages.

Legally, tips are a form of compensation. But they are treated somewhat differently than regular wages, as a legal matter. Here are the rules.

Tip basics. The basic rule of tips is that they belong to employees, not the employer. Employees can't be required to give their tips or any part of them to the company, except as part of a valid tip pooling arrangement (see "Tip Pooling," below)—and even then, the tip pool must be divided only among certain other employees. The employer can't be part of the pool.

It's not always easy to figure out exactly how much of what a customer pays is a "tip." Take, for example, bills paid by credit card: If the employer has to pay the credit card company a processing fee, some states allow the employer to subtract a proportionate amount of the designated tip to cover its expenses. Other states—most notably, California—say that the employer has to give the employee the full tip indicated by the customer and pay the fee itself.

Mandatory service charges. What about those mandatory service charges often tacked on to bills for large tables of diners, private parties, and catered events? Under federal law and in most states, this isn't considered a tip. Even if the customer thinks that money is going to the wait staff and doesn't leave anything extra on the table, the employer can keep any money designated as a "service charge." The law generally considers this part of the contract between the patron and the establishment, not a voluntary acknowledgment of good service by an employee. Many employers give at least part of these service charges to employees, but that's the employer's choice—employees have no legal right to that money.

A couple of states have different rules, however, intended to make sure customers know what they're paying for. For example, New York's highest court recently found that companies have to give all mandatory service charges to their employees unless they make it clear to customers that the company is keeping the money. And, the state of Washington requires companies to tell customers—on menus and receipts—what portion of a mandatory service charge goes to the employee who served the customer.

Tip credits. Under federal law and in most states, employers may pay tipped employees less than the minimum wage, as long as employees receive enough in tips to make up the difference. This is called a "tip credit." The credit itself is the amount the employer doesn't have to pay, so the applicable minimum wage (federal or state) less the tip credit is the least the employer can pay per hour. If employees don't earn enough in tips during a given shift to bring their total compensation up to at least the applicable minimum wage, their employer has to pay the difference. Although most states allow employers to take a tip credit, some don't, including California, Minnesota, and Oregon.

Tip pooling. Many states allow employers to require tip pooling. All employees subject to the pool have to chip in a portion of their tips, which are then divided among a group of employees.

An employee can't be required to pay more into the pool than is customary and reasonable, and the employee must be able to keep at least the full minimum wage (that is, the employee can't be required to pay any part of the tips the employer is counting toward the minimum wage into a tip pool).

Only employees who regularly receive tips can be part of the pool. Employees can't be required to share their tips with employees who don't usually receive their own tips, like dishwashers or cooks. And no employers are allowed in the pool: Tips from a tip pool can't go to employers or, in some states, managers or supervisors.

Related terms: Fair Labor Standards Act; minimum wage.

Title VII

Title VII is the section of the federal Civil Rights Act of 1964 that prohibits employment discrimination.

What's prohibited? Title VII outlaws employment discrimination on the basis of race, color, national origin, sex, and religion in any aspect of employment, from hiring to firing (and everything in between, such as compensation, fringe benefits, job assignments, and promotions). These traits are called "protected characteristics."

Title VII also prohibits harassment based on a protected characteristic, although the term "harassment" doesn't appear in the law. In fact, harassment wasn't recognized as illegal—and a form of discrimination—until the mid-1970s, when a federal court for the first time issued an opinion finding that firing a woman for refusing to have sex with her boss was a violation of the antidiscrimination provisions of Title VII. The U.S. Supreme Court did not issue a single decision on harassment—and formally acknowledge that harassment was a form of illegal discrimination—until the 1986 decision of *Meritor Savings Bank v. Vinson*, 477 U.S. 57. In that case, the Court said, "courts have uniformly held, and we agree, that a plaintiff may establish a violation of Title VII by proving that discrimination based on sex has created a hostile or abusive working environment."

Title VII also prohibits employers from retaliating against an employee for making a complaint of harassment or discrimination (whether internally, to a government agency, or in a lawsuit), participating in an investigation or other proceeding, or otherwise opposing harassment or discrimination.

Who's covered? The following employers have to follow Title VII:

- the federal government
- state and local governments
- private employers with at least 15 employees
- private and public employment agencies
- labor organizations, and
- joint labor/management committees.

Title VII protects all applicants and current employees of a covered employer. This includes covered nationals working for a covered employer, even if the employee is not authorized to work in the United States. Such an employee still has rights under Title VII, although his or her available remedies may be limited. For example, although reinstatement is a common remedy for an employee who is fired for discriminatory reasons, a foreign national may not be reinstated to a job in the U.S. without authorization to work in this country.

Title VII also protects U.S. citizens working outside the U.S. for employers that are incorporated in the U.S., based in the U.S., or controlled by a U.S. employer.

Introducing the Equal Employment Opportunity Commission. Title VII also created the Equal Employment Opportunity Commission (EEOC), the federal agency responsible for interpreting and enforcing Title VII and other federal laws that prohibit discrimination, such as the Age Discrimination in Employment Act, the Americans with Disabilities Act, and the Genetic Information Nondiscrimination Act. The first Chairman of the EEOC was Franklin D. Roosevelt, Jr.

And a little history. President John F. Kennedy sent the Civil Rights Act to Congress in June of 1963; his brother Robert, who was the Attorney General at the time, was the first witness to testify to Congress about the proposed legislation, to the Senate Judiciary Committee. He referred to our nation's long history of race discrimination, saying, "This bill springs from the people's desire to correct a wrong that has been allowed to exist too long in our society. It comes from the basic sense of justice in the hearts of all Americans."

Within days of President Kennedy's assassination, President Lyndon Johnson made clear to Congress that the civil rights bill remained a top priority: "No memorial oration or eulogy could more eloquently honor President Kennedy's memory that the earliest passage of the civil rights bill for which he fought so long .... I urge you ... to enact a civil rights law so that we can move forward to eliminate from this Nation any trace of discrimination and oppression that is based upon race or color." After the longest debate in Congressional history, the Civil Rights Act finally passed and was signed by the president in July 1964.

Any ladies in the house? You might have noticed that the quotations above refer to race and color, but not to sex. The prohibition on sex discrimination was added to the bill in the House of Representatives, by a Congressman who apparently thought his amendment was so controversial and ridiculous that it would scuttle the legislation in its entirety. The effort was a failure, however: Sex was added as a protected characteristic, and the bill eventually passed.

Related terms: Equal Employment Opportunity Commission; harassment; protected characteristic; retaliation; sexual harassment.

tort

A tort is a civil legal claim to recover for personal injuries. Many common types of lawsuits are tort claims. Some examples include a lawsuit against a tobacco company for the harm caused by smoking, a claim against a driver resulting from injuries in a traffic accident, a lawsuit over a damaged hip from slipping in a supermarket, an action against a doctor for medical malpractice, or a suit against an auto company for injuries resulting from a faulty brake system.

What makes tort claims so attractive to plaintiffs and their lawyers are the potential damages available to the injured party. Someone who wins a tort claim can be awarded not only out-of-pocket losses (in an employment claim, these often include lost wages, lost benefits, and so on), but also damages for emotional distress and punitive damages: damages intended to punish the defendant for acting badly and deter others who might consider doing the same. Attorney fees and court costs are also available. All told, this makes a winning tort case worth significantly more than a contract claim, many types of statutory claims (such as claims under the Equal Pay Act, Fair Labor Standard Act, or Age Discrimination in Employment Act, which allow employees to recover their lost pay and benefits, an equal amount in liquidated damages if the employer acted willfully, and attorney fees and costs, but not punitive damages or damages for pain and suffering and other emotional distress), and even discrimination claims under Title VII, which caps (limits) the punitive and emotional distress damages an employee may be awarded.

Here are some of the most common tort claims that might arise from the employment relationship:

- **Defamation.** To prove defamation, the plaintiff (the employee) must show that the defendant (the employer or an individual manager) made a false statement of fact, with malice, that harmed the plaintiff. Defamation claims often come up in the context of job references, if the employee believes a false and malicious statement by a former employer led a prospective employer not to hire the employee.

- **Negligent hiring, retention, or supervision.** Under these legal theories, employers can be sued if they knew or should have known that an applicant or employee was unfit for the job yet did nothing about it. These claims often come up in the context of dangerous employees whose jobs put them in a position to cause serious harm to others. For example, a company that hires a delivery driver whose driver's license has been revoked because of repeated DUIs could face a negligent

The Anatomy of a Multimillion-Dollar Punitive Damages Award

Question: What makes a jury decide to render a huge punitive damages award? Answer: evidence that a company placed its own financial interests over the dignity or safety of others. Remember the exploding gas tank Ford Pinto lawsuits, in which the evidence showed that Ford decided saving 180 lives wasn't worth the extra $11 per car it would have cost to fix the defect? An analogy in the employment law arena is the case of *Weeks v. Baker & McKenzie*, 63 Cal.App.4th 1128 (1998).

Rena Weeks started working as a secretary to Martin Greenstein, a partner in the law firm of Baker & McKenzie, in July of 1991. Greenstein treated Weeks boorishly right from the start, reaching into her breast pocket, grabbing her rear end, asking her about "the wildest thing" she'd ever done, and pulling her shoulders back so he could see "which breast is bigger." Weeks complained almost immediately. The firm transferred her to another position, but she still felt uncomfortable. Shortly thereafter, she left the firm after her performance was questioned. Her complaint about Greenstein was never investigated.

Her economic losses were relatively small: She was a short-term employee, working as a secretary. However, when the punitive damages award was added in, the bill came to almost $4 million dollars, not including her attorney fees. Here's why: Before Weeks came along, Greenstein had been accused by at least seven other women of sexual harassment, and the firm had never done a thing about it. There was no documentation in Greenstein's file, he was never disciplined, and no investigation was ever conducted. What's worse, many of the women who complained were transferred or fired.

Perhaps the final blow to the law firm's defense was the fact that Greenstein himself was finally fired, in the midst of the lawsuit no less—but not for sexual harassment. He was fired immediately when the firm learned that he had been improperly dating documents. Apparently, this was an offense that merited firing, but propositioning and fondling a long line of female subordinates was not. When faced with the relative value the firm put on Greenstein's rainmaking skills versus the safety and job security of its female employees, the jury evidently decided to rebalance the scale.

T

hiring lawsuit from a pedestrian whom the driver injures while driving under the influence. Or, a moving company could be liable if one of its employees had a criminal record for sexual assault and attacked a customer in her home.

- **Fraud.** Fraud occurs when an employer knowingly makes a false statement or promise, with the intent of convincing an employee (or more typically, prospective employee) to act in reliance on the statement, and the employee acts accordingly and is injured as a result. Fraud claims often arise in the context of hiring, particularly when a company makes big—and false—promises to entice an employee to leave a steady job (and sometimes uproot his or her family), then fails to come through on any of its commitments.

- **Intentional infliction of emotional distress.** An employer that commits extreme and outrageous conduct against an employee, with the intent of inflicting emotional distress or with reckless disregard as to whether such distress would result, and who does actually cause such distress, can be sued under this legal theory. Conduct has to be pretty bad to qualify as extreme and outrageous: threats of violence, assault, battery, or abuse are generally required.

- **False imprisonment.** When an employer restrains an employee against his or her will, and there's an actual or implied threat that force will be used to require the employee to stay, that's false imprisonment. These claims typically come up in the context of workplace investigations or interviews regarding misconduct.

- **Wrongful termination.** Depending on state law, wrongful termination (firing an employee for reasons that are illegal or violate public policy) may be a tort claim.

Related terms: damages; defamation; false imprisonment; fraud; negligent hiring; negligent retention; wrongful discharge.

Toyota Motor Manufacturing v. Williams

See Americans with Disabilities Act Amendments Act.

trade secret

A trade secret is a formula, pattern, device, or compilation of information that is used in business, is not generally known, and gives the owner an opportunity to obtain an advantage over competitors who do not know it. Each state has its own trade secret law, designed to protect this confidential information from disclosure. Although these laws vary in the details, most states have adopted some version of the Uniform Trade Secrets Act, so there's a lot of consistency in trade secret law from one state to the next.

What's a trade secret? Generally speaking, a trade secret is information that has the following characteristics:

- **Value.** The information must have economic value to the owner because competitors don't know it. (In other words, it's valuable because it's a secret.) Information that doesn't give the owner a competitive edge is not a trade secret.
- **Secrecy.** The information must not be generally known nor easy to discover. If a competitor could learn the same information easily without much work or ingenuity, it's probably not a trade secret. Similarly, if competitors already know the information, then it's not a trade secret.
- **Effort.** The trade secret owner must take reasonable steps to keep the information as secret as possible. For example, if a company posts the information in a place where anyone, including employees, customers, and vendors, can see it, then it's probably not a trade secret. Similarly, information posted on a company's public website wouldn't qualify as a trade secret.

Some examples of trade secrets are:

- a formula for a sports drink
- survey methods used by professional pollsters
- recipes
- a new invention

- marketing strategies
- manufacturing techniques, and
- computer algorithms.

No registration required. Unlike other forms of intellectual property such as patents, copyrights, and trademarks, trade secrecy is basically a do-it-yourself form of protection. Companies don't register with the government to secure their trade secrets; the company simply keeps the information confidential. Trade secret protection lasts for as long as the secret is kept confidential. Once a trade secret is made available to the public, trade secret protection ends.

Ownership rights. A trade secret owner has the right to prevent the following people from copying, using, and/or benefiting from its trade secrets, or from disclosing them to others without permission:

- people who are automatically bound by a duty of confidentiality not to disclose or use trade secret information, including any employee who routinely comes into contact with the employer's trade secrets as part of the employee's job
- people who acquire a trade secret through improper means such as theft, industrial espionage or bribery
- people who knowingly obtain trade secrets from people who have no right to disclose them (for example, a company that hires a competitor's employee and then intentionally tries to exploit that employee's knowledge of the competitor's trade secrets)
- people who learn about a trade secret by accident or mistake, but had reason to know that the information was a protected trade secret (for example, a company that hires a competitor's employee and accidentally learns information from the employee that turns out to be a trade secret), and
- people who sign nondisclosure agreements (also known as "confidentiality agreements") promising not to disclose trade secrets without authorization from the owner.

However, a company cannot protect its trade secrets from use by people who discover the secret independently (that is, without using illegal means or violating agreements or state laws). For example, it is not a violation of trade secret law to analyze (or "reverse engineer") any lawfully obtained product and determine its trade secret.

You took my secret! If someone steals a trade secret, the trade secret owner can ask a court to issue an order (an injunction) preventing further disclosure or use of the secrets. A trade secret owner can also collect damages for any economic injury suffered as a result of the trade secret's theft and use.

To prevail in a trade secret infringement suit, a trade secret owner must show (1) that the information alleged to be confidential provides a competitive advantage and (2) the information really is maintained in secrecy. In addition, the trade secret owner must show that the information was either improperly acquired by the defendant (if the defendant is accused of making commercial use of the secret) or improperly disclosed by the defendant (if the defendant is accused of leaking the information).

Related terms: independent contractor; nondisclosure agreement.

travel time

Travel time refers to the time an employee spends in transit for work. Employees are entitled to be paid for some of their travel time, but not all of it. Employees don't have to be paid for the time they spend commuting from their homes to their worksites or back home again at the end of the day. However, employers have to pay for travel time that's part of the job. For example, if employees are required to go out on service calls, the time spent traveling to and from the customers must be paid. Also, if employees are required to take employer-provided transportation from a central location to the worksite, this time may have to be paid. And, even an employee whose job does not ordinarily involve travel may be entitled to pay for travel time if the employee is required to come to the workplace at odd hours to deal with emergency situations.

Special rules apply to employees who occasionally travel to another location for business. The rules depend on whether the trip includes an overnight stay.

All in a day's work. An employee who goes on a one-day business trip must be paid for the time the employee spends traveling. However, the employee doesn't have to be paid for the time it takes the employee to get to the airport or public transportation hub. That time is categorized as unpaid commuting time, even if it takes the employee longer than his or her ordinary commute to the worksite.

> EXAMPLE: Tom lives in Greenbrae, California, and regularly commutes to his job in San Francisco. His commute takes about ½ hour each way by bus. His employer sends him to Los Angeles for a business trip. Tom leaves home at 6 a.m. to catch an 8 a.m. flight. He spends all day with a customer in Los Angeles, then dashes off to the airport to catch his 6:30 p.m. flight, which lands at 8 p.m. Tom arrives home by 9 p.m. He is entitled to be paid for 12 hours of work; the time he spends commuting between his home and the airport is considered unpaid commuting time, even though it's quite a bit longer than his usual commute.

Overnight trips. When an employee spends more than a day out of town, the rules are different. Of course, the employee is entitled to be paid for all of the time actually spent working. However, whether the employee must be paid for time spent in transit depends on when the travel takes place.

Employees are entitled to pay for time spent traveling during the hours when they regularly work (the period of the day they regularly work), even if they ordinarily work Monday through Friday but travel on the weekend. For example, if Tom usually works 9 to 5, and leaves the office at 3 p.m. to catch a flight for an overnight business trip, he should be paid for the two remaining hours in his day, but not for the rest of the time he spends traveling that evening. But if Tom returns home on a 10 a.m. Saturday flight that takes four hours, he is entitled to be paid for all of that time. Even though he traveled on the weekend, the flight took place during his ordinary hours of weekday work.

Related terms: hours worked

T

undue hardship

Under the Americans with Disabilities Act (ADA), an employer must provide a reasonable accommodation to allow a qualified individual with a disability to do a job—unless providing the accommodation would pose an undue hardship. An accommodation creates an undue hardship if it would involve significant difficulty or expense for the employer or if it would fundamentally alter the nature or operation of the business.

Whether an accommodation creates an undue hardship depends on a number of factors, including:

- the accommodation's cost
- the size and financial resources of the business
- the business structure, and
- the effect the accommodation would have on the business.

An undue hardship may be financial, but it doesn't have to be. For example, a library clerk with a hearing disability might request that a loud bell and speaker be added to the telephone, which would enable the employee to hear and answer calls. This accommodation is probably not expensive, but it would certainly disturb library patrons and destroy the quiet atmosphere of the library. It's probably an undue hardship.

Related terms: Americans with Disabilities Act; qualified individual with a disability; reasonable accommodation.

unemployment benefits

Unemployment benefits provide financial assistance to those who are temporarily out of work through no fault of their own. Workers who lose their jobs and meet their state's eligibility requirements may collect benefits from the state's unemployment fund. Unemployment is a joint federal-state program: States set the rules on eligibility, benefit amounts, and so on, within a general framework established by federal law.

Unemployment eligibility. Employees generally must meet three requirements to qualify for benefits:

- **They must be out of work through no fault of their own, as defined by state law.** In every state, an employee who is laid off for economic reasons, lack of work, or organizational changes within the company (for example, a decision to close a plant or stop offering a particular product or service) is eligible for unemployment. Generally, employees who are fired for reasons other than serious misconduct (for example, because they are simply a poor fit or lack the skills necessary for the job) will also be eligible. Employees who are fired for serious misconduct are not eligible, but each state defines this term differently. An employee fired for theft, criminal activity, or failing a drug test is unlikely to be eligible anywhere. However, an employee who is fired for breaking a workplace rule or policy may be eligible in some states and not in others.

What If You Quit?

In every state, an employee who quits without good cause won't be eligible for benefits. The definition of "good cause" varies from state to state. Quitting to pursue another line of work or find a job that offers better opportunities to advance might make good sense, but it doesn't add up to good cause of the type that results in an unemployment check. Some states allow employees to collect unemployment only if they quit for job-related reasons, such as intolerable working conditions or a serious disability that prevents them from working. In other states, employees who quit for compelling personal reasons, such as to care for an ill family member, to escape domestic violence, or to move with a spouse, will also be eligible.

U

- **They must have worked a minimum number of hours, earned a minimum amount, or both during a set period of time called the "base period."** In almost every state, the base period is the earliest four of the last five complete calendar quarters before the employee became unemployed. The employee's hours, wages, or both during this time must meet the state's threshold amounts. The base period requirement ensures that only employees who have been working relatively recently can collect unemployment. People who have been out of work for a long time—such as stay-at-home parents who haven't worked in years—aren't eligible for unemployment benefits until they have rejoined the workforce for a period of time.

- **They must be able, available, and actively seeking work.** In other words, the employee cannot collect benefits if a mental or physical disability would prevent the employee from taking a job, or if the employee couldn't take a job if one were offered because the employee is attending sschool, handling child care full time, or otherwise is unavailable. Employees must also make an effort to look for work to be eligible.

How much do you get—and for how long? Unemployment is intended to partially replace lost wages, so the weekly benefit amount depends on the employee's prior earnings. Each state sets a maximum benefit amount. A typical formula pays half the employee's prior wages, up to a cap that's tied to the average earnings in that state. Benefits currently also include an additional $25 per week kicked in by the federal government during the economic downturn.

In a normal economic climate, most states offer unemployment benefits for up to 26 weeks, or half a year. In these anything-but-normal times, however, the total period for which a former employee can receive benefits has been lengthened several times, through two separate programs. Depending on when and where the employee began collecting unemployment, an employee who exhausts all regular benefits and all benefits available under these extension programs could collect benefits for up to 99 months (as of 2010).

Related term: base period.

U

unfair labor practice

Unfair labor practices are actions taken by employers or unions that are illegal under the National Labor Relations Act (NLRA) and other labor laws.

Unfair employer practices. Employers are prohibited from taking actions tending to inhibit employees' right to organize, such as refusing to bargain collectively with a union, interfering with an employee's right to organize or engage in protected concerted activities, dominating or providing illegal assistance to a union, or discriminating or retaliating against union supporters.

Unfair union practices. Unions are prohibited from such things as coercing employees to support or not support a union, refusing to engage in good faith collective bargaining, engaging in strikes that have an illegal purpose, or restraining or coercing an employer in its choice of bargaining representative.

Related terms: collective bargaining; National Labor Relations Act; strike.

unforeseeable leave

Under the Family and Medical Leave Act (FMLA), unforeseeable leave is time off that's, well, unforeseeable. For example, an employee who is in a car accident, goes into premature labor, or has a heart attack isn't able to plan ahead to take time off: The employee needs time off immediately, without advance notice or warning.

Generally, employees are required to provide at least 30 days' notice of the need to take FMLA leave. However, the law recognizes that this isn't always possible. So, for unforeseeable leave, employees are required only to give notice as soon as is practicable, which typically means the same business day or the next business day after the employee learns of the need for leave. If the employee is unable to give notice (for example, because the employee is undergoing emergency surgery or has fallen seriously ill), the employee's family member or another spokesperson may give notice.

Related terms: Family and Medical Leave Act; foreseeable leave; serious health condition.

uniforms

Many different types of employers require employees to wear uniforms. Restaurants, delivery companies, car dealerships, big-box stores, gas stations, fitness centers, and many more companies require employees to wear clothing that clearly identifies their affiliation with the company. Some employers dictate the full outfit while others take more of a "dress code" approach (for example, that waiters must wear dark pants and a white dress shirt) or require only certain identifying clothing, such as a vest, polo shirt, or jacket with the company's logo.

For the most part, employers are free to require employees to dress in a particular way, including wearing a uniform, as long as those requirements aren't discriminatory or otherwise illegal. Under California law, for example, an employer may not prohibit female employees from wearing pants. So, a uniform requirement that required dresses or skirts for women would be illegal in the Golden State. A uniform that is difficult for an employee with a disability to put on and take off may have to be modified for that employee's use (for example, by replacing buttons with Velcro closures). (For more on these issues, see: dress codes.)

Who pays for the uniform? Federal law allows employers to deduct the cost of supplying and maintaining a uniform (for example, having it cleaned and pressed) from an employee's paycheck, as long as the employee's wages after the deduction don't fall below the minimum wage. (The federal minimum wage is $7.25.) If an employee earns the minimum wage, the employer may not require the employee to pay for a uniform, through payroll deductions or otherwise.

Some state laws are stricter. For example, some states—such as New Jersey—prohibit employers from charging employees or requiring employees to buy a uniform that has a company logo or

U

can't be used as street wear. And, a number of states don't allow employers to charge employees for uniforms at all. In these states, an employer that wants to require a uniform must supply it to employees free.

Related term: minimum wage.

Uniformed Services Employment and Reemployment Rights Act

Since 1940, federal law has guaranteed certain employment rights to employees who serve in the military. In 1994, following the Persian Gulf War, Congress substantially revised this law, now called the Uniformed Services Employment and Reemployment Rights Act (USERRA). USERRA prohibits discrimination against employees or applicants who are members of the uniformed services; requires employers to reinstate employees to the position they would have held if not for serving, with benefits, upon their return from up to five years of leave for military service; and protects employees who have returned from military service from being fired, except for cause, for up to a year.

Who is covered by USERRA? USERRA covers all employers of all sizes, public and private. It protects all employees and applicants who serve or have served in the uniformed services. However, the employee's entitlement to the reinstatement and job security provisions of USERRA is cut off if the employee:

- is separated from the service under other than honorable conditions (such as a dishonorable discharge or bad conduct discharge), or
- in the case of a commissioned officer, is dropped from the military rolls because of an absence without authority of more than three months or imprisonment by a civilian court, is dismissed from the uniformed service in a court martial, or is dismissed by order of the president in time of war.

Discrimination provisions. Employers may not discriminate against members of the uniformed services or retaliate against workers who

U

exercise their USERRA rights. This includes, for example, firing an employee for taking time off for National Guard training exercises, demoting an employee who is called to active duty, or refusing to hire those who have served in the military.

Reinstatement. Employers must reinstate employees when they return from up to five years of leave for service in the uniformed services. (The five-year period can be extended in some circumstances.) To be protected, the employee must give the employer notice, before taking leave, that the time off is for military service, and must report back or apply for reinstatement within specified time limits that depend on the length of the employee's service. The employee must be reinstated to the "escalator position": the position the employee would have held if he or she had been continuously employed rather than taking leave. If the employee isn't qualified for the escalator position, the employer must make reasonable efforts to help the employee get qualified.

Benefits. While the employee is on leave, the employer must continue to provide health insurance for up to two years. If the employee is absent for 30 days or less, the employer may not require the employee to pay more than the usual employee share (if any) for such coverage. If the employee is absent for more than 30 days, the employer may require the employee to pay up to 102% of the full premium for such coverage. For other benefits, the employer must follow the same practice as for workers in similar positions who take a leave of absence for other reasons.

Once the employee returns, the employer must reinstate his or her health insurance immediately (if it lapsed), generally without an exclusion or waiting period. Employees are entitled to the seniority, and any rights and benefits based on seniority, that they would have had if they had been continuously employed. A reinstated worker's time on leave must be treated as service with the employer for purposes of pension plans. USERRA provides detailed rules on other treatment of pension plans, including how employees may make up contributions.

Job security. Once an employee returns to work after military leave, he or she may not be fired, except for cause, for one year if the worker served for more than 180 days, or for 180 days if the worker served for a shorter period (but at least 31 days). In this context, "cause" means a legitimate, nondiscriminatory reason for firing or laying off the employee. USERRA cases recognize two types of cause: employee misconduct (such as theft) and legitimate business reasons unrelated to the employee's military service (such as layoffs necessitated by business declines). An employer who fires an employee during the protected period of job security must show that the discharge was reasonable and that the employee had notice that his or her conduct was cause for discharge.

Related terms: escalator position; good cause; military leave.

union

A union is a group of workers who join together to collectively bargain with their employer to secure better wages, benefits, working conditions, job security, and so on.

Related terms: bargaining unit; collective bargaining; National Labor Relations Act.

union security agreement

A union security agreement is a contract between an employer and a union requiring workers to make certain payments (called "agency fees") to the union as a condition of getting or keeping a job. Although it is illegal to require an employee to join a union, workers may be required to instead pay agency fees if such an agreement is in place. Union security agreements are prohibited in right-to-work states

Related terms: agency shop; closed shop; open shop; right-to-work laws.

U

USERRA

See Uniformed Services Employment and Reemployment Rights Act.

U

vacation

Vacation is paid time off work to be spent as the employee pleases. No law requires employers to give their workers paid vacation days, but most companies do: More than three-quarters of all private industry employers provide paid vacation, at least for some employees, according to 2010 figures from the federal Bureau of Labor Statistics.

Because employers don't have to offer vacation, those that do have a lot of legal leeway in setting the rules on who is eligible, how vacation time accrues, when vacation may be used, and so on. Employers can provide only a few paid days off a year or a couple of months' worth. Employers are also free to offer vacation to some employees and not to others. For example, they are legally allowed to reserve paid vacation only for full-time employees. And many do: The Bureau of Labor Statistics reports that, while 91% of full-time employees in private industry receive some paid vacation, only 37% of part-time employees do. Employers may not discriminate illegally in determining who gets vacation—that is, they may not base paid vacation decisions on protected characteristics such as race, religion, or disability.

Companies are also free to adopt schedules for vacation accrual. For example, company policy might provide that an employee earns one vacation day per month or a certain number of hours per pay period. Some companies impose a waiting period before new employees may begin accruing vacation time. And some companies allow employees to accrue more vacation days when they have more tenure at the company.

It is also legal for companies to cap how much vacation time employees can accrue, and many companies take advantage of this right to encourage employees to use their vacation time regularly.

Once employees reach the limit set by the cap, they can't earn any more vacation time until they use some and bring themselves back down below the cap.

In some states, it is illegal for employers to impose "use it or lose it" policies, by which employees must forfeit vacation time they have already accrued unless they take it by a certain time. In these states, vacation time is considered a form of compensation, which must be cashed out when the employee quits or is fired. A policy that takes vacation time away is therefore seen as illegally failing to pay employees compensation that they have already earned. Although the difference may seem fairly technical, an accrual cap is legal in these states because it prohibits the employee from earning vacation time in the first place, rather than taking away vacation time after the employee has earned it.

Vail letter

The Vail letter was a staff opinion letter, issued in 1999 by the Federal Trade Commission, that threw the procedures for workplace investigations into turmoil for a few years. In the Vail letter (so-called because it was a response to a question from a lawyer named Judi Vail), the FTC said that a sexual harassment investigation conducted by an outside party (such as a law firm or workplace investigation specialist) was subject to the Fair Credit Reporting Act (FCRA). Among other things, this meant that the employer had to tell the employee about the investigation and get the employee's written consent to the investigation in advance, and give a copy of the investigation report to the employee—and wait for a reasonable period—before taking any adverse action based on its findings.

FACTA to the rescue. The Vail letter left employers unsure how to proceed if, for example, the accused employee refused to "consent" to the investigation, or the investigation report included confidential information that the accused employee should not be privy to. Congress resolved the situation in 2003 when it passed the Fair and Accurate Credit Transactions Act (FACTA). Among many other things, FACTA created special rules that apply to workplace investigations. Under these rules, an employer that hires an outsider to investigate no longer has to inform the accused employee or get his or her consent. If the employer decides to take action against the employee as a result of the investigation, it has to provide only a summary of the report, and need not identify the employees who were interviewed as part of the investigation.

Related terms: consumer report; investigative consumer report; Fair Credit Reporting Act; investigation.

volunteer

A volunteer is someone who donates his or her time to an organization, working without pay. Volunteering is perfectly legal—unless it's a subterfuge an employer uses to avoid having to pay people who should actually be classified as employees. Under the Fair Labor Standards Act (FLSA), those who work for for-profit private employers may not be classified as volunteers—and not paid. However, volunteers may donate their time to public employers (such as schools, libraries, prisons, and animal shelters) and to nonprofits.

Who Volunteers—and What They Do

According to 2009 data from the Bureau of Labor Statistics, more than 63 million people—26.8% of the population—did volunteer work for at least one organization in the prior year. Women were more likely to volunteer than men, and volunteering was most likely among those aged 35 to 54. Not surprisingly, parents of minor children were significantly more likely to volunteer than their childless peers. And those with a paying job are more likely to volunteer than the unemployed.

The median time spent volunteering in a year was about 50 hours. The most common way people spent these hours were fundraising or selling items to raise money (11.3%); collecting, preparing, distributing, or serving food (10.3%); and tutoring or teaching (9.4%).

V

Related term: Fair Labor Standards Act.

voting leave

Voting leave is time an employee takes off work to cast a ballot. Almost every state prohibits employers from disciplining or firing an employee who takes time off work to vote. In many states, an employer must grant a certain number of hours of voting leave, but only if the employee is unable, because of the employee's work schedule or the distance the employee must travel to cast a ballot, to vote outside of work hours. Most of these states require employers to pay for this time.

V

wage

Wages refer generally to the compensation an employee receives in exchange for work. Whether the employee is paid an hourly rate, a salary, a piece rate, commissions, tips, or some combination, the employee's earnings are referred to as wages. Overtime also qualifies as wages. In some states, accrued vacation hours are also considered wages.

Related terms: hour worked; living wage laws; minimum wage; overtime; salary basis; tips.

wage garnishment

A wage garnishment is a court order requiring an employer to withhold a set amount of an employee's pay and send it to the person or institution named in the order. Wage garnishments are issued when an employee has an outstanding debt for child support, student loans, or unpaid taxes, or when an employee has lost a court judgment and has been ordered to pay damages. The rules for how garnishments work and how much money can be withheld depend on the reason for the garnishment.

Wage garnishments for court judgments. If an employee loses a lawsuit and is ordered to pay damages, the person or entity that won the lawsuit can garnish the employee's wages by providing a copy of the court order to the local sheriff or marshal, who will send it to the employer. The employer must then notify the employee of the garnishment, begin withholding part of the employee's wages, send the garnished money to the creditor, and give the employee information on how to protest the garnishment.

Unless an employee owes child support, back taxes, or student loans, creditors must get a court order before they can garnish an employee's wages. If an employee has defaulted on a loan, stopped paying a credit card bill, or run up huge medical bills, those creditors can't just start garnishing the employee's wages. They must first file and win a lawsuit against the employee and get a court order requiring the employee to pay the debt.

For court judgments, the maximum amount that can be garnished is 25% of the employee's disposable earnings (what's left after mandatory deductions) or the amount by which the employee's wages exceed 30 times the minimum wage, whichever is lower. Some states set a lower percentage limit.

An employee may not be fired or otherwise retaliated against because of a wage garnishment to pay one debt. Less protection is available if more garnishments are in play. Under federal law, an employee whose wages have been garnished by more than one creditor is not protected from retaliation, nor is an employee who is subject to more than one garnishment by the same creditor. Some states offer more protection.

To protest a wage garnishment based on a court judgment, the employee must file papers with the court to get a hearing date. At the hearing, the employee must present evidence that the garnishment is leaving the employee less than he or she needs to pay living expenses. The judge can terminate the garnishment or leave it in place.

Wage garnishments for child support and alimony. Since 1988, all child support orders include an automatic wage withholding order. (If child support and alimony are combined into one family support payment, the wage withholding order applies to the whole amount owed; however, orders involving only alimony don't result in automatic wage withholding.) Once the court issues a child support order, the court or the child's other parent sends a copy of the order to the debtor's employer, who will withhold the ordered amount from the employee's paycheck and send it to the other parent. If the employee is required to maintain health insurance coverage for the child, the payment for that will be deducted as well.

More of an employee's paycheck can be taken to pay child support. Up to 50% of the employee's disposable earnings may be garnished to pay child support if the employee is currently supporting a spouse or a child who isn't the subject of the order. If the employee isn't supporting a spouse or child, up to 60% may be taken. An employee may not be fired, disciplined, or otherwise retaliated against because of a wage withholding order to pay child support.

Wage garnishments for student loans. In 2006, Congress passed a law that allows the U.S. Department of Education (or any agency trying to collect a student loan on its behalf) to garnish up to 15% of an employee's pay if the employee is in default on a student loan. No lawsuit or court order is required for this type of garnishment.

At least 30 days before the garnishment is set to begin, the employee must be notified in writing of:

- the amount of the debt
- how to get a copy of records relating to the loan
- how to enter into a voluntary repayment schedule, and
- how to request a hearing on the proposed garnishment.

The law specifies only one basis for objecting to the garnishment: that the employee returned to work within the past 12 months after being fired or laid off.

Wage garnishments for back taxes. The IRS can take a huge chunk of an employee's wages, and it doesn't have to get a court order first. The amount the employee gets to keep depends on how many dependents the employee has and the employee's standard deduction amount. The employer will pay the employee a fairly low minimum amount each week and give the rest to the IRS.

State and local tax agencies also have the right to take employee wages. In many states, however, the law limits how much the taxing authority can take.

W

waiver

See release.

Wards Cove v. Atonio

See business necessity.

WARN Act

See Worker Adjustment and Retraining Notification Act.

weight discrimination

Weight discrimination (sometimes also referred to as size discrimination) occurs when someone is treated differently because of his or her weight. No federal law prohibits weight discrimination in employment per se, and Michigan is currently the only state that explicitly prohibits weight discrimination; a handful of local governments (including San Francisco and the District of Columbia) protect employees from weight discrimination.

Hooters: Where the Largest Uniform Is a "Small"

In 2010, Cassandra Marie Smith sued Hooters for weight discrimination. Because she worked in Michigan, Smith was able to make an explicit weight discrimination claim rather than proceeding under a disability discrimination law. And a good thing for her, as no court is going to diagnose morbid obesity in someone who is 5'8" and tipped the scales at 132.5 pounds on the sad day when she was put on "weight probation" by the notorious restaurant chain. According to her complaint, she was advised to join a gym so she could fit into the company's "extra small" uniform; apparently, the uniforms only come in small, extra small, and extra, extra small. To add insult to injury, Hooters told coworkers and customers about Smith's weight probation status.

Disability protections. In places where no weight discrimination law applies, some employees and applicants bring claims of disability discrimination, arguing that they were treated differently due to the disability of obesity (or other weight-related health problems), or that their employer incorrectly perceived them as having a disability because of their weight.

Weingarten rights

Weingarten rights refer to a union member's right to have union representation at any interview or meeting that could lead to disciplinary action. The name comes from the Supreme Court case of *National Labor Relations Board v. Weingarten*, 420 U.S. 251 (1975).

The case of the four-piece bucket. In the *Weingarten* case, an employee at a lunch counter (Leura Collins) was suspected of stealing, and was called into an interview with the store manager and a loss prevention specialist. The company believed Collins had taken a large box of chicken but paid only for a small box. Collins said that she took only four pieces of chicken—the amount customers receive in a small box—but had to put it in a large box because the store was out of small boxes. Her story checked out, and Collins was cleared.

During the interview, Collins asked several times for her union rep or shop steward, but the company wouldn't grant her request. Although management asked Collins to keep the interview to herself, Collins told her shop steward about it and the union filed an unfair labor practice charge against the company.

The Supreme Court found that an employee who reasonably believes that an investigatory interview could lead to discipline is entitled to union representation. The employee must request such representation in the first instance. Once the request is made, the employer may allow the rep and continue the interview, or refuse the rep and discontinue the interview, carrying on its investigation

W

through other means. The employer has no duty to bargain with the union rep; the rep is present only to assist the employee, and the employer is free to insist that the employee provide his or her own version of events.

Weingarten rights in the nonunion workplace. For a few years, employees who were not in a union were also entitled to ask that a coworker be present at investigatory interviews. In 2000, the NLRB issued a decision extending *Weingarten* rights to all employees, whether or not they were in a union. (*In re E.I. Dupont,* 289 NLRB Case No. 187.) Four years later, the NLRB reversed itself, stating that this right applied only to union members. (*In re IBM Corporation*, 341 NLRB Case No. 148.)

whistleblower

A whistleblower is someone who reports a company's crimes or misconduct, usually to government officials or other regulators outside of the company. Sometimes, whistleblowing refers to any publicizing of a company's wrongdoing (for example, in the media or online—sometimes referred to as "whistleblogging").

An employee who blows the whistle may be protected from reprisals by a number of laws. For example, an employee who files a complaint of harassment, discrimination, unsafe working conditions, or wage and hour violations with a government agency is protected from discipline or discharge by laws that prohibit retaliation. Many industrial safety and corporate malfeasance laws include explicit whistleblower protections, which provide that employees who come forward to report, for example, unsafe business practices, improper use of hazardous substances, or accounting fraud, may not be punished by their employers.

Related term: retaliation.

Blowing the Whistle on YouTube

Michael De Kort, an engineer at Lockheed Martin, was concerned about design flaws in work the company was doing to refurbish patrol boats for the Coast Guard. The flaws included blind spots in the boats' surveillance systems, security problems with the communications systems, and possible equipment malfunction in cold weather.

De Kort spoke to his supervisors, government investigators, and even members of Congress. He felt that his concerns weren't being taken seriously, so he posted a video of himself talking about them on YouTube. Six months later, a government report confirmed some of his complaints. And, in January 2008, he received an award from the Society for Social Implications of Technology, for "high ethical standards in protecting or promoting the interests and safety of the public." Lockheed apparently didn't share the love for De Kort, however: He was fired shortly after posting the video, for what the company said were cost-cutting reasons.

white-collar employee

White-collar employee is a catchall phrase for anyone who works in an office setting. Under the Fair Labor Standards Act, administrative, managerial, and professional employees—categories of employees who are not entitled to earn overtime—are sometimes lumped together and referred to as white-collar employees. The term most likely comes from the white-collared dress shirts traditionally required of male office workers.

Related terms: administrative employee; Fair Labor Standards Act; manager; overtime; professional employee.

W

work for hire

A work for hire is a type of creative work that has special status under copyright law. When an employee produces a creative work within the scope of employment, the copyright to that work belongs to the employer. When a company hires an independent contractor to produce a creative work, the rules are different. The independent contractor will own the copyright unless (1) the contractor assigns the copyright to the hiring firm, or (2) the work qualifies as a work for hire and the contractor and hiring firm have signed a written agreement to that effect, which ensures that the hiring firm owns the copyright.

Work-for-hire categories. Only nine types of creative work legally qualify as works for hire:

- a contribution to a collective work, such as a magazine or literary anthology
- a part of an audiovisual work
- a translation
- a supplementary work, such as an appendix, bibliography, or chart
- a compilation
- an instructional text
- a test
- answer material for a test, and
- an atlas.

Related term: independent contractor.

Worker Adjustment and Retraining Notification Act

The Worker Adjustment and Retraining Notification Act (WARN) requires certain larger employers to give some advance notice of an impending plant closing or mass layoff that will result in job loss for a specified number or percentage of employees. The law is intended to help ease the transition for workers who lose their jobs in these circumstances. WARN requires employers to give notice not only to employees and unions that will be affected by the job cuts, but also to state government agencies that provide assistance to dislocated workers.

Who has to follow WARN? Public employers aren't covered by WARN, and only large private employers must comply. The law applies to private employers with:

- 100 or more full-time employees, or
- 100 or more full-time and part-time employees who work a combined total of at least 4,000 per week.

Employees who are on leave or temporary layoff count towards the total, if they have a reasonable expectation of returning to work. Independent contractors don't count.

What are mass layoffs and plant closings? Not every large reduction-in-force qualifies as a mass layoff under WARN, and not every facility shutdown or relocation counts as a plant closing. The law defines these terms as follows:

- A **mass layoff** is a reduction in force that isn't the result of a plant closing and results in an employment loss (job loss or reduction in hours by more than half) for (1) 500 or more full-time employees, or (2) 50 to 499 full-time employees, if the number of employees laid off makes up at least one-third of the employer's active workforce. Only mass layoffs that take place at a single site of employment—one geographical location of an employer's operations, such as a building, suite of offices, or campus or industrial park—can be counted toward the total.
- A **plant closing** is the permanent or temporary shutdown of a single site of employment, or one or more facilities or operating units within it, which results in employment loss for 50 or more full-time employees.

Timing rules. Generally, a plant closing or mass layoff must take place within a 30-day period for WARN to apply. However, layoffs or plant closing that occur in stages over a 90-day period are also covered. For example, an employer with 150 employees would not have to comply with WARN if it laid off 20 workers in a 30-day

W

period, because this would not meet the numerical requirements set forth above. However, if the same employer laid off 20 more workers in each of the next two months, these combined layoffs would total more than one-third of its workforce—and therefore, would count as a mass layoff under WARN. The purpose of this rule is to prevent employers from getting around WARN's requirements by conducting a series of smaller layoffs.

Required notice. For layoffs covered by WARN, the employer must give written notice of the layoff, 60 days in advance, to each affected employee (except union members), the bargaining representatives of all affected employees who are union members, the state's dislocated worker unit, and the local government. If an employer doesn't give the required amount of notice and no exception applies (see below), employees can sue for compensation for each day of the violation (up to 60).

Exceptions. Employers don't have to provide any advance notice of a mass layoff or plant closing if it results from a strike or an employer lockout, or if it resulted from the closure of a temporary facility or the end of a temporary project, if the employees knew when they were hired that their employment was limited to the duration of the temporary project or facility.

Employers may comply with WARN by giving as much notice as possible under the circumstances—even if the employer can't give 60 days' notice—in these situations:

- **Natural disasters.** An employer may give less than 60 days' notice if the layoff or closing results from an earthquake, hurricane, or other natural disaster.
- **Unforeseeable business circumstances.** If the closure or layoff is caused by business circumstances that weren't reasonably foreseeable when the employer should have given 60 days' notice, a shorter notice period is allowed.
- **Faltering company.** If a company is struggling financially when it should have given 60 days' notice of a plant closing (only; this exception doesn't apply to mass layoffs), it can give a shorter period of notice. However, the company must show

that it was actively seeking business or money that would have allowed it to avoid or postpone the closing, and that it reasonably believed, in good faith, that giving 60 days' notice would have precluded it from obtaining the necessary business or money.

Consider Yourself WARNed, FOREWARNed, and ALERTed

As the economic downturn results in increasing numbers of jobs lost, Congress has looked at amending the WARN Act to protect more workers (thus far, none of these amendments has passed). Apparently, the chance to come up with more acronyms was also quite appealing. For example, the Alert Laid-off Employees in Reasonable Time (ALERT) Act would expand the definition of a mass layoff to include combined job losses at more than one employment site, and would increase the damages available to employees. The Federal Oversight, Reform and Enforcement of the WARN Act (FOREWARN Act) would apply to employers with at least 75 employees (down from the current minimum of 100), lower the number of employees who must lose their jobs to qualify as a mass layoff or plant closing, and increase the amount of notice required from 60 to 90 days, among other things.

Related terms: layoff; mass layoff; plant closing.

workers' compensation

Workers' compensation (often shortened to "workers' comp") is a state-mandated insurance program that provides compensation to employees who suffer job-related injuries and illnesses. While the federal government administers a workers' comp program for federal and certain other types of employees, each state has its own laws and programs for workers' compensation.

In general, an employee with a work-related illness or injury can get workers' compensation benefits regardless of who was at

W

fault—the employee, the employer, a coworker, a customer, or some other third party. The benefits typically include payment for medical expenses, some wage replacement (about two-thirds of the employee's usual salary), and perhaps some vocational rehabilitation benefits. An employee who is permanently unable to do his or her regular job, or to work at all, may also be eligible for a lump-sum compensation payment. In exchange for these guaranteed benefits, employees usually do not have the right to sue the employer in court for damages for those injuries. (This arrangement, by which employees have no right to sue for injuries covered by workers' comp, is sometimes referred to as the "compensation bargain.")

Only work-related injuries and illnesses are covered by workers' comp. Usually, if an employee is injured or becomes ill as a result of something the employee was doing for the employer, workers' comp applies. This includes accidents that occur during work-related travel (such as a business trip) or at company-sponsored events (like the softball game at the annual picnic). On the other hand, an injury that takes place off-site during nonwork hours is probably not covered, unless the employee was working at the time. For example, if an employee is asked to drop off supplies on the way home, and is injured while performing the errand, the injury is probably covered by workers' comp.

workplace violence

Although workplace violence—assaults, homicides, and other intentionally harmful incidents at work—may not be as common as the news might lead us to believe, it is a major problem in the United States. Government studies estimate that there are about two million assaults and threats of violence made against workers each year. According to the Workplace Violence Research Institute, workplace violence costs businesses more than $36 billion each year.

Outsider violence. The great majority of violent workplace incidents are perpetrated by outsiders—strangers intending to commit a crime—rather than employees. According to the federal

W

Bureau of Labor Statistics, for example, most workplace homicides are committed by robbers trying to steal from the business. Motives for stranger violence run the gamut from robbery to revenge to a misguided sense of honor or principle. For example:

- In 1994, Paul Hill killed a doctor and one of the doctor's escorts as they arrived at the Pensacola Ladies Clinic. Hill claimed that he killed the doctor to prevent him from performing abortions.
- In 1993, Gian Luigi Ferri, a former client of the law firm Pettit & Martin, entered the firm's offices at 101 California Street in San Francisco. Ferri killed eight people and wounded six more before taking his own life.
- In 2000, seven workers at a Wendy's restaurant in Flushing, Queens, were shot and five of them killed during a robbery. One of the men convicted in the shooting was a former employee.

High-Risk Occupations

Government statistics certify what most of us might guess: Workers who deal with the public are more likely to fall victim to outsider violence. Those at particularly high risk include workers who exchange money with the public, deliver goods or services, work alone or in small numbers during the late evening/early morning hours, or work in jobs that require extensive public contact. Certain professions—such as health care, security (including police officers), and retail—are targeted more frequently than others.

Domestic violence. According to the American Institute on Domestic Violence, more than 18,000 acts of violence are committed by intimate partners and spouses (current and former) every year against women in the workplace. And sometimes, these incidents go beyond the intended victim to harm other employees as well. For more information, see: domestic violence leave.

W

Violence by employees. Sometimes, employees and former employees are the perpetrators of workplace violence. These acts may be related to frustrations and anger over work decisions (such as layoffs, cuts in benefits, perceived harassment, and so on) or may be the result of other pressures. For example:

- After the receptionist at the Housing Authority in Richmond, California, was fired, he pulled out a gun and opened fire on his coworkers. He was fired after a coworker reported that the receptionist had said he felt like committing a mass murder. The incident occurred after the receptionist was fired, but was allowed to return to his desk—where he kept his gun—on the way out the door.

- Moments after being told he would have to resign or be fired for theft, Omar Thornton opened fire at a beer distributor in Connecticut, killing eight and injuring two; Thornton called 9-1-1 and said that he had been harassed and treated differently because of his race.

- Timothy Hendron shot several coworkers and took his own life at ABB Group in St. Louis; he was part of a group of employees that were suing the company and its trustee for charging excessive fees in connection with their retirement benefits.

- Michael McDermott, a software developer, killed seven coworkers with an assault rifle at Edgewater Technology in Wakefield, Massachusetts; McDermott was having financial problems, he had just been hit with a wage garnishment, and his car was repossessed from the company parking lot on the day of the shootings.

Employer liability for violence. Generally, employers are legally liable for workplace violence only if they failed to take reasonable steps to prevent or discourage it. Courts have allowed victims of workplace violence (and their survivors) to recover under several different theories:

- **Occupational Safety and Health Act (OSH Act) violations.** The OSH Act requires employers to provide employees with a workplace free of recognized hazards that are causing or likely to cause serious harm or death. Although this requirement has traditionally applied primarily to hazards created by machinery, poor ventilation, dangerous chemicals, and so on, OSHA has also said that workplace violence may constitute a hazard. This means that employers who don't take reasonable steps to prevent or abate a recognized violence hazard can be punished by OSHA.

- **Harassment laws.** In some situations, workplace violence and threats may constitute illegal harassment or discrimination. For example, an employee who touches a coworker against her will or threatens to harm her if she dates someone else may be guilty of both sexual harassment and violence. Or, an employee who gets in a fistfight with another worker after calling him racist names could be committing both racial harassment and violence.

- **Negligent hiring, retention, and supervision.** Someone who is injured by an employee may be able to sue the employer if it failed to take reasonable care in selecting and retaining its workers. Under the legal theories of negligent hiring, retention, and supervision, employers can be sued if they knew or should have known that an applicant or employee was unfit for the job yet did nothing about it. These lawsuits are not allowed in every state, but the clear trend is to allow injured parties to sue employers for hiring or keeping on a dangerous worker.

- **Workers' compensation claims.** Some incidents of workplace violence may be covered by workers' compensation. This means that the employee victims may not sue their employer for their injuries (although they may be able to sue the person who attacked them), but they can bring a claim for workers' compensation. If, however, the violence is committed by a supervisor, manager, or officer of the company, or if the company has ignored threats to an employee or retained an employee who has already acted violently, the incident

W

probably won't be covered by workers' compensation. This means that the victim can't file a claim, but can sue the employer directly under one of the theories discussed above.

Related terms: discrimination; domestic violence leave; harassment; negligent hiring; negligent retention; Occupational Safety and Health Act; restraining order (for employer); workers' compensation.

wrongful discharge

Wrongful discharge (sometimes called "wrongful termination") is a general term that refers to any illegal firing. The firing may be illegal because it violates antidiscrimination laws, because the employee had an employment contract requiring good cause for termination, because the employee was fired for exercising a legal right (such as taking leave under the Family and Medical Leave Act or complaining of unsafe working conditions), or because the firing otherwise violated federal or state law. For example, the Uniformed Services Employment and Reemployment Rights Act prohibits employers from firing employees for up to one year after they return from military service, except for cause. If an employer fires such an employee without cause, that would be wrongful discharge. Similarly, Montana prohibits employers from firing employees at will once the employee has completed an initial probationary period or worked for the employer for six months. An employer that fires a long-term employee without good cause has committed wrongful discharge under this statutory provision.

Related terms: at-will employment; discrimination; employment contract; good cause; harassment; retaliation.

wrongful termination in violation of public policy

An employer violates public policy when it fires an employee for reasons most people would find morally or ethically wrong. Typically, these claims allege that the employee was fired for:

- exercising a legal right, such as voting, joining a union, filing a workers' comp claim, or refusing to take a lie detector test
- refusing to do something illegal, such as submit false corporate tax returns, defraud customers or service providers, sell faulty equipment, or lie on government reports, or
- reporting illegal conduct or wrongdoing by filing a complaint with a government agency (whistleblowing) or, in some states, reporting misconduct of public concern to higher management within the company—for example, complaining to the company's CEO that employees are lying to government officials or endangering the public by selling products that don't meet applicable safety standards.

The Origins of the *Tameny* Claim

In California, claims of wrongful termination in violation of public policy are referred to as "*Tameny*" claims, after the 1980 California Supreme Court case that recognized an employee's right to sue under this theory—and to collect tort damages (including punitive damages and damages for pain and suffering) if victorious. In the *Tameny* case, Gordon Tameny claimed that he had been fired after 15 years because he refused to participate in an illegal scheme to fix gasoline prices among franchisees that were supposed to be independent service stations. The Court found that Tameny could proceed with his lawsuit: "We hold that an employer's authority over its employee does not include the right to demand that the employee commit a criminal act to further its interests, and an employer may not coerce compliance with such unlawful directions by discharging an employee who refuses to follow such an order. An employer engaging in such conduct violates a basic duty imposed by law upon all employers, and thus an employee who has suffered damages as a result of such discharge may maintain a tort action for wrongful discharge against the employer."

Tameny v. Atlantic Richfield Co., 27 Cal.3d 167 (1980).

W

Not every state allows employees to sue for public policy violations. Those that do have different rules about what constitutes a public policy. The federal government and some states have laws explicitly prohibiting employers from firing employees for doing certain things, such as reporting a health and safety violation or taking medical leave. Some states allow employees to file public policy lawsuits even when no statute spells out exactly what the employer can and cannot do.

Related terms: retaliation; tort; whistleblowing.

W

yellow-dog contract

A yellow-dog contract was a contract between an employer and an employee in which the employee agreed, as a condition of employment, not to join a union, or to resign from a union if the employee was already a member. These contracts were outlawed by the National Labor Relations Act in 1935, which recognized an employee's right to join a union, and made it an unfair labor practice for employers to interfere with this right.

Related term: National Labor Relations Act.

zero-tolerance policy

A zero-tolerance policy is an employment policy that says employees will be fired for any violation of the policy; in other words, the company will not tolerate a single step across the bright line established by the policy. Zero-tolerance language is typically reserved for serious misconduct that the company wants to highlight as particularly unacceptable. For example, many companies have zero-tolerance policies on workplace violence or use of illegal drugs at work.

Related terms: drug testing; progressive discipline; workplace violence.

1. Go to Nolo.com/newsletters to sign up for free newsletters and discounts on Nolo products.

   - **Nolo Briefs.** Our monthly email newsletter with great deals and free information.

   - **Nolo's Special Offer.** A monthly newsletter with the biggest Nolo discounts around.

   - **BizBriefs.** Tips and discounts on Nolo products for business owners and managers.

   - **Landlord's Quarterly.** Deals and free tips just for landlords and property managers, too.

2. Don't forget to check for updates at Nolo.com. Under "Products," find this book and click "Legal Updates."

Let Us Hear From You

3. Register your Nolo product and give us your feedback at Nolo.com/book-registration.

   - Once you've registered, you qualify for technical support if you have any trouble with a download or CD (though most folks don't).

   - We'll also drop you an email when a new edition of your book is released—and we'll send you a coupon for 15% off your next Nolo.com order!

DRHR1

The Small Business Start-Up Kit

A Step-by-Step Legal Guide

$29.99

How to Write a Business Plan

$34.99

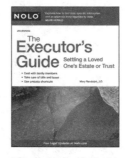

The Executor's Guide

Settling a Loved One's Estate or Trust

$39.99

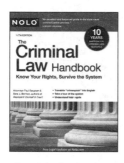

The Criminal Law Handbook

Know Your Rights, Survive the System

$39.99

Patent It Yourself

$49.99

Make Your Own Living Trust

$39.99

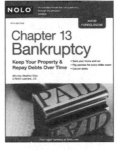
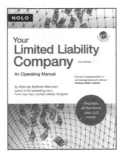

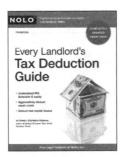

⚖ NOLO *Online Legal Forms*

Nolo offers a large library of legal solutions and forms, created by Nolo's in-house legal staff. These reliable documents can be prepared in minutes.

Create a Document

- **Incorporation.** Incorporate your business in any state.
- **LLC Formations.** Gain asset protection and pass-through tax status in any state.
- **Wills.** Nolo has helped people make over 2 million wills. Is it time to make or revise yours?
- **Living Trust (avoid probate).** Plan now to save your family the cost, delays, and hassle of probate.
- **Trademark.** Protect the name of your business or product.
- **Provisional Patent.** Preserve your rights under patent law and claim "patent pending" status.

Download a Legal Form

Nolo.com has hundreds of top quality legal forms available for download—bills of sale, promissory notes, nondisclosure agreements, LLC operating agreements, corporate minutes, commercial lease and sublease, motor vehicle bill of sale, consignment agreements and many, many more.

Review Your Documents

Many lawyers in Nolo's consumer-friendly lawyer directory will review Nolo documents for a very reasonable fee. Check their detailed profiles at **Nolo.com/lawyers**.

⚖ NOLO *Lawyer Directory*

Find an Employment Attorney

- *Qualified lawyers*
- *In-depth profiles*
- *A pledge of respectful service*

When you want professional help with serious employment concerns, you don't want just any lawyer—you want an expert in the field, who can give you and your family up-to-the-minute advice. You need a lawyer who has the experience and knowledge to answer your questions about discrimination and harassment claims, wages and hours issues, independent contractor status, firing for cause, health and safety concerns, and all the other employment law issues that can affect your business.

Nolo's Lawyer Directory is unique because it provides an extensive profile of every lawyer. You'll learn about not only each lawyer's education, professional history, legal specialties, credentials and fees, but also about their philosophy of practicing law and how they like to work with clients.

All lawyers listed in Nolo's directory are in good standing with their state bar association. Many will review Nolo documents, such as a will or living trust, for a fixed fee. They all pledge to work diligently and respectfully with clients—communicating regularly, providing a written agreement about how legal matters will be handled, sending clear and detailed bills and more.

www.nolo.com